JOURNAL FOR THE STUDY OF THE OLD TESTAMENT
SUPPLEMENT SERIES
30

Editors

David J A Clines

Philip R Davies

Department of Biblical Studies

The University of Sheffield

Sheffield S10 2TN

England

THE
ESTHER
SCROLL

The Story of the Story

DAVID J.A. CLINES

Journal for the Study of the Old Testament
Supplement Series 30

For Dawn

γενέθλιος δόσις

Published by
JSOT Press
Department of Biblical Studies
The University of Sheffield
Sheffield S10 2TN
England

Printed in Great Britain
by Redwood Burn Ltd.,
Trowbridge, Wiltshire.

British Library Cataloguing in Publication Data

Clines, David J.A.
    The Esther scroll.—(Journal for the
    study of the Old Testament supplement series,
    ISSN 0309-0787; 30)
    1. Bible. O.T. Esther—Criticism, Textual
    I. Title   II. Series
    222'.904   BS1375.2

    ISBN 0-905774-66-3
    ISBN 0-905774-67-1 Pbk

CONTENTS

PREFACE

Different parts of this book will probably appeal to different people. Septuagintalists will appreciate most Chapter 7 on the non-Septuagintal Greek Esther; source-critics may find Chapter 9 interesting, where it is maintained that our ability to analyse sources is not a sufficient reason for concluding they existed; redaction-critics will turn rather to Chapters 3 and 4 where a proposal is made for peeling off late editorial layers from the end of the Scroll; while literary critics may find Chapters 1 and 10 (noting the inclusio) more to their taste, and savour the qualities of this intriguing tale, not only in the final form of the text, but in the various shapes in which it still exists or apparently once existed.

With the needs of different readers in mind, I have tried to signpost the beginnings and ends of chapters with some account of the argument, so that the complete interlocking thesis of the book can be comprehended without reading every chapter right through. The story has its own 'story'—the phases through which it passed—and each of the phases of that story has its own 'story'—its design, pattern, and meaning. I shall not be surprised if there are those who have no wish to trace all these stories within stories, but would still like to know the general drift of the book; I hope I have enabled them to discover that.

A word of explanation about the Greek text and its translation printed at the end of the monograph is in order. In the course of my research I came to believe that the Greek Esther story known as the A-text was a very important witness to a pre-Masoretic form of the story. But this text has never been translated into any language, and the Greek itself is not easily accessible. So I decided to incorporate it here, along with a translation. But I would not like it to be thought that this text is the focus of the present study.

The idea behind this book came to me when I was at work on a commentary on Esther for the New Century Bible series, and so I want to thank Professor R.E. Clements, the editor of the Old

8

Testament volumes, for his invitation to contribute the volume *Ezra, Nehemiah, Esther* to that series. Dr C.A. Moore of Gettysburg, Pennsylvania, and Dr E. Tov of Jerusalem very kindly offered comments and encouragement, especially on aspects relating to the Greek versions. The Sheffield Biblical seminar with colleagues and postgraduate students heard an early version of the argument and strengthened my hands, and other colleagues at the IOSOT Congress in Salamanca, August, 1983, heard another version and gave me a fresh impetus to complete the work. Dr Philip Davies commented judiciously and constructively on the penultimate form of the text, and invented a subtitle that took my fancy. Mrs Sally Parker, together with Mrs Melinda Fowl, typed the book, and Mrs Pauline Climpson typeset it. To all of these I am most grateful.

This book is dedicated to my wife on a day which she, like Esther, might well call ἡμέρα ἐπισημός μοι (AT 6.14); no word, however, need be said here of any celebratory δεῖπνον πολυτελές (AT 6.16).

Sheffield, April 24, 1984   D.J.A.C.

Chapter 1

THE STORY OF ESTHER IN ITS MASORETIC FORM

The story of Esther, in its Masoretic Hebrew form, has a structure in
which beginning, middle, and end are clearly marked out. Chapters 1
and 2 form the exposition, chapters 3 to 9.19 the main action (the
complication and its resolution), and 9.20–10.3 the conclusion.

I

1. *Exposition (1.1–2.23)*
The exposition or setting of the stage in the first two chapters unfolds
a series of situations each precedent to the main action of the book—
a series in which each successive situation is more germane and more
crucial to the development of the main plot. There are seven scenes
into which the exposition falls:

1. the royal banquet for the officials (1.1-4)
2. the royal banquet for the citizens of Susa (1.5-9)
3. Vashti's refusal on the seventh day (1.10-22)
4. the king's decision to seek a new wife (2.1-4)
5. Esther's admission to the court (2.5-11)
6. Esther's accession to the throne (2.12-18)
7. Mordecai's discovery of the eunuch's plot (2.19-23)

These scenes are progressively indispensable prerequisites for the
plot of the main section of the book; and at the same time they are
each foreshadowings of some aspect of it.

To take the progressive character of these opening scenes first:
without implying a mechanistic progression of the plot, or even a
conscious intention of the author to arrange the scenes in a scale of
ascending importance, we may observe the effect of such a sequence.
The unrewarded service Mordecai renders the king in scene 7 will in

the end prove to be the essential presupposition for fundamental data of the basic plot of the book: (i) the installation of Mordecai as vizier with his consequent authority to stave off the force of Haman's letter of destruction against the Jews (8.9), (ii) Mordecai's becoming in his own person the primary reason why the Persian officials throughout the empire aligned themselves with the Jewish cause (fear of Mordecai had fallen on them, 9.3), and (iii) Mordecai's continuing power and fame exercised as a permanent safeguard for the Jewish people under Persian rule (9.4; 10.3). Even the coronation of the Jewish girl Esther as Persian queen, told in scene 6, and her heroic and skilful intercession on behalf of her people, rank as marginally less significant for the ultimate purposes of the plot.

If then scene 6 of the exposition is marginally less indispensable for the remainder of the story than is scene 7, scene 5 portraying the means by which the Jewish Esther gains access to the Persian court is in its turn somewhat less indispensable than scene 6; for there must be more ways of attracting the king's attention than being rounded up in an empire-wide beauty contest, and we can easily imagine alternative stories of how a Jewish girl found herself favoured by a Persian monarch. However, given that the story does depict a search for the most beautiful maidens of the empire (scene 5) it does not have to present antecedently a scene devoted to the king's decision to undertake such a search (scene 4). Further, if the story is to portray the appointment of talent scouts to find a queen for the king (scene 4), it is by no means necessary to presuppose that the queen sought is to replace one deposed (scene 3); the plot of the Esther story would be no different if there had been no Vashti. And if a queen has been deposed (scene 3), it need not have been because of a misdemeanour at a royal banquet (scene 2); there must be plenty of opportunities for the wife of an autocrat to earn his displeasure. And finally, if there has been a royal banquet for the citizens of Susa (scene 2), it need not have been preceded by a banquet for all the officials of the empire (scene 1).

Yet over against the scale of ascending indispensability for the main plot in which these prefatory scenes are arranged lies another significance all the scenes have in common: the more or less equal appropriateness of each of them for the tale that is yet to begin. Even those scenes that are most dispensable as far as the plot is concerned are charged with the atmospherics of the Persian court. The world they set forth is a world of conflicts, open and hidden, explicit and implicit: between Ahasuerus and Vashti; between his power over his empire and his impotence to bend his wife's will; between one nubile contestant for the royal favour and another; between the conspiracy of the eunuchs and the security of the king's person. It is a self-consciously multiracial world, in which it is imperial policy that all nations should live together harmoniously under the *pax Persica* and should observe the same laws (cf. 1.3, 20, 22), and yet in which the hard facts are these: that the Medo-Persians are the master race (cf. 1.14, 18); that the Persian administration has inherited from its Neo-Babylonian predecessors potentially disaffected members of an exiled people (Mordecai, he of the distinguished lineage, actually residing at the seat of government in Susa [2.5] and apparently himself a palace official [2.19]); that, for whatever reason, it is not always wise (? or safe) for a Jew to disclose his (or, at least, her) racial origins (2.10, 20); and that a scroll composed in one of the minor languages of the one hundred and twenty-seven provinces can fail signally to take the flower of Persian gentility at their own valuation and can with a faint maliciousness make Persian splendour and dignity—to say nothing of the mysteries of the seraglio—an object of fun. It is a world where the wish of the king instantly attains the status of law, and where the king's wish is often his whim (his anger [1.12; 2.1] or his pleasure [1.21; 2.4]). It is a world ruled by law and regulation, in which the serving of wine is the subject of royal edict (1.8), the bedfellow of the king is determined by a complex administrative machinery (2.12-14), and the authority of every man in his own house throughout the empire is regulated by a multilingual decree (1.20, 22). It is a world in which even the king himself can be caught in the web of irreversible law: when the wrath of Ahasuerus against Vashti has abated and he 'remembers' her (2.1) he must perforce also remember 'what had been decreed against her' (2.1) by the unalterable law of the Persians and Medes (1.19), so that any second thoughts are completely out of the question. It is a world that takes itself so seriously, perhaps with the nervousness of the parvenu, that every event and decision has to be recorded in writing: it must be written down that Vashti is to come no more before Ahasuerus (1.19), that every man be master in his own house (1.22), that the name of Mordecai, informer concerning a plot against the king, be entered in the royal chronicles (2.23).

In every one of these elements adumbrations of the main plot are disclosed and the area within which it will have freedom to move is being staked out.

2. Main action (3.1–9.19)

The plot itself, in the central section of the book (3.1–9.19) develops
from a kernel in which two of these elements combine: courtly
conflict and the question of obedience to the king. Mordecai refuses
homage to the newly-elevated Haman, and thereby provokes a
conflict of courtiers, thus setting the plot in motion. But there is
another dimension to Mordecai's refusal: he refuses the obeisance
that the king had commanded for Haman (3.2)—and so his action
sets up a tension not only between himself and Haman but also
between himself and royal law. Haman, however, chooses to ignore
the most obvious remedy open to him to redress Mordecai's insubordination: he does not invoke the law of the king or the king himself.
He devises a worse fate for Mordecai than that which befell Vashti
for *her* refusal. Mordecai will not suffer alone for his misdeed, as did
Vashti, but will drag down the whole race of the Jewish people along
with him in his fall. A conflict of courtiers, no unusual matter at the
Persian court (one gathers), becomes instantaneously the ground of a
threat to the survival of a whole nation. Haman 'disdained' to lay
hands on Mordecai alone, says the story (3.6).

From that point on, the plot retains this double dimension: it
remains the story of Mordecai vs. Haman, as the scene of Mordecai's
symbolic elevation in ch. 6 will show and the ultimate gift of the royal
ring which Haman had worn will remind us (8.2). But at the same
time it is the story of the decree against the Jewish people and their
deliverance from it, as the entreaties of Esther (4.8; 7.3-4) and the
issuance of the second decree (8.5-14) make plain. The second
dimension is of course the more momentous: it continues to fuel the
progress of the story well beyond the time when the conflict of
Haman and Mordecai has ceased, with Haman impaled on the pole
prepared for Mordecai (7.10). Even when Haman has lost decisively
and has been 'promoted' to the height of fifty cubits, his decree
against the Jewish people still stands and its averting must be
besought with tears (8.3) and carried into effect with legal nicety
(8.11). So there must be more than one 'ending' to the tale: the little
report of Mordecai's elevation in 8.1-2 forms, as W. Dommershausen
remarks, only a 'resting-point' in the narrative,[1] while 8.15-17 and
9.19 in different ways bring the other element of the plot (the fate of
the Jews) to its conclusion.

The plot of the central section of the book presents itself as the
interaction of the four principal characters, Ahasuerus, Haman,

Mordecai, and Esther. In each of the distinct scenes of the narrative a different grouping of the protagonists develops the action. So we find the following disposition of principal characters:

Scene 1.	3.1-6	Haman, Mordecai
Scene 2.	3.8-15	Ahasuerus, Haman
Scene 3.	4.1-3	Mordecai
Scene 4.	4.4-17	Mordecai, Esther
Scene 5.	5.1-8	Ahasuerus, Esther
Scene 6.	5.9-14	Haman
Scene 7.	6.1-14	Ahasuerus, Haman, Mordecai
Scene 8.	7.1-10	Ahasuerus, Haman, Esther
Scene 9.	8.1-17	Ahasuerus, Mordecai, Esther.[2]

This constantly shifting grouping of the protagonists (a schema not necessarily deliberately so devised by the narrator) gives opportunity for the fundamental story elements adumbrated in the opening scenes of chs. 1–2 to appear again in various guises. Those elements we may now consider more closely.

1. Conflicts of interest, purpose, and expectation are manifest at every point: between Haman and Mordecai over the question of proskynesis (ch. 3), between Mordecai and Esther over the feasibility of an intervention by Esther (ch. 4), between Ahasuerus' conventional unapproachability and Esther's unsummoned appearance before him (ch. 5), between the king's expectation of who it is that he will honour and Haman's expectation (ch. 6), between Esther (and, ultimately, Ahasuerus) and Haman in the scene of his downfall (ch. 7).

2. The question of racial identity also, of course, immediately becomes a fundamental plot element, as the Jewish people becomes the object of Haman's character assassination in the presence of the king and has the sentence of genocide against it rubber-stamped by royal authority. So much for the famed royal hospitality which has gathered ethnarchs and provincial governors (Jews included, no doubt) from all over the empire for a hundred and eighty days of expenses-paid imperial junketing (1.3); under the surface there is potential animosity between the king's interest and 'a certain people' (3.8), though the citizens of Susa, who presumably only know Jews as people and have not been educated to think strategically, are shocked to learn of the planned genocide (3.15) and mightily relieved when its shadow is lifted (8.15).

Even so, the conflict between Persian and Jew is not the only racial tension in the plot: the very much less explicit conflict between the Agagite and the Jew(s) is in a way even more fundamental. It is an alert reader who at the first mention of Haman sees that the most important word in 3.1 is 'the Agagite' and casts the plot that is yet to develop as a re-working of the old traditions of Israelite animosity toward the Amalekites, personified as Agag and Amalek in Balaam's oracles (Num. 24.7, 20) and represented by Agag king of the Amalekites in 1 Samuel 15 in his confrontation with Saul. But when at the second time of reading Haman is pronounced 'the Agagite, the enemy of the Jews' (3.10), the realization may dawn that this is not some titulature Haman has recently acquired, along with his new promotion to the freedom of bargaining with the king over his subjects' lives (3.8-10), but a role that he was born to. The true state of affairs becomes plainer when Haman complains to his family that his honours do him no good so long as he sees 'Mordecai the Jew' sitting at the king's gate; if it had been 'Mordecai the neo-Babylonian', we suspect, it would injure his vanity, but it would not poison his life. Finally, all becomes clear when Haman's confidants and his wife, for all the world as if they were a Greek tragic chorus, respond to the news of his unwilling display of Mordecai's honour in the city square by intoning, 'If Mordecai, before whom you have begun to fall, is of the Jewish people, you will not prevail against him but will surely fall before him' (6.13). The fall of the Agagite before the Jew is fated, genetically determined. It is the Jews who are the master race, the Jews who in the bloodbath of ch. 9 'get the mastery over their foes' (9.1), finding that 'no one could make a stand against them' because 'the fear of them', as if some numinous dread, has fallen upon all other races (9.2).

In the end, with the dénouement of the plot, we find that the Agagite-Jewish racial hostility was the only one really worth talking about—though we do wonder, in ch. 9, who the seventy-five thousand provincials with whom the Jews 'did as they pleased' (9.5, 16) may have been. The *Persian*-Jewish tension was all a big mistake: has not the Persian king got himself yet a nice Jewish girl for a queen, has he not promoted Mordecai to second rank in the kingdom because of the Jewish connection (8.1), and is not the royal message 'write as you please with regard to the Jews, in the name of the king' (8.8)? Yes, in the end all is sweetness and 'light' (8.16), but the telling of the story ensures that it can never be forgotten that the mistake *was* made, and not everyone in the empire has converted to Judaism (8.17)—which would be the only sure way of eliminating racial conflict from the future. The narrative points to a social-political reality beyond its own plot.

3. The theme of the king's unassailable will also becomes a significant element of the plot. However indecisive our Ahasuerus may be, relying on courtly advice for every decision (1.13-14; 2.2-4; 3.8-11; 6.6; 7.9-10; 8.5-8), once a suggestion 'pleases' him it must immediately be carried into effect, whether it is the feckless dispatch of a whole people that is settled upon before cocktails (3.15), the acting out of Haman's little fantasy about being king for a day by wearing the king's very own clothes (6.7-9), or the ultimate execution of his prime minister (7.9-10). Above all, what will hang on the king's whim are two most crucial junctures in the plot.

The first is the issue of how the king will react when Esther, 'against the law' (4.16), enters his presence unbidden (unreasonable though the law may be, as the narrator hints by stressing that it is *Queen* Esther, in her *royal robes* who thus approaches him [5.1-2]). In the event, the passage from the inner court, where the king first glimpses Esther standing, to the throne room inside the palace is negotiated without accident—but just because Esther happens to have 'found favour' in the king's eyes (5.2). In another mood, indeed in the mood that had excluded her from his presence for the past thirty days (4.11), her life would have been forfeit, and deliverance for the Jews would perforce have had to arise from another quarter (4.14)—*and* there would have been no Esther story.

The second juncture at which it is crucial which way the king will jump is the moment of Esther's uncloaking of Haman (7.6). A safe passage here is not so quickly assured, for the king's first instinct is to escape the revelation Esther is forcing upon him. He must step into the palace gardens for a breath of fresh air because more than the wine (7.2) has made him dizzy. If Esther were home and dry, the king would make no exit. He is going outside because he is going to have to choose between his prime minister, whom he himself has publicly promoted (3.1), and his queen, a girl of uncertain ancestry who has nothing much to recommend her except her good looks and her cookery. We have no way of telling just yet whether his wrath is against Haman or against Esther—or not perhaps against the disaster this dinner party has become. At a previous banquet he could invoke the advice of his seven princes over how to handle his wife (1.13-15), and such, we have read, was his usual practice (כן דבר המלך, 1.13).

But to whom can he now appeal to judge between the queen and the
vizier? Hardly to the seven princes of Persia and Media, who in ch. 1
saw the king's face and sat first in the kingdom (1.14), since their
noses have no doubt been put out of joint by his promoting the non-
Persian, Haman the Agagite, 'above all the princes who were with
him' (3.1). As things turn out, it is providence rather than the king
that decides the issue, for on returning from the garden with who
knows what intention the king finds his mind made up for him by the
compromising position Haman has unwittingly got himself into.[3] At
the banquet of ch. 1 Ahasuerus had had his dignity affronted by the
non-arrival of Vashti; at this banquet he sees his property assaulted:
in his 'own' presence, in his 'own' house, he chooses to see the queen
(he might as well have said his 'own' queen) assaulted (7.8), and—
ignorant though he may be on the finer points of Persian law (1.15)—
he knows where he stands as far as his property rights are concerned.
The matter being thereby settled, Haman is immediately led to
execution.[4] Not his wicked plot, but the king's outrage costs him his
life: that is the way things are at the Persian court. A pity for Haman
that he never realized that Esther was Jewish; he might have been a
little less tickled at being invited to a private dinner party by 'Queen
Esther' (5.12).

4. The issue of legality casts its shadow everywhere in the plot. It is
on the ground that Jews do not keep the king's laws (3.8) that Haman
contrives their annihilation, and, conveniently for his case, both
Mordecai (3.3) and Esther (4.16) explicitly defy the law of the king.
The question from the Jewish point of view is of course whether mere
legality should triumph over attested concern for the king's safety
(Mordecai) or over self-sacrificing intercession on behalf of one's
kinspeople (Esther). More radically, the question is whether legality
is the same as justice. Legal the decree against the Jews may be,
written in the name of King Ahasuerus and sealed with his ring
(3.12), but how can it be just when it is based upon a lie and a bribe?

The plot has another twist to the issue of legality. In the prologue
of chs. 1–2 we were prepared, by the triviality of the matters
determined by law in the Persian court, for a complication in which
every development would accord with law. The reality is otherwise:
the plot undermines law (Persian law, at any rate). Not only does
Mordecai by falling prey to Haman escape the king's wrath for his
law-breaking, but Esther nullifies the universally dreaded law (4.11)
by entering the king's presence unscathed and proceeds to trivialize it

by making the purpose of her intrusion nothing more sensational than a dinner arrangement—the king himself, awed by the sanctions of his own legality, being decidedly wrong-footed in imagining the stakes must be in the half-a-kingdom range (5.3). Even more, the plot undermines law by ignoring it: the crucial moments—Esther's acceptance, Mordecai's elevation, Haman's unmasking—have nothing to do with law and go to show that Persian legality, despite the lengths to which it reaches, is really something of a facade; human affairs, even issues of life and death, can be conducted without reference to it at all. The issue in the end is not a matter of law but a matter of good and evil, as the 'recognition' scene will reveal: 'This wicked Haman' (7.6) is the moral, not the legal, verdict agreed upon by Jew and Persian together (even if the king could only see the wickedness for what it was when it affected his own property). It is a story of the crushing of evil, not the triumph of law; indeed, it is a story of the crushing of evil even when it is enshrined in the law.

5. We have been well prepared in the prologue for the theme of the irreversibility of Persian law (1.19). It will not again be spoken of explicitly until 8.8, the moment at which the decree that brings deliverance to the Jews is authorized. It is not even alluded to at the time of proclamation of the first decree, though everything else is there: there are secretaries and couriers bearing its news to satraps, governors and princes; there are copies of the document in every script of every province and every people in every language, and there are orders commanding the oral proclamation of it on the day appointed; there are specifications of what is to be done to Jews—destroy, slay, annihilate, plunder their goods—and of which Jews are its target—young, old, women, children—and of which day it is to become effective—the thirteenth day of the twelfth month, which is Adar (3.12-14). There is more said of this decree than we need to know, but the one aspect of it that will prove most constructive for the plot is left unsaid: there is no reversing it. That silence can be left precisely because there is no doubt about it—but it has the function of compelling the readers to figure out for themselves that this is another of those 'laws of the Persians and the Medes that cannot be altered' (1.19). When Vashti fell foul of such a law, she could only be remembered with regret (2.1).

The next time that Persian law is spoken of (4.11) the theme of irreversibility is not at issue; for the law in question in ch. 4 contains within itself an escape clause: the king *may* hold out the golden

sceptre. Yet the very fact of its not being at issue actually raises the
issue in an oblique fashion; for if some Persian laws have built-in
escape clauses that very provision reminds us that the edict against
the Jews has no such clause, so that the Jews are locked onto a
collision course with annihilation. So long as the attention of the plot
is focussed on Esther and her brush with danger, on Haman and his
grisly plan for Mordecai, on Mordecai and his peripeteia, on Esther's
denunciation of the wicked Haman—so long is the real horror of the
Persian decree driven underground. At the very moment when
Haman is dispatched and his property has been tidily distributed to
the Jewish protagonists (8.1-2)—and, one might have thought—the
end of the tale is in sight, the issue of the irreversible decree rises
spontaneously to the surface again, and has the triumphant Esther
on her knees in tears, and, presently, deploying all her rhetorical gifts
(8.5-6; cf. 7.3-4) against its malignancy. The simple fact is that
Haman's death has solved nothing, relieved nothing. He himself may
be dead, but his evil is very much alive. And it lives on under the
banner of unalterable Persian law.

Now for the second time in the story, the king finds himself
trapped by his own law. Mordecai's words to Esther, 'Think not that
in the king's palace you will escape' (4.13) can have an ironic
application also to the king himself. Vashti's removal, though it could
not be rescinded, could be largely compensated for by the importation
of a bevy of maidens; but now, when the truth about Esther's
involvement in the decree of annihilation has been unveiled, there
seems to be no possible escape from the web of irreversible law. The
narrative offers only an ambivalent comment on this complication of
the plot. On the one hand, it has the king giving Esther and Mordecai
perfect freedom to write as they please in the king's name concerning
the Jews (8.8a)—which seems the answer to every Jewish prayer and
the penultimate step before the final and complete deliverance of the
Jewish people. And, at the first hearing, the clause that follows it
gives calm and authoritative encouragement to think just that: 'for an
edict written in the name of the king and sealed with the king's ring
cannot be revoked' (8.8b). Esther and Mordecai have only to dictate a
letter, it seems, and the deed of Haman will be undone, his letters will
be revoked, just as Esther had requested (8.5), and the new decree of
revocation will carry permanent and irreversible royal authority.
But, on the other hand, those very last words of the sentence, 'cannot
be revoked' (אין להשיב), as they sink into the consciousness, renew the

tension all over again.[5] For, with the best will in the world, the king has brought into the open his powerlessness to do what Esther has asked; the first decree perfectly fulfilled the conditions for legal irreversibility: written in the king's name, sealed with the king's ring (3.12). The perfect freedom that the first half of the verse has ostensibly granted is severely limited—on this occasion, fatally limited, so it would seem—by the reminder the second half gives of the restricted area within which that freedom may operate.[6] Write what you like, says the king, as long as it doesn't overturn, revoke, or contradict anything previously written. Write what you like to Jewish advantage, says the king, as long as you realize that Haman's decree still stands. Write what you like, says the king, it will bear my seal; but remember that so does every other official document, including Haman's letter. Write what you like, says the king, for I give up; the conundrum of how to revoke an irrevocable decree, as you, Esther have asked, is beyond me; but feel free to write what you like—if you can think of a way to reverse the irreversible.[7]

The tension in the 'national' dimension of the plot here reaches its climax. The king is as much defeated by law as is Darius in Daniel 6, where also it is (three times) spelled out that the edict against which Daniel offends is the unchangeable law of the Medes and Persians (6.8, 12, 15), and the king must accept Daniel's being cast into the den of lions. In the Daniel story the decree of the king is in the end nullified by a higher authority than the Persian law: God sends his angel to shut the lions' mouths (6.22). But in the Esther story we have been given not the slightest encouragement to expect any divine intervention, and nothing will prevent the due arrival of the thirteenth of Adar—so Mordecai and Esther will have to devise a strictly legal means of escape from their den of lions.[8]

The countervailing device adopted by Mordecai to thwart the effect of the first decree without rescinding its wording is of course to allow the Jews to defend themselves (8.11). We are to presume that under the first edict self-defence would have been illegal, as well as futile; for if the royal command is to annihilate the Jews, any Jew who tried not to be annihilated would be 'transgressing the king's command' (to borrow the idiom of 3.3). Now, however, the illegality is removed, if the first decree is—not revoked, but—*supplemented*, not by a further command, but by a very modest permission (נתן, 8.11) to the Jews, for one specified day only (8.12), to gather (להקהל, 8.11) and make a stand for their lives (לעמד על־נפשם)—which seems

reasonable enough—and to 'destroy, slay, annihilate' any armed
force that might seek to attack them, their wives, or children, or
might attempt to seize their goods.[9] Not a word is said of who these
anonymous armed forces might be, not a hint is given that they
would be acting under express royal direction, their orders no less
authoritative than the permission granted the Jews.[10] Such reserve is
all a legal delicacy, of course, to avoid an explicit confrontation of the
two decrees; but it is also a delicacy of the plot, which for the moment
will leave to the imagination the reception of the second decree and,
more interesting, the unguessable manner of their operation.

The theme of the irreversibility of Persian law is not yet exhausted,
not until we have witnessed the outworking of the two incompatible
but equally irreversible decrees. We first notice that the 'permission'
immediately becomes a 'decree' (דת, 8.13), 'the king's word and
decree' (דבר־המלך ודתו, 8.17; cf. 9.1, 13); for while Mordecai conceives
it as permission, the moment it is sealed, dispatched, posted, and
proclaimed it can only be perceived as royal law—an autocrat has no
other mode of communication.[11] We secondly observe that the
announcement of the second decree is celebrated by its recipients as
if it had effectively cancelled out the first: wherever the king's edict is
announced, there is gladness and joy among the Jews, a feast and a
holiday (8.17). It can hardly be thought that mere permission (or
even royal command) to defend oneself—as best one can—against
imperially-organized armed forces (כל־חיל, 8.11) can have provoked
such celebration. What has happened is that the second edict, issued
as it is by the grand vizier Mordecai the Jew, has made the first
ridiculous and unthinkable. It has not rescinded it, but it has made it
impossible for any loyal subject of the king to carry it out. For the
chief target of the decree against the Jews must necessarily be the
chief Jew, Mordecai (and have we not known all along that it was
against him that it was principally aimed?), but he is the king's
plenipotentiary. The illegality of not obeying the first decree falls into
the background beside the madness of attempting to carry it out.
There is, fortunately for those caught in the dilemma, a simple and
prudent course of action available: they can entirely avoid the
responsibility of failing to carry out the first decree by making
themselves the subjects of the second. No Jew can be expected to
execute the first, insane, decree; is it surprising that 'many from the
peoples of the land declared themselves Jews' (8.17)? The fear of the
Jews had fallen upon them, says the text; the fear, that is, of what

would happen if they should find themselves in the opposing camp—not 'enemies' of the Jews necessarily, but simply *non*-Jews, required by Haman's decree, whatever their rank or office, to ready themselves against the thirteenth of Adar for the annihilation of all Jews (3.13-14).

There is yet more of this plot to unravel. In ch. 9 three unexpected developments transpire. First, not a single non-Jew has the courage to obey the first decree: 'no one could make a stand against them' (9.2), since the fear of the *Jews* has fallen on them. Secondly, *all* the imperial officials, princes of the provinces, satraps, governors and royal placemen side with the Jews, because the fear of *Mordecai* has fallen on them (9.3). Thirdly, the Jews understand the second decree to permit them not simply to *resist* (for there is no one to resist), but to smite their 'enemies' with the sword, doing as they please to 'those who hated' them (9.5), and in general 'getting the mastery over their enemies' (9.1). There is a puzzle here; for, if the first decree is not put into effect, neither, we should suppose, may the second be. What in fact is put into effect is *not* the second decree but a new initiative of the Jews against opponents not previously envisaged: the 'enemies' of the Jews, those who 'hate' them, not by any means the same as 'any armed force' of 8.11. What this goes to show is that if you have your countryman in the highest office in the land, Persian laws, reversible or otherwise, tend to go by the board, and you seize the opportunity for a pre-emptive strike—for a limited period only, if you care about your image—against any who may be harbouring designs to eliminate you on a future occasion, viz. your 'enemies', unarmed and unable to stand though they may be at the moment (9.2). In short, the diplomacy of Mordecai as bureaucratic draughtsman (ch. 8) has been quite overshadowed by his symbolic significance as representative of Jewish interests (ch. 9). The tail end of the plot in ch. 9 suggests that citizens should not make too much of the pitting of one decree against another, and that what life is about in Susa is not documents but power. Mordecai embodies power, 'great in the king's house', and growing 'more and more powerful' (9.4)—and it is power, not law, that decides the day. The plot, in the end, is subversive of Persian law's claim to irrevocability—just as earlier it had undermined Persian law's claim to justice.

There is no harm, of course, in making out that power is legal, that the Jewish initiative in ch. 9 against weak-kneed opponents is the exercise not of *force majeure* but of strict legality; Esther wholeheartedly adopts this viewpoint in requesting that 'the Jews who are in Susa be allowed tomorrow also to do according to this day's edict' (9.13). As it happens, the Jews have on the thirteenth of Adar not been acting according to *any* edict (דת) that we have been told about—since they have been going far beyond 'self-defence'—so neither will they be on the fourteenth. But if the king makes a further edict (דת, 9.14) then the activities of the fourteenth are covered by royal law, even though the opponents of the Jews will have no legality to fall back on if they attempt to defend themselves against the Jews. If the Jews could not defend themselves against Haman's decree except by the promulgation of Mordecai's decree giving them permission, now on the fourteenth of Adar the 'enemies' of the Jews in Susa will find themselves in the same situation as the Jews had been: defenceless against an imperial edict. It is a strange and questionable ending to the tale, in which, with the best will in the world, we are inclined to judge the Jewish author to have done a disservice to his compatriots' honour. Perhaps, however, it is the very reversal that the plot—and 'poetic' justice—demands and that has been adumbrated by the language of 9.1: 'the very day when the enemies of the Jews hoped to get the mastery over them . . . had been changed to a day [now we must understand: days] when the Jews should get the mastery over their foes'. What the story has shown us, though it has never said so *expressis verbis*, is that Persian law, for all its professed irrevocability, is immensely malleable, and that (from the Jewish viewpoint) justice or deliverance—whatever you prefer to call it—can be achieved despite every outward appearance of inflexibility in the law.

6. Finally, we may examine the motif of writing. No part of the Old Testament story is more overtly oriented towards the practice of keeping written records of events and decisions (though Ezra and Daniel come close). In Esther, reality tends towards inscripturation, and attains its true quality only when it is written down. What is written is valid and permanent; what happens merely happens and is thereupon cast to the winds—unless it is recorded. The Esther story is of course a mirror of its times in this respect, and a reflection of Persian bureaucratic practice. But it is more than that: it has adopted the Persian perspective on this issue as its own.

Everything in the Masoretic story of Esther tends towards the recording of its events and the issuance of the decrees of Mordecai and Esther in ch. 9. The sentence in 9.20 is crucially significant:

'Mordecai recorded these things, and sent letters to all the Jews who were in all the provinces of King Ahasuerus'. I take it that Mordecai's record was of the events now told in the narrative of the Book of Esther.[12] It is not envisaged as the Book itself because the act of recording is contained *within* the Book; it will naturally refer to the kind of records mentioned as the Book of the Chronicles (דברי ספר הימים, 2.23) or the 'book of memorable deeds, the chronicles' (ספר הזכרנות דברי הימים, 6.1). The story of Mordecai and Esther is as naturally written into the Persian record as was the story of Mordecai and the eunuchs' plot (2.23), except that now it is Mordecai's responsibility, as chief minister of state, to supervise the recording of events.

But not only are the events recorded in the Persian annals, they are contained, in capsule form, within the letter of Mordecai to the Jews, as it seems.[13] Jews as well as Persians need to have the realities of the Haman affair permanently enshrined in written form.

Another written goal to which the events of the Esther story lead is the institution, in writing, of the festival of Purim. The deliverance from Haman's threat brought about by Jewish self-'defence' leads to 'resting' and feasting on the fourteenth (or fifteenth) of Adar—which in turn leads to the letters of Mordecai (9.20-22 [? 25]) and Esther (9.29-32), written documents 'enjoining' (לקים, 9.21, 29) the continued observance of the festival thus begun. The deliverance prompts the spontaneous festival-making; but writing is what preserves the festival and transports its occasion into every future generation.

It was writing, for that matter, that posed the threat to the Jews in the first place. Haman's hatred of Mordecai could only be successfully extended to the whole race of the Jews through the medium of secretaries, translators and couriers (3.12-13). To reach into every corner of the empire and ferret out every Jew for destruction is a design hard to encompass without writing, but is obviously practicable when the imperial scriptoria are at one's disposal.

All that intervenes between the first decree and the second is oral—of course, for nothing in chs. 4–7 is settled or finalized. Only when the flux of conversation, negotiating, and executing has come to an end will the secretaries be summoned again (8.9) and the imperial pleasure be set down in the diverse scripts of the empire. The very act of writing—quite apart from the fact that it is irreversible Persian law that is being written—makes matters certain and makes them everywhere accessible; it is almost as if it is the writing itself that effects the deliverance: 'in every province and in every city, wherever the king's command and his edict came, there was gladness and joy among the Jews, a feast and a holiday' (8.17).

There is a final act of writing, not mentioned in the Book of Esther because it *is* the Book of Esther. It has a special relationship with writing in being the only book of the Hebrew Bible (apart from Chronicles) known, by its familiar title of the Scroll, the Megillah, as a *writing*. Torah, Psalms, Proverbs, Prophets Former and Latter conjure up oral literature or its creators.[14] The Scroll, designed as a *written* story, is the appropriate ultimate respository for a narrative which has centred on the two written decrees and has itself concluded with the writing down of two written messages. The 'confirmation' or 'establishment' (קים) that the letters of Mordecai and Esther urge for the festival of Purim is finally effected by their incorporation in the Megillah, the writing.

3. *Conclusion (9.19–10.3)*

The conclusion to the book, 9.19–10.3, contains four elements:

1. 9.20-22	(+ perhaps vv. 24-25)	Mordecai's letter
2. 9.23-28	(– perhaps vv. 24-25)	Jewish response
3. 9.29-32	Esther's letter	
4. 10.1-3	epilogue on the greatness of Mordecai.	

These elements are strictly supplementary to the narrative itself, projecting the significance of the story beyond the confines of the relatively short period of nine years within which it has developed (the third to the twelfth years of Ahasuerus; cf. 1.3 and 3.7, 8.9, 9.1).

The letters of Mordecai and Esther envisage a perpetual memory of the events of the book, Mordecai especially projecting the spontaneous joyful celebrations that had accompanied the deliverance (9.17-19) and Esther the spontaneous lamentation rituals that had accompanied the initial threat (4.1, 3).

The record of the response of the Jews to Mordecai's letter is itself, from a narrative point of view, supplementary to Mordecai's letter; the agreement of the Jewish people to celebrate a holiday—one which moreover they themselves had initiated—is something that could be taken for granted by the most suspicious reader. But its formal expression stamps the conclusion to the book with unusual solemnity and fixedness. The principle of the irreversible law of the Persians and Medes seems, by an ironic turn, to have taken root on Jewish soil: the Jews 'ordained and took it upon themselves and their descendants and all who joined them, that without fail they would keep these two days according to what was written at the time appointed every year, that these days should be remembered and kept throughout every generation, in every family, province and city, and that these days of Purim should never fall into disuse among the Jews, nor should the commemoration of these days cease among their descendants' (9.27-28). No Persian bureaucrat could have phrased it more impeccably.

Likewise the final element, in 10.1-3, delivers an encomium upon Mordecai that is worthy, in its grandiloquence and imprecision, of the best of any civil service. Again, it projects the book beyond the narrated period; not, as with the previous three elements, by envisaging the observance of the festival throughout future generations, but by focussing upon the future achievements of Mordecai, next in rank to the king, great among the Jews, popular with the multitude of his brethren, seeking the welfare of his people and speaking peace to all his people (10.3).

Two ends are served in the projections of these concluding elements: the role of Mordecai, archetypical for the potential relation of Jew and Persian, Jew and Gentile, is represented as ultimately beneficial to Jew and Persian alike—despite the desperate straits to which racial differences had previously led in the narrative. This last element attempts to put to rest any lingering disquiet over the possibility of harmony or co-operation between Jew and non-Jew. And the projections of the first three elements (9.20-32) envisage a survival of the Jewish people, untouched in the future by threats to its existence, busying itself not with self-defence or gaining the mastery over its foes, but with solemn and joyful memories of a past threat; perhaps not for ever past—else why the fasts and lamenting?— but unlikely to be ever so comprehensively genocidal again—else why the feasting and giving of gifts?

The tale of Esther, in other words, is not in the Masoretic book left as a closed-off ancient narrative from which its readers may glean as best they can whatever advices or encouragement they may wish; rather, it has—in its conclusion—inbuilt its own hermeneutical rules, specifying how it is to be read and thus what it really means.

II

Up to this point in the chapter we have analysed the shape of the book and explored some prominent elements of its plot. Is it possible now to say anything more comprehensive about its plot?

A word of hesitation about the connection of the plot with the festival of Purim should first be expressed. I have above designated those verses in which the continuance of festival observance is enjoined, and therewith the terming of those days Purim (9.26), as supplementary to the main plot. And I want to stick by that despite what seems to be said in the standard handbooks. Brevard S. Childs, for example, begins his chapter on Esther with the sentence: 'There is general agreement that the major purpose of the book of Esther is to provide the historical grounds for the celebration of the feast of Purim'.[15] Several decades ago S.R. Driver could write in very similar terms: 'The aim of the Book of Esther is manifest: it is to explain the origin of the Feast of Purim, and to suggest motives for its observance'.[16] I have no doubt that Childs is right about the general agreement this view finds, but I consider this opinion of the 'purpose' or 'aim' of the Masoretic book not evidently helpful in coming to understand the *plot* of the story. The problem is, I think, that questions of 'purpose' are essentially historically oriented; and I would rather suggest that we should first attempt to seize the narrative shape and direction before asking what purpose the narrative shaped in this way may be supposed to have served. The literary question must precede the historical.

What then is the essential plot of the Esther story? As I read it, it goes something like this: The plot is of a dual threat to the existence of the Jewish people and of a representative Jew, Mordecai, which is averted by a chain of (providential) coincidences combined with acts of human courage and sagacity. The point at which the threat is posed is very plain: Haman's anger at Mordecai and his letter against the Jews in ch. 3. But where is the threat averted? Is it not first at the moment when Haman is led to be executed and secondly when the letter of Mordecai in ch. 8 is sent, effectively cancelling out the former letter? If we focus on the threat to the Jews—which is the major dimension, as we have noted—we can narrow down the threat more precisely to the letter of Haman as the instrument or even the substance of the threat, and to the letter of Mordecai as the averting of the threat. The one is the complication, the other the resolution.

There is a nice ironic balance in such a plot: a reversal of fortune towards deliverance that uses the same means that had set in train the impending disaster. But the moment we consider the contents of the letters, a certain asymmetry becomes apparent. For the second decree does not itself reverse the first; it does not nullify, contradict or set to one side the decree of Haman. Rather, it assumes its continuing validity and—formally at least—can only represent itself as supplementation. To put it concretely: The story reaches its resolution at the moment when permission—nothing more—is given to attempt to avert the threat![17] Most self-respecting stories of deliverance from danger retain their tension until the moment of effectual and actual deliverance; any attempt at averting the threat usually requires no permission and usually is merely the precondition of the deliverance, not the deliverance itself.

The text of the narrative strongly supports this analysis of the structure of its plot. For the most elaborated scene of rejoicing at the deliverance is narrated—not after the massacre of ch. 9 (which is at first sight the moment of deliverance), but—immediately after the announcement of the second decree. Not a word suggests that the rejoicing of 8.15-17 is purely anticipatory or primarily hopeful of forthcoming deliverance. The day of resolution is the day when the city of Susa—Jew and Gentile alike—rejoices, when the Jews have light and gladness and joy and honour, when they make a feast and a festival, when Gentiles in religious awe spontaneously convert to Judaism. The very shape of the paragraph 8.15-17, moving in its focus from Mordecai to the citizens of Susa, from them to the Jews throughout the empire, and from them to the citizens of the entire empire, creates an emphatically conclusive impression. It not only sounds like a concluding paragraph, but by the range of its contents actually draws together the principal threads of the plot.[18]

Given the point to which the story has run by the end of ch. 8, what possibilities for its further development exist? The decree for the annihilation of the Jews still stands, but now they are allowed to defend themselves. The most mundane expectation is that they will suffer losses but will not be totally exterminated, but will live to fight another day. We recall that the edict calls for a pogrom upon one day only, and we can hardly be intended to imagine that the Jews, fighting for their lives, can be entirely wiped out in a single day. Since genocide is now out of the question the narrative tension has been greatly reduced. We wonder what kind of climax can be projected when the original threat—which was unquestionably genocide—has

already been averted. Can the tension lie in the question, How many
Jews must die in the cause of Jewish survival? It may sound a trifle
cynical to reflect in this setting that 'the sword devours now one and
now another' (cf. 2 Sam. 11.25), but when all is said and done this is
not the first or last time that Jews will be killed for being Jews, and
there will have to be something unique about this occasion to make it
worth the telling. If the thirteenth of Adar is still likely to see a huge
number of Jewish fatalities, we will as readers be expectant of a
narrative resolution of our question. But if it is likely to be few, we
will not be so interested (however strong our attachment to the
Jewish cause). If, of course, we cannot see whether the loss of life is
likely to be great or small, we may find that very uncertainty the
source of narrative tension—and go on reading. The text of 8.15-17,
however, saps the tension out of all such questions. We learn first
that Mordecai's appointment as vizier is greeted with acclaim and
gladness by the citizens of Susa—Jew and Gentile alike—and so we
are actively discouraged from imagining that any significant hostility
to the Jews will now arise within the Persian capital. And we learn
last of all in this paragraph that 'many from the peoples of the
country declared themselves Jews'—which speaks for the pro-Jewish
feeling throughout the empire—outside the capital. Converting to
Judaism is the most extravagant way of demonstrating sympathy
with the Jews. If many actually convert, how many more must have
no intention of harming the Jews, and how many others must be
quite indifferent to the Jews and equally pose no kind of danger? The
only question the text leaves open is whether there will be any kind of
enthusiasm in favour of the first decree, issued nearly three months
previously.

This is the neatest irony of all: the second decree, in its wording so
circumspect to avoid confrontation with the first decree, in its effect
denatures the first decree. Who will want to risk his own life by
pitting it against a Jew fighting for *his* life, a Jew moreover that is
bathed in religious awe (פחד, v. 17)? By the end of ch. 8 the plot has
told us—though the text has never said so in so many words—that
the outcome must be stalemate. The narrator does not want any of
his compatriots hurt, but then neither does he have any particular
hatred of Persians (Haman excepted, and he has already been dealt
with—and he is in any case not a Persian). The story is effectively
over. This is why there is no anticipation, hope, or tension in 8.15-17:
there is no crucial action to follow.

If this were the end of the story, it is true, we would never be assured that the thirteenth of Adar passed peacefully, with the threat of Jewish force counterbalancing the threat of anti-Jewish force, with the attempt at annihilation being stifled by the attempt at defence, with the first and second decrees attaining their only possible joint fulfilment by neither being executed, with obedience to the king's wishes being paid by disobedience to both his decrees. Yet any narrative statement of such non-events would be bound to be banal, and it is perhaps not difficult to envisage an artful narrator leaving the 'history' of the thirteenth of Adar to the imagination of his readers.

I said earlier that the text of the narrative of chs. 1–8 supports an analysis of its plot as reaching its resolution at the end of ch. 8. The text of ch. 9 points in the same direction. For here the narrative of the Masoretic text strikes out in new directions which have not been prepared for and sometimes run counter to the plot of chs. 1–8. For example, it is a novelty of ch. 9, not harmonious with chs. 1–8, that the thirteenth of Adar is represented as 'a day when the Jews should get the mastery over their foes' (9.1), for the most the second decree had envisaged was Jewish slaughter of any armed force that should attack them (8.11). We are somewhat surprised that 'none could make a stand against them' (9.2) as if the Jews were on the offensive; the tendency of the plot hitherto had been to suggest that no one could find it in them to take up arms against the Jews. The one-day extension of the decree in favour of the Jews (9.13) likewise belongs to a conception of the thirteenth of Adar as a day of Jewish attack rather than defence. The introduction of discrepancy between the thirteenth and the fourteenth of Adar (9.15, 17-19) can hardly be thought an improvement on the crisp notations of 3.13 and 8.12, 13 that restrict the pogrom and the resistance thereto to 'one day' throughout all the provinces. Finally, the clear disjunction of Jews and 'enemies of the Jews' without any recognition of the group of Jewish sympathizers which 3.15 and 8.15 have alerted us to runs against the plot of earlier chapters.

Moreover, within ch. 9 itself there is a conflict of conceptions of the thirteenth of Adar. For although in vv. 1-15 it is principally a day of victory, 'mastery', and slaughter, in v. 16 it is presented as a day of 'relief' or 'rest' (נוח); this is not, admittedly, an incompatibility but it does evidence a difference of conception. In vv. 17 and 18, to complicate the conception further, the day *after* the killing, whether the fourteenth or fifteenth, is regarded as the 'rest' (נוח). This downplaying of the 'victory' idea matches the emphasis in vv. 10, 15, and 16 that 'they laid no hands on the plunder'—which phrase only serves to highlight the weakness of the plot's conception, with the Jews doing as they pleased with the persons of those who hated them (9.5) but leaving their property inviolate.

The suggestion to which this study of the plot of the Masoretic narrative of Esther leads is that the dynamics of the story require its conclusion at the end of ch. 8 with the issuance of the second decree, the acclamation of Mordecai, the rejoicing of the Jews, and the conversion of Gentiles. The further suggestion that will be developed in subsequent chapters of this study is that the story of Esther in an earlier phase ended at that point, and that chs. 9–10 consist of additions made to provide a more conventional ending for the tale and to link it with the Purim festival with which it probably had no connection originally.

These suggestions will be supported in Chapters 3 and 4 by evidence of distinctly inferior narrative artistry in chs. 9–10 compared with chs. 1–8, and of disagreements between these later chapters and preceding chapters of the book. I will further attempt to support these suggestions by arguing in Chapter 7 that the Greek version known as the A-text provides testimony to an earlier Hebrew Esther story that concluded at about this point. But first, in Chapter 2, I will draw attention to some examples of the narrative skill of the author of the core of the Masoretic Esther story (chs. 1–8) as a backdrop to an analysis of the literary and narrative weaknesses of chs. 9–10.

Chapter 2

THE LITERARY ART OF THE ESTHER SCROLL

Many writers have praised the literary art of the Esther narrative, some perhaps too highly, but all with good cause. In his monograph, *Die Estherrolle. Stil und Ziel einer alttestamentlichen Schrift,*[1] Werner Dommershausen can begin his own appreciation of the book's literary worth by quoting the enthusiastic impressions of several generations of scholars who have praised its skilful construction, its strong characterization, and its dramatic tension.[2] Such summary judgments, while perhaps predisposing the uncommitted reader to a willingness to feel admiration, are no substitute for a candid and sustained scrutiny of the narrative itself. But since my purpose in this chapter is solely to provide a standard by which the ending of the book may in subsequent chapters be judged, I think it enough to focus upon no more than three segments of the narrative which display superior literary skill and which, indeed, emerge with credit—to put it no higher than that—from the critical probings of a more self-consciously literate and psychologically alert age such as our own.

I

The opening scenes of the book in ch. 1 are, as we have noted, by no means indispensable for the story of Esther proper, but they serve the purpose of establishing a tone of voice for the narrative as a whole and for displaying to the reader certain significant facts about Persian mores and values.

The tone of ch. 1 is satirical—of that there can be no doubt. The point at which it ends, with royal letters being sent to all the royal provinces, to each province in its own script and to each people in its own language, giving command that every man should be master in his own house, is the point of unmistakable glee at Persian foolishness to which the whole chapter has been moving. The amusement was not lost on readers of the story in ancient times: bMegillah 12b comments, 'What does he mean by sending us word that every man should rule in his own home? Of course he should! Even a weaver in his own house must be commander!'[3] The narrative has descended from the sublimity of imperial pomp to the most ridiculous and unprepossessing aspect of domestic life: the attempt of husbands to shore up an 'authority' they do not have, by an appeal to custom and consensus. The emperor himself, who lives in unparalleled wealth and exercises well-nigh universal dominion, is shown up to be, at bottom, an utterly unselfconscious male chauvinist who is astonished to be worsted in the battle of the sexes when on every other front he is masterfully supreme.

The satire is against the king, Persians, men. The king is a vain man, delighted to be able to show off 'the riches of his royal glory and the splendour and pomp of his majesty for many days' (1.4), but taken aback when his queen will not submit to being shown off in the same way as another piece of his property (1.11). The king, though he is a monarch, does not know how to handle his recalcitrant wife—or rather how to disengage himself from a situation in which he has lost face and in which he rather than Vashti has become the spectacle. He must ask advice of his courtiers, 'wise men who know the times', those 'versed in law and judgment' (1.13)—although the answer they will give him will have no relation to astrological lore or even to legal forms or precedents. They too, for all their standing—to say nothing of their 'sitting first in the kingdom' (1.14)—lose their wits and their dignity in their hysterical asssumption that Vashti's disobedience is just the signal their own wives ('the ladies of Persia and Media', 1.18) have been waiting for to rise in rebellion against them. Vashti, they unitedly determine, must be dethroned from her office of state in the interests of avoiding 'contempt and wrath in plenty' (1.18) on the purely domestic scene, that is, contempt on the women's part and wrath on the men's—who know no better than Ahasuerus how to behave when their male supremacy is threatened.

The decree against Vashti has its own special irony, prescribing as her punishment what is really her own decision: she is 'to come no more before King Ahasuerus' (1.19). Memucan the courtier assumes that not to appear before the king is the worst possible fate that can befell Vashti, but we have been encouraged to suspect that Vashti may think otherwise. The final irony in the Vashti saga will be that the royal decree to all the provinces announcing Vashti's dismissal will give more publicity to Vashti's deed—and her cause—as well as to the king's embarrasssment than could ever have been achieved by the mere rumour his courtiers had feared (1.17).

Chapter 1 is more openly satirical than anything else in the book. Of course, the narrative of the disposable Vashti's downfall can afford to be more amusing that can the account of the much graver threat to the life of the Jewish people. But the opening chapter has set a tone that cannot be forgotten, conditioning the reader not to take the king, his princes, or his law at their face value, and alerting the reader to keep his eyes open for ironies that will doubtless be implicit in the story that is yet to unfold. Without the rather obvious satire of the first chapter we might well be in more doubt over the propriety of ironic readings in the body of the book. Chapter 1 licenses a hermeneutic of suspicion.

II

We may next consider a scene which has immense importance for the development of the plot and which at the same time presents narrative and dialogue of the utmost delicacy.

Chapter 4, in the first place, performs an important structural function in the development of the narrative. In it a transition must be effected from the figure of Mordecai, who has set the plot in motion by his refusal to do obeisance to Haman, to the figure of Esther, who must come to adopt a central place in moving the complication of the plot towards its resolution. The locus of responsibility for what will happen next must shift from the one to the other; but the movement must happen naturalistically, credibly, and—for preference—subtly. The passing of responsibility must not be narrated briefly, for it is a crucial moment in the total narrative. And the narrative must not simply *replace* Mordecai by the figure of Esther, since Mordecai must retain a significant role in the story as a whole. For this is not to be a tale of how a shrewd and pretty woman rescues her gauche and haughty kinsman from a disaster of his own making, but rather of how each of the Jewish protagonists contributes his and her best talents to the salvation of their people. Esther must not achieve prominence at the expense of Mordecai; but by the end of the scene the next move must be firmly in her hands. At its simplest, the chapter must 'pan' from Mordecai, who with Haman was the subject of the previous chapter, to Esther, who with Ahasuerus will be the subject of the following one; it must 'track' from the acropolis of Susa (3.15) and the city itself (4.1) to the king's palace (4.13) and its inner court (5.2).

These desiderata for chapter 4 are—of course—retrojections from the narrative that lies before us; but by posing them as desiderata we are alerted to the busy structural functionality of this narrative which may seem, on the surface, to be more talk than action.

This highly meaningful movement from Mordecai to Esther is accomplished by three scenes of communication between Esther and Mordecai, each more developed than the former, a signal that the communication is becoming effective, that the barrier of the king's gate (4.2, 6) is being breached. In v. 4 no words are spoken and the token of communication between Esther and Mordecai—the gift of clothes—is rejected. In vv. 5-9 a messenger is sent by Esther to Mordecai, and a message, both oral and written, is delivered from Mordecai to Esther; but no words are reported. In vv. 10-17, a still more developed scene, a three-speech dialogue of Esther, Mordecai, and Esther economically moves the action forward by argument, counter-argument and resolution. In the three scenes there is a movement from ignorance to understanding and from understanding to decision. The balance of *responsibility* for the final crucial decision to approach the king is nicely shared between Mordecai and Esther. The real progress in the unfolding of the plot throughout this act is created by Mordecai (his mourning garb provokes Esther's sympathetic reaction; his news of the king's decision and his own challenge to her to approach the king provokes her initial involvement; his argument that subdues her resistance provokes her courageous decision). At the same time responsibility for future progress of the plot is being shifted to Esther: on the one hand, the three initiatives in communication are primarily hers, though they are also responses to others, and on the other, she begins to take decisive charge, a symbol of which is that the whole episode concludes with Mordecai doing what Esther has commanded (v. 17).

We should add to this mastery of structural function some details of narrative subtlety. We can concentrate first on the objects of 'sending'. Against the colourfully painted backdrop of the edict's being 'sent' by couriers throughout the empire (3.13), in 4.8 we find Mordecai sending into the palace not just the news of the decree but a written copy of the edict. It is a physical counterpart of the clothes that Esther has sent out in the previous communication scene (v. 4), but unlike the clothes, the edict is a token that cannot be refused. This is because with clothes Mordecai has a choice, but with the edict there is no choice. There is no counter-edict (though there is a 'counter' set of clothes)—at least there is no counter-edict yet. When there is, Mordecai will wear palace clothes, royal robes of blue and white (8.15), and, proleptically, even before there is, but as soon as the balance has begun to tip in the Jews' favour, Mordecai will have the use of royal robes temporarily, for a day. Now, in ch. 4, the edict is the clothing that Esther must 'wear'.

Here too in 4.8 we find Mordecai 'commanding' (צוה) Esther for the third time, with clear resonances of the first two occasions. In 2.10, on entering the palace, Esther did not make known her kindred or race, since Mordecai had 'commanded' (צוה) that she should not. We are reminded of his command and her obedience again at 2.20 as being of continuing validity during her reign since she 'obeyed Mordecai just as when she was brought up by him'. In ch. 2, as in ch. 4, Esther's obedience is precisely over the issue of her ethnic identity. Then it was to be concealed, now it is to be revealed, and Mordecai is to be the arbiter of the right time and the right place. Now the Jews are to be regarded as *her* people, now she must identify herself as a Jew to the king. Esther will 'obey' Mordecai but now she is not just his adoptive daughter but a Jewish leader on whose behalf the Jews are to hold an exceptional fast, and so Mordecai must 'obey' Esther (4.17).

We stay a moment longer with ch. 4 to observe the rhetorical brilliance of Mordecai's famous speech (vv. 13-14). To Esther's understandable reluctance to enter the king's presence unbidden (v. 11), Mordecai responds, 'Think not that in the king's palace you will escape any more than all the other Jews' (v. 13). This is not so much a threat or a reproach as the other pan of the balance in which Esther's fate is being weighed. It is ironic that staying out of the king's presence is no less dangerous than entering it—an irony that Vashti had indeed already encountered in her own way. One queen stays out when bidden, the other will enter when unbidden; but whereas Vashti risked only the wrath of the king Esther risks the king's sentence of death or else a divine punishment on her and her family. 'Relief and deliverance will rise for the Jews' from some quarter or other—of that Mordecai is convinced—but the providence

that has set a Jewish queen on the Persian throne at 'such a time as
this' will doubtless be sorely displeased to find its instrument dumb
('if you keep silence . . . '). Contrary to common opinion, we should
remark, it is not likely that 'from another quarter' is an indirect way
of referring to God; for deliverance through Esther and deliverance
from God cannot be contrasted, and if 'quarter, place' signifies 'God'
(as in later Hebrew), what does 'another quarter' mean?[4] Mordecai,
still Esther's substitute father, laces his rhetoric with an unambiguous
hint at the wrath of the God conspicuous by his absence from the
pages of the story. Esther can hardly fail to be converted by appeal to
her religious susceptibilities as well as to her national consciousness
and her family feeling for her 'father's house' (among whom is not
least her adoptive father, who will no doubt be the first to fall to
Haman).

III

A brief notice may finally be taken of the accounts of the banquets
prepared by Esther. Their very existence sustains the ironic note
evident at many points in the book, but at the same time they contain
a subtle development of the plot. Banqueting has been presented to
us as the Persian pastime *par excellence*: the king has arranged two
for himself (1.3, 5), and one for Esther (2.18), and Vashti has had her
private banquet for the ladies (1.9). Then, too, Haman and Ahasuerus
have sealed their bargain with a ceremonious drinking (3.15).
Banqueting is the Persians' opportunity for conspicuous consumption,
for displays of wealth, and, evidently, for the drinking (שתה) that lies
at the heart of banqueting (משתה) (cf. 1.7-8; 5.6; 7.2).[5] The Jews, on
the other hand, have only been represented as going without food: in
4.3, wherever the king's command and his decree came, there was
great mourning among the Jews, with fasting. In 4.16 Esther has
bidden Mordecai 'gather all the Jews to be found in Susa, and hold a
fast on my behalf, and neither eat nor drink for three days, night or
day. I and my maids will also fast as you do.' Persians feast
extravagantly, for one hundred and eighty days (1.4), Jews fast
extravagantly. This is a fast of quite exceptional severity. A fast was
usually from morning to evening (Judg. 20.26; 2 Sam. 1.12), and a
longer fast, like one of seven days (1 Sam. 31.13), will hardly have
been a night and day fast. This fast even—so it seems—abolishes the
celebration of Passover, despite the law of Exodus 12; for the last

notation of time (in 3.12) has revealed that the edict of Haman was
sent out on the thirteenth day of the first month, and the three-day
fast begins the same day, on the eve of Passover. Esther herself, both
Jewish girl and Persian queen, moves directly from one sphere to the
other, from her Jewish fast to her Persian feast—which, we should
remind ourselves, she was 'preparing' (5.4) for the king and Haman
even while she was fasting! It is a complex irony that while the Jews
fast at Esther's bidding because of the king's decree that has put them
in the power of Haman their Jewish protectress at the Persian court
prepares banquet after banquet for the twin engineers of her own and
her people's doom.

As for the two banquets themselves, it is often thought that the
reason why Esther does not state her business directly at the first
banquet is merely to prolong the suspense. That it certainly does; but
there is a more subtle narrative reason. At the first banquet, upon the
king's invitation to her to state her request (5.3), Esther's first
response has been to invite him to a second banquet (5.4). But her
second response (5.7-8) is to oblige the king in advance to 'grant [her]
petition and fulfil [her] request'—sight unseen—and to signify his
obligation publicly by attending that second banquet with Haman.
Unlike the first banquet, which she said she had already prepared,
the second will be prepared only when the king has agreed—by his
acceptance of the invitation—to meet the demand Esther will make.
Esther has at the first banquet given notice (to the reader who
ponders the story) that—contrary to courtly etiquette—she intends
to take the king's generosity more or less literally and ask for the
'half' of his kingdom in asking for the life of his 'second', Haman.
And by the end of her speech Esther has been able to represent what
she wants as a matter of doing 'what the king has said' (v. 8), as
though it were she rather than he who was doing the favour. The
dialogue of vv. 3-7, we see, has all been a delicate play of bargaining
in which Esther manages to achieve her goal without ever disclosing
the object of the play.[6] The text of the narrative is immensely rich
and subtle, evidencing at every point the craftsmanship of the
narrator.

It is only against the narrative skill and rhetorical delicacy of the
narrator that what we must frankly call the hamfistedness of chs. 9–
10 can fairly be measured. It has frequently been argued that 9.20-32
and 10.1-3 have the air of secondary additions, and those arguments

will have to be rehearsed, together with a riposte to a recent writer
who has denied that there is anything strange or secondary about
9.20–10.3 (Chapter 4). But first I will suggest (Chapter 3) a number
of reasons why the preceding verses also, the narrative of 9.1-19,
should be regarded as secondary to that of chs. 1–8, a thesis that has
not before been argued, so far as I am aware.[7]

Chapter 3

THE ENDING OF THE ESTHER SCROLL (9.1-19)

Once we are prepared to entertain the possibility of a break between
ch. 8 and ch. 9 we are able to consider the story of ch. 9 (vv. 1-19 in
the first place) as narrative in its own right, and probe its narratival
and psychological logic. When we do so, I believe that we find that,
far from presenting a vivid, subtle and dramatic story such as chs. 1–
8 contained, 9.1-19 is striking for its poor construction, its inferior
narrative development, and its logical weaknesses. It is not easy to
demonstrate inferior narrative skill, since to some extent a judgment
in that area may be a matter of taste, but in the area of narrative logic
there are certain qualities of self-consistency and coherence that are
common to all kinds of straightforward linear narratives. And it is in
this area that the sequence 9.1-19 is markedly deficient. Among the
logical narrative weaknesses of 9.1-19 the following six items must be
mentioned.

1. By the end of ch. 8 it is clear that the two opposing decrees are
both valid. As Paton put it, 'According to the irrevocable law of 3^{13},
the heathen are to kill the Jews; and, according to the equally
irrevocable law of 8^{11}, the Jews are to kill the heathen. Lively times
are to be anticipated.' On the contrary, however, lively times do not
ensue in ch. 9, where no one in the empire takes a stand on the first
royal decree, and no Jew is killed—or even attacked. The conceptual
or documentary crisis (the conflict of the two decrees) of ch. 8 is not
played out, but ignored, in the narrative of ch. 9. The narrative would
have been the same if the first decree had indeed been revoked.[1]

2. The second decree gave permission to the Jews 'to destroy, to
slay, and to annihilate' any armed force that might attack them[2] or
their wives or children (8.11).[3] In ch. 9, however, there is no mention
of any attack upon the Jews, but to the contrary it is the Jews who
appear to take the initiative, and the objects of their slaughter are

never spoken of as an armed force (as חיל in 8.11 signifies) but simply as 'those who hated them' (שנאיהם, 9.1), 'those who sought their hurt' (מבקשי רעתם, 9.2), 'their enemies' (איביהם, 9.5), 'those who hated them' (שנאיהם, 9.5), 'their enemies' (איביהם, 9.16), 'those who hated them' (שנאיהם, 9.16).[4] These are much more general terms that envisage anti-Jewish feeling among communities in the empire rather than an officially inspired and organized act of aggression. The narrator of ch. 9 has presented a Jewish massacre of anti-Semites rather than Jewish self-defence against an imperially sponsored pogrom. It cannot have served his purpose either as storyteller or as propagandist to have made this massacre the sequel of the conflicting decrees, and we can only conclude that the author of ch. 9 imperfectly understood the thrust of the plot of chs. 1–8. He knew chs. 1–8 only superficially as a story of Jewish triumph over a heathen plot—which indeed it is—and lacked the subtlety to imagine a victory that could not be quantified by a body-count.

3. In his endeavour to repair what he must have seen as a regrettable deficiency in the book, he used phrases and motifs from chs. 1–8 in the service of his conception of how the story should end. But he was no match for the practised author of the original tale, and the maladroitness of his graffing in shows.

Thus the motif of the 'fear of the Jews' which he uses in 9.2 is borrowed from 8.17, but to very different effect. The fear of the Jews which in 8.17 fell upon 'many from the peoples of the land', i.e. from the various nations of the Persian empire, was a religious awe. It was a fear that had nothing to do with any perceived military prowess of the Jews, but rather with the sensitivity of these proselytes to the religious significance of the events that had befallen. The reversal of fortune of the Jewish people that had been achieved by a series of implausible coincidences (from the human point of view) infallibly displayed where truth lay in matters of religion. The phrase is of course derived from older biblical texts, perhaps primarily from Joshua 2.9ff. where Rahab says:

> I know that Yahweh has given you the land, and that the fear of you has fallen upon us, and that all the inhabitants of the land melt away before you. For we have heard how Yahweh dried up the water of the Red Sea before you when you came out of Egypt, and what you did to the two kings of the Amorites . . . And as soon as we heard it, our hearts melted, and there was no courage left in any man, because of you; for Yahweh your God is he who is God in heaven above and on the earth beneath.

Cf. also Exodus 15.16 and Psalm 105.38. Even by comparison with the Joshua text, where it is both God's mighty act against the natural order and his deed of valour against the hostile kings that evoke this language, Esther 8.17 is further demilitarized and it is solely the non-violent, political capability of the Jews and their God that provokes this rash of proselytism.

As such, there is a kind of spiritual plausibility about 8.17. By contrast, 9.2 is crass, materialistic and unbelievable: when the Jews have gathered, combat-ready, in their cities, 'no one could make a stand against them, for the fear of them had fallen upon all peoples'. The awe that had enlightened the Gentiles, gathering others to the Lord besides those already gathered (as the prophet would say), has here materialized into a fear that—incredibly—prevents 75,000 anti-Semites from raising a hand in self-defence against the massed ranks of Jewish hit-squads. We are in a quite different thought-world in ch. 9.

If we do not distinguish in this way between chs. 8 and 9, but try to read them harmoniously, as has previously been done, misunderstandings are inevitable. Thus Paton comments on 8.17: 'So completely were the tables turned, that it was now dangerous not to be a Jew'.[5] This reading does not arise naturally from 8.17, but is palpably a retrojection of ch. 9, for at 8.17 it is not danger but enlightenment that brings about proselytism; it is not a matter of universal trembling in the face of Jewish might (as it is in 9.2) but of discriminating decision ('many from the peoples'); and it is not a question of enforced and unwilled passivity on the part of anti-Jews (as in 9.2) but of a deliberate action on the part of some Gentiles (who are not necessarily 'enemies of the Jews') of declaring or making themselves Jews (מתיהדים).[6] Moore likewise misses the point of 8.17 in remarking that 'In light of the subsequent statistics concerning the slaughter of the Jews' enemies (ix 16), their fear of the Jews was quite justified'.[7] Or again, we find Gerleman expressing surprise that the simple permission given to the Jews to defend themselves should arouse such enthusiasm for Judaism among Gentiles;[8] but it is not the simple permission, nor even a prudential fear of the Jewish people, that is accountable, but the פחד, religious awe, that has fallen upon them. It is not indeed a fear precisely of the Jews, though the narrator is obliged to say that because he is avoiding specifically religious language, but of the God of the Jews, as Hoschander,[9] Ringgren,[10] and Dommershausen,[11] among others,[12] have seen.

Things are altogether different in ch. 9, where the fear is quite simply fear of the Jews themselves and the might they evince; in just the same way the author of ch. 9 can present 'the fear of Mordecai', which is no numinous dread, but a simple, undeniably this-worldly, anxiety not to displease a higher-ranking imperial official. It is fear of Mordecai that is the motivation for the princes, satraps, governors and royal officials to 'help' the Jews (v. 3). The strikingly different conceptions of 'fear' should make it plain that no one who had written 8.17 could also write 9.3.

4. Other aspects of the wording of 9.1-5 are strange if they come from the author of chs. 1–8. The first is the set of references to the 'enemies' of the Jews and 'those who hated' them. For in chs. 1–8 there are no *enemies* (in the plural!) of the Jews.[13] Haman is the *only* enemy of the Jews. He is so called by the narrator at 3.10 and 8.1, and so accused by Esther at 7.6. The plot to destroy the Jewish people is Haman's own, and it is explicitly portrayed as his personal act of revenge against Mordecai for refusing to do courtly obeisance to him; he 'disdained to lay hands on Mordecai alone' and so set about to destroy 'all the Jews, the people of Mordecai' (3.6). The people of the Persian empire, on the other hand, are never depicted as opposed to the Jews. When the edict of Haman is issued, 'the city of Susa was perplexed', or, 'thrown into confusion' (NEB) (3.15), i.e. the metropolis of Susa as distinct from the acropolis where the palace is.[14] Paton remarks: 'That the people of Susa would feel any great grief over the destruction of the Jews is improbable. The author here ascribes his own emotions to them.'[15] But that he could not do if he regarded them as anti-Semites, even potentially so! Persian distress at the first edict is matched by Persian rejoicing at the second: when the decree is issued 'in Susa the acropolis' and Mordecai is clothed in royal robes 'the metropolis Susa shouted and rejoiced' (8.14f.).[16] It is perhaps a little cynical to suggest, as Moore does, that 'the cheering of the Gentiles may have been more an expression of their dislike and rejection of Haman than of their approval of Mordecai'.[17] Even if they have no especially warm personal regard for Mordecai, whom the populace can recognize only as the object of the recent conspicuous but somewhat foolish display of honour, they certainly appear to have no objection to the fact that he is Jewish.

Perhaps it is in the light of Persian sympathy with the Jews that we should understand Mordecai's evident confidence that if the Jewish queen does not save her people, 'relief and deliverance will rise for the Jews from another quarter' (4.14); is he banking on the goodwill of the inhabitants of the empire as the instruments of a reliable divine providence?

Haman is the only enemy the Jews have. Even his family are not portrayed as anti-Jewish, just anti-Mordecai. Zeresh his wife indeed recommends that Haman should arrange for Mordecai to be impaled on a 75-foot pole in their courtyard (5.14), but this advice seems more to humour her husband who confesses that every honour does him no good, 'so long as I see Mordecai sitting at the king's gate' (5.13), rather than out of any settled hatred of the Jewish people as such. The other passage where Zeresh comments on Mordecai is specially significant. When Haman reports to his family how he has been humiliated by having to honour Mordecai (Mordecai has indeed been elevated, but not in the manner or in the place that Haman had intended), his wise men and his wife say to him, 'If Mordecai, before whom you have begun to fall, is of the Jewish people, you will not prevail against him but will surely fall before him' (6.13).

It is at first hard to see why this seemingly temporary reverse to Haman's plans should evoke such an alarmist response from his wife and his 'advisors' (as his 'friends' of 5.10, 14; 6.13 have become now that deep issues are on the agenda). It can only be that they see in the elevation of Mordecai a symbol of a fate to which they know he and his people are destined, a fate which involves the overthrow of Haman. Their response is not a simple fatalism nor even a shrewd calculation that since Mordecai's star is in the ascendant Haman's must be in decline—for that would not explain the reference to the Jewish people. In the background must lie the ancestry of Haman, the Agagite (3.1), descendant of Agag the Amalekite (1 Sam. 15), as against the ancestry of Mordecai, descendant of the Benjaminite Kish (is he Saul's father?).[18] The reference may perhaps be to the conflict between Saul (son of Kish) and Agag the Amalekite in 1 Samuel 15, but it is more probably to the Balaam oracles of the downfall of Amalek:

> Amalek was the first of the nations,
>> but in the end he shall come to destruction (Num. 24.20).

> His [Jacob/Israel's] king shall be higher than Agag,
>> and his kingdom shall be exalted (24.7).

Of course it is impossible that Haman's family and friends should have known Jewish literature so well, as Paton not over-subtly remarks. But the important point, which the commentators miss, is that Haman's associates evince no indelible anti-Jewish sentiment but capitulate to the Jewish side as soon as Haman suffers no more than a symbolic rejection. They were eager enough to have Mordecai impaled when Mordecai's continued tenure of office was taking the edge off Haman's delight in hobnobbing with the royals (5.13f.), but the moment Haman tells them of the rather farcical charade in which he—still 'one of the king's most noble princes' according to his own job description (6.9)—has paraded Mordecai through the streets they meekly accept that their patron has no chance before the unstoppable Jewish people. Haman is out in the cold, where he has always really been, *the* enemy of the Jews, their one and only.

Haman's problem is that he is not a Persian. Persians are—according to the evidence of the story—vinous, pompous, sexist, choking to death on their bureaucratic red tape, incapable of making decisions without consultations, prone to tantrums and decidedly feckless about the welfare of the subject peoples of the empire. But they are not evil.[19] It is Haman the Agagite who is the genocidal maniac. Haman has talked the king into permitting the massacre of the Jewish people—on quintessentially racist grounds ('it is unAryan[20] to tolerate them')—and the king, though morally responsible for what is done in his name, has nothing against the Jews. He doesn't even know that there is an edict against them, nor that his queen is a member of the proscribed race. Haman stands alone in his atavistic hatred of them.

The author of the Greek Addition E to the book also saw clearly how sharply Haman is to be distinguished from Ahasuerus in his attitude to the Jews. In his fictitious letter of Artaxerxes inserted after 8.12, he recounts how 'Haman . . ., a Macedonian, certainly not of Persian blood, and very different from us in generosity . . . hoped to catch us defenseless [by depriving us of Mordecai and Esther] and to transfer the rule of the Persians to the Macedonians' (E 10, 14 NAB). A note in the NAB appropriately comments that the supplementer 'used the designation *Macedonian* . . . to express, after Macedonia's conquest of Persia, the most odious kind of man that a Persian ruler could be supposed to think of'.

If none of the other principal characters of the book beside Haman is portrayed as anti-Jewish, what of those minor characters, the court officials who reported to Haman Mordecai's non-compliance with the courtly custom of obeisance (3.3f.)? Surely their informing on him cannot be an act of friendship? The narrative here is highly nuanced and—no doubt for that reason—commonly misunderstood. Mordecai's refusal to bow down is not, as some have thought, unmotivated and irrational, and narrated only to provide some literary reason for Haman's hostility to Mordecai,[21] nor because Mordecai as a Jew refused homage to any but God,[22] but simply because as a Jew he would not bow to an Agagite.[23] Mordecai can hardly have held down any job in the Persian bureaucracy without frequent routine bowing down; but no problem of proskynesis arises before Haman is promoted over Mordecai. Mordecai's fellow-officials are therefore faced with a novel anomaly of behaviour, and, being bureaucrats, naturally endeavour to bend Mordecai to the norm. Says Paton, reasonably enough, 'the courtiers bear Mordecai no grudge, and give him fair warning of his danger';[24] and Mordecai obviously pleads in his defence that he is a Jew (3.4). Whether he highmindedly tells them only that or further explains why being a Jew makes him unable to contemplate bowing to Haman we do not know; it is perhaps not accidental that the clause 'for he had told them that he was a Jew' (כי־הגיד להם אשר־הוא יהודי, v. 4) does not come (in some form or another) at a more natural place but follows 'they told Haman, in order to see whether Mordecai's words would stand (הֲיַעַמְדוּ)'. It is as if they have given up seeing the issue as a conflict between courtier and protocol and have come to see it, as does Mordecai, as a conflict between Jew and Agagite.

Does not their interest in whether Mordecai's words would prevail signify their suspicion (like that of Haman's advisers in 6.13) that the Jew is the one they favour to win this contest? For if there is not something special about Jewishness, why should they suppose that there is any question of Mordecai's attitude prevailing? He has against him court ceremonial and Haman's status—but above all, the commandment of the king, which is explicitly stated in v. 2, and obedience to which is made the point of issue in the courtiers' question to Mordecai (v. 3). This is the unalterable law of the Medes and Persians that Mordecai is up against; if the courtiers find it worth speculating whether Mordecai may prevail against that, either life at the Persian court is very boring or else the courtiers have a sneaking suspicion that the Jew is going to get away with his insubordination. Even if we simply believe that the courtiers tire of Mordecai's non-conformity, 'become irritated and resolve to bring him to his senses by calling Haman's attention to him',[25] we are far from any notion of an anti-Jewish conspiracy. Here too we fail to find any hint that the Jews, as Jews, have enemies in the Persian empire.

Where then have the 75,000 or more enemies of the Jews in ch. 9 appeared from? We can only reply: From a different author's conception of the story, for there is not a trace of them in the main body of the narrative.

5. Other minor conflicts of wording between 9.1-5 and chs. 1–8 include:

(i) The events of Adar 13 are presented as a matter of the Jews' enemies' hoping to get the mastery (שלט) over them, and of the Jews' getting the mastery (שלט) over their foes (v. 1). The term is not used in chs. 1–8, where the issue is represented rather as annihilation of the Jews versus their freedom to defend themselves and in so doing to destroy any armed force that should attack them.

(ii) No indication is given in chs. 1–8 that the Jews dwell in particular cities, as 'in their cities' in 9.2 implies.

(iii) The officials of the empire are classified in 9.3 as 'princes of the cities, or, regions' (שרי המדינות), 'satraps' (אחשדרפנים), 'governors' (פחות), and 'officials' (עשי המלאכה). In 3.12 and 8.9, however, they are 'satraps', 'governors' and 'princes', in that order, the correct order of rank. There are indeed minor variations between 3.12 and 8.9, but they are legitimate alternative ways of indicating the functions of the three ranks: thus in 3.12 the satraps are 'royal satraps' (אחשדרפני־ המלך), in 8.9 just 'the satraps' (האחשדרפנים); in 3.12 the governors are 'the provincial/city governors' (הפחות אשר על־מדינה ומדינה), in 8.9 just 'the governors' (הפחות); in 3.12 the 'princes' are 'the princes of all the peoples' (שרי עם ועם), i.e. ethnarchs or tribal chieftains, in 8.9 'the princes of the regions/cities' (שרי המדינות). Bardtke attempted to account for the different order in ch. 9 by arguing that in 3.12 and 8.9 the officials are viewed as recipients of imperial decrees and are consequently named in order of rank; whereas in 9.3 they are viewed from the perspective of the Jews, the more local officials ('ethnarchs') being named first, and those of higher rank second.[26] He admitted, however, that he could not on this principle explain why the highest officials, satraps, are mentioned before governors, nor why a fourth category, 'officials', was included. It seems more probable that another author who wrote rather more loosely of such matters was responsible for ch. 9. His use of the term 'officials' (עשי המלאכה) was no doubt borrowed from 3.9, where it was used in a non-specific sense; but he did not realize that it was a general term that could not be properly added to the three established categories.

6. A motif adapted none too cleverly from chs. 1–8 by the author of ch. 9 is that of the king's generosity. The depiction in ch. 9 is quite other from the scenes in 5.3, 6; 7.2, where the king's offer to fulfil Esther's request is in each case grounded in a previously narrated request made by the queen. In 5.3 the request has been made silently by the queen's entering his presence unbidden; in 5.6 the king's offer is a response to Esther's invitation to her first banquet; in 7.2 it is his response to her invitation to her second banquet. In 9.12, on the other hand, it is unmotivated by any request on Esther's part: it is when the king hears that five hundred men have been slain in the acropolis of Susa that he asks Esther what her request is. Why should he suppose she has any request? Has she not received in full the request she has already made, for the second decree to be issued, authorizing the Jewish people to defend themselves?

Further, it does appear that the king is astonished[27] (though not angry, as b. Megillah makes out[28]) at the news, especially when he attempts some mental arithmetic over the extent of the massacre when extrapolated to the whole empire. Why then should he invite a further request from Esther? Has the woman not done enough damage already?

Further, why does the king take—for the first time in the book—a significant initiative without any courtly advice? Elsewhere we have had this ruler depicted as unable to decide what to do about the recalcitrant Vashti without the wisdom of his lawyers (1.13ff.), unable to devise a plan for obtaining for himself a new queen (2.2ff.), unable to see that a man who is willing to pay 10,000 talents for the king's signature may not be doing the king as big a favour as he is doing himself (3.8ff.), unable to concoct any scheme for rewarding a hitherto overlooked benefactor and reliant upon the first busybody whom the insomniac monarch happens to hear shuffling about in the lobby, incapable of seeing through Esther's little banquet routine in which his prime minister will be served up as the main course, unable to decide what to do with Haman once he has been unmasked, unable to compose a decree that will ameliorate, though it cannot undo, the dreadful fate his fecklessness had foisted upon the kinsman of his queen. We wonder whether it is the same king who now takes the initiative in extending the *carte blanche* to the Jewish people to continue 'doing as they pleased to those who hated them'.

Can we explain this novel behaviour on the part of the king? Is it perhaps a token of surrender? Has Esther too, like her people, gained the upper hand, despite her lord's masterful language ('it shall be granted to you', v. 12)? Is the king as much at her mercy to stop the killing as she was at his to start it? Is he really still the same indecisive Ahasuerus as we have known all along, appealing to his queen now for advice for his next move? Have perhaps too many of his courtiers succumbed to the Jewish attack? If this were to be the appropriate reading, ch. 9 would not be out of tune with chs. 1–8. But there is one further factor that weighs against such a reading.

This is the response of Esther. Her request is that the Jews in Susa 'be allowed tomorrow also to do according to this day's edict' (v. 13). This request lacks any narrative motivation, i.e. it is illogical in the context of the book as a whole. The decree *against* the Jews applied only to the thirteenth of Adar, and the decree allowing Jewish self-defence makes sense only against the background of the first decree. If on the fourteenth the Jews suffer any attack, it will be an illegal attack and the Jews will need no royal permission to defend themselves. But if the author of this chapter can be distinguished from that of chs. 1–8, we can soon conclude that he reckoned essentially with only one decree which—far from merely allowing Jews to defend their lives—gave them a free hand to deal with their opponents as they would (vv. 1, 5). Esther's request then, in this narrower context, becomes intelligible as a boon that will further Jewish supremacy at the heart of the Persian empire. There has been enough blood-letting in the provinces to put the fear of God—so to speak—into their inhabitants, but in Susa the capital[29] it will pay to stamp out more anti-Semites.

The alternative to this disjunction of ch. 9 from the preceding chapters can only be to admit that the second day of slaughter indeed lacks narrative motivation and has solely a liturgical motivation, i.e. it exists to explain how it came about that the Jews of Susa, unlike Jews elsewhere, celebrated the fifteenth of Adar as the day of festival. If they did not celebrate till the fifteenth—so the logic must have run—they must still have been fighting on the fourteenth; if they were fighting on the fourteenth, they must have had the permission of the thirteenth extended; if permission was extended, it must have been extended by the king.[30] The liturgical anomaly has quite simply created out of nothing this element of the narrative. Dommershausen, too, who is most alert to the finer nuances of the

text, throws in the towel at this point and pronounces the reason for
Esther's request to be really 'aetiological-literary'; that is to say, 'The
Jewish author wishes to explain and account for a custom existing in
his own day: why Jews of the countryside begin the Purim festival on
Adar 14 and Jews of Susa on Adar 15 ... He puts no value upon
causal, psychological or, indeed, moral elements.'[31] Dommershausen
compares two other places where there has been the repetition of a
scene—2.19, 'when the virgins were gathered a second time', and 8.3,
'then Esther spoke again to the king'—and remarks that in all three
cases this device of 'repeated narrative' has an air of the improbable,
the doubtful and the awkward about it. 'One has the impression that
the author chose an inappropriate means for the expression of his
thought.'[32] 2.19 and 8.3 are to be understood differently from
Dommershausen, but his instinct about 9.12f. seems correct, as is his
confession that 'Ein höherer Sinn ist darum dieser Szene schwerlich
abzugewinnen'. Gerleman similarly judges that 'The second day of
massacre, which is from a narrative and artistic perspective superfluous
and intrusive, is necessary to explain and account for the two days of
the festival (18f.)'.[33]

This narrator, we may judge, is not the craftsman of chs. 1–8. Even
if it were true to say that the Esther story is essentially a 'Purim-
legend'—that is, a liturgically conceived narrative—it would be far
more than that: it is a coherent story in its own right, quite
independently of any Purim connection.

Chapter 4

THE APPENDICES OF THE ESTHER SCROLL (9.20–10.3)

I

We have already seen sufficient reason for denying the first nineteen verses of ch. 9 to the primary narrator of the Esther scroll. 9.1-19 has been defective as a story by comparison with the preceding chapters; and things do not improve thereafter. In fact, from 9.20 onwards, it is downhill all the way, from a dramatic, narrative, or even logical, point of view. It is not surprising that many commentators have regarded 9.20-32 or 9.20–10.3 as secondary to the rest of the book. So first, it seems, Michaelis;[1] then Bertheau, Kamphausen, Wildeboer, and Paton.[2] Most of the more recent studies, however, it must be admitted, take the opposite view: Anderson[3] thinks the arguments against the book's unity indecisive, Bardtke[4] and Gerleman[5] find no good reason to 'deny' the verses to the original narrator, and Moore[6] thinks the evidence for different authors far from conclusive. Dommershausen, for his part, opines that the whole story owes its conception to the Purim festival[7]—which of course necessitates treating ch. 9 as integral to the narrative—and Berg argues that even if vv. 29-32 (the verses she is principally concerned with) stem from a later hand, their 'author is sensitive to the style and spirit of the tale'.[8] These more recent writers appear to have been largely influenced by the Purim factor: viz. the presumption that the book as a whole has been composed in order to create a *hieros logos* for the Purim festival. If indeed it was Purim that brought the story into existence, it would seem not unreasonable to ascribe the passage, however banal and crudely written, describing the actual institution of Purim to the author of the narrative. But we have now seen sufficient reason for separating ch. 9 (from its very beginning) from chs. 1–8 and thus for severing the Purim connection altogether—which will enable us in due course to reconstruct a different genesis and history for the Esther story.

Among the difficulties presented by 9.20–10.3 are the following:

1. Verses 20-22 give an alternative account to v. 19 of how the festival in the month of Adar came to be celebrated annually by the Jews. 9.19 implies that the celebration of Adar 14 had become a practice among Jews—at least among those of the 'villages'—which had developed spontaneously over a period of years; 9.20-22, on the other hand, implies that the observance of Adar 14 (and 15) by the Jews (whether in Susa or in the provinces) was in response to Mordecai's instruction.

This difficulty is relieved by supposing that v. 19 is a gloss.[9] Its introductory words עֹל־כֵּן may offer a hint of that; and there can be little doubt that it is an awkward verse, especially in its concentration upon the Jews of the 'villages' and their custom without regard for Jews elsewhere. The LXX plus at the end of v. 19, 'And those who dwell in the cities (ἐν ταῖς μητροπόλεσιν) also celebrate the fifteenth of Adar with good cheer (εὐφροσύνην ἀγαθὴν ἄγουσιν), sending portions also to their neighbours', would cope with the latter problem if the clause could be thought a witness to a fuller MT of v. 19; but the clause itself seems to be secondary in the LXX, for two reasons. (i) 'Fifteenth' is represented in Vaticanus and several miniscules by τὴν ε′ καὶ ι′ (or τὴν ιε′),[10] whereas 'fourteenth' appears as τεσσαρεσκαιδεκάτην (or variants) in all but one miniscule; this may be evidence that the clause was originally a gloss in a Greek MS. (ii) It is a little strange to say that those in the cities sent portions 'also to [their] neighbours' (καὶ τοῖς πλησίον) where the previous clause has said that the Jews in the villages sent portions 'each to [his] neighbour' (ἕκαστος τῷ πλησίον [singular]).[11] So the LXX plus hardly relieves the MT v. 19 of awkwardness.[12]

If then v. 19 is to be designated a gloss, Mordecai's letter fits well with vv. 17-18 as Mordecai's resolution of what he sees to be an impending disagreement among the Jews. And v. 23 would mean that the Jews formally agreed to 'make customary' (קִבֵּל) *both* what they had begun to do (אֵת אֲשֶׁר־הֵחֵלּוּ לַעֲשׂוֹת), i.e. to celebrate the deliverance with a holiday, *and* what Mordecai had instructed them to do (וְאֵת אֲשֶׁר־כָּתַב מָרְדֳּכַי אֲלֵיהֶם). Otherwise, if v. 19 is to be envisaged as preceding v. 23 chronologically, 'what they had begun to do' would seem to refer to the continuing *commemoration* of the deliverance, on the *fourteenth*—which would be different from what 'Mordecai had written to them'.[13]

2. The connection of vv. 24-26a with their context, and their

function in the book, are far from evident. In Chapter 1, where the Masoretic book was being viewed as a whole, I suggested that the best reading of these verses was to take them as part of Mordecai's letter to Jews throughout the empire, who would otherwise not have known that the first decree was the work of Haman, that lots had been cast in connection with the pogrom, or that Haman had suffered execution and impalement. But when we consider the wording more closely with a redaction-critical eye, we find that such an explanation of the function of these verses in the book as it stands will not satisfy any enquiry about origins, viz. how they come to be where they are. They offer, it is true, a brief summary of the plot of the story, but it is inadequate to label these verses merely a recapitulation of the plot—on three grounds: (i) If they are a recapitulation, some reason has to be advanced why the plot should need recapitulating. (ii) Some explanation must be given for why this summary of the plot is introduced by כי, 'for', as though the summary was being adduced as an explanation for something which was not already clear. (iii) The summary differs from the narrative of the book in a number of details.

On the first point, no readers of the book learn anything from this summary that they do not know already. There is no narrative or logical reason why the plot should be summarized, so the suspicion arises that these verses are not integral to the primary story of the book but have their origin elsewhere.

On the second point, the כי ostensibly introduces the plot summary as an explanation for why the Jews undertook to celebrate the days of deliverance according to Mordecai's command (לקים עליהם, v. 21). But in fact, the proximate cause of the Jews' undertaking commemorative celebration is Mordecai's charge—and beyond that, their own instinctive reaction after the day of deliverance—and beyond that, the events that led to the danger. All of these causes, proximate and remote, the reader is already familiar with, so the verses are completely otiose. Superfluity is not in itself a sign of diverse authorship, but it helps to sustain the suspicion raised by several aspects of these verses.

On the third point, it is unnecessary to be hypercritical about such divergences between the narrative and the summary as may arise simply from the exigencies of compression. Nevertheless, the following points of difference cannot be overlooked:

a. The summary presents as the primary issue of the plot the decree of Haman and its fatal consequences for himself. This differs from the plot of chs. 1–8, where the issue is the relationship of the two decrees, and even differs from the plot of 9.1-20, where the issue is the Jews' massacre of their enemies in accord with a royal edict authorizing them to take revenge on those who hated them.

b. The casting of Pur, the lot, was in 3.7 performed simply to determine an auspicious day to fix for the destruction of the Jews. It could not be said—as it is in this summary—from the narrative of ch. 3 that Pur was cast in order to destroy the Jews. Indeed, the fixing of the day plays such a minor role in ch. 3 that, from the perspective of that chapter, it probably deserves no place at all in any two-sentence summary of the whole narrative.

c. It appears from vv. 24-26a that the king had no knowledge of Haman's plan, but that at the moment it was brought to his attention he gave orders for Haman's execution. Such a summary significantly misrepresents the tempo of the narrative's development.

d. In the narrative, unlike the summary, the king did not give orders 'in writing' for the execution of Haman or the impalement of Haman and his sons.[14]

e. In the narrative, unlike the summary, it is not Haman's plot against the Jews that comes upon his own head, but his plot against Mordecai.[15]

f. In the summary, Esther's part in the development of the narrative is completely ignored, and it appears that it is solely the king's sense of justice or goodwill towards the Jews that has delivered them from Haman's decree. Despite the Vulgate, Peshitta, Targums, AV, RSV, NAB, and various commentators[16] the Hebrew makes no reference to Esther in v. 25: וּבְבֹאָהּ must mean 'and when it (the matter) came (before the king)', since there is no mention of Esther in the context.[17]

g. Of lesser significance is the fact that the summary gives the impression that Haman and his sons were impaled at the same time, whereas in the narrative some months have intervened between the two events. The compression of the two events is understandable in a summary.[18]

These points are evidence that these verses are the work of a different author from that of chs. 1–8. It is not clear that they show that vv. 20-32 as a whole are secondary, since it is hard to imagine a single author linking vv. 24-26a to v. 23 with כִּי.

Some scholars, nevertheless, maintain that vv. 24-26a make good sense in their present position. Bardtke describes them as a recapitulation of the prehistory of the Purim festival, designed to explain the meaning of the name Purim, and he smooths over the discrepancies between this summary and the Esther narrative with the disarming but tendentious comment that the summary is so short that differences between it and the narrative are bound to exist[19] (tendentious because there can be no question, in the nature of the case, but that a summary will differ from what it summarizes; he means that the differences can all be explained as due to the necessities of summarizing—but that is to beg the question).

An original attempt to explain the connective particle כי with which v. 24 begins has been made by Dommershausen.[20] He argues that these verses continue the letter of Mordecai whose contents have been reported in indirect speech in vv. 21-22. They are a continuation not in indirect speech but in direct speech, as *erlebte Rede*,[21] a technique designed to enliven the presentation of events. But if we compare other examples of *erlebte Rede* in Biblical narrative, it is difficult to believe that the author of the 'catechism-like' verses[22] would have employed one of the more subtle rhetorical devices of the fluent narrator. And Dommershausen does not offer any explanation for why the report of v. 23 should intrude into an account of Mordecai's letter.

We should conclude that vv. 24-26a form a substantial piece of evidence that ch. 9 contains secondary material.

3. The logical connections in v. 26 are hard to discern. The first על-כן purportedly presents the preceding verse(s) as an explanation of why the Jews called their days of celebration Purim. Plainly, however, the author of these verses felt the connection to be somewhat opaque, since he found it necessary to add 'on account of the term Pur'. If the summary of the plot had been satisfactorily constructed around the term Pur, it would have been enough to say 'Therefore [= on account of what has just been narrated] they called these days Purim' (על-כן קראו לימים האלה פורים). Only if the connection of the על-כן clause with what precedes was not sufficiently express need it be added, על-שם הפור, 'on account of the term Pur'—since that phrase is logically prior to the introductory particle על-כן. The difficulty also remains why the days are called Purim, 'lots' in the plural, when only one lot, Pur, was cast (v. 24).

The second על-כן is rather more difficult. It presents what precedes it as the explanation for why the Jews undertook to keep the two days of Purim in all generations. But the reason cannot be that given in v. 26a: 'they called these days Purim'. Perhaps the reason could be the summary narrative of vv. 24-25; though in that case we would expect 'and therefore' (וְעַל־כֵּן)—which is indeed what RSV finds it necessary to say. It seems, however, that here too the author has been aware that עַל־כֵּן is not a very appropriate connective, for he has digressed syntactically immediately after the particle to introduce a two-fold account of what the real explanation of the observance of Purim was. The initial 'therefore', in the process, loses its force completely; for if the reason *follows* עַל־כֵּן, it cannot also *precede* it. Needless to say, it can hardly be a normal use of עַל־כֵּן to refer to what follows it; the writing is simply clumsy.[23] The awkwardness can usually be covered up by translating, for example, 'Thus, because of all that was contained in this letter, and because of what they had witnessed and experienced in this affair, the Jews established...' (NAB); but it remains the fact that 'thus' does not refer to anything in particular.

4. Verses 26b-28 add so little, and at such length, to what has preceded, that this segment is open to suspicion as a second attempt to fashion a suitable ending for the book as the story of the origin of Purim. The use of אִגֶּרֶת (v. 26) for 'letter' instead of סְפָרִים of v. 20, to which 'this letter' of v. 26 refers, may be a pointer towards differing authorship.

It is true that the segment vv. 26b-28 is more explicit than the preceding verses in one respect: it prescribes observance of Purim for future generations of Jews and for proselytes, who indeed had not been mentioned previously; but it can hardly be imagined that Mordecai's letter of vv. 20-22 intended to exclude either descendants or proselytes. In all respects, therefore, these verses are nothing but an elaborate and formal repetition[24] and expansion of previous material.

5. The account of Esther's letter, vv. 29-32, appears to be yet another ending to the book. Verses 27-28 have evidently brought the book to a solemn and rhetorically satisfying conclusion; v. 29 is an unexpected resumption of the narrative. Unlike vv. 26b-28, it does introduce a new aspect into the observance of Purim; but it is an aspect that in a unified narrative would much more naturally have been incorporated at an earlier point. Verses 29-32 can most reasonably be regarded as an addition later even than vv. 20-28.[25]

The LXX text of vv. 29-32 may point to a different origin of these verses from that of vv. 20-28. For while in vv. 20-28 LXX is in general a quite faithful version of the Hebrew, in vv. 29-32 it deviates from it quite seriously and presents some completely unintelligible sentences. Whether this state of affairs signifies that the text of vv. 29-32 was still 'in a fluid state' at a time when the wording of vv. 20-28 was well established, as Loewenstamm suggests,[26] is hard to determine; but the essential fact of the differing character of LXX 9.20-28 and 9.29-32 is indisputable.[27]

However secondary vv. 29-32 may be, they themselves have been subjected to at least one further revision, apparently in an attempt to share the responsibility for authorization of Purim observance equally between Mordecai and Esther. In the first place, the words 'and Mordecai the Jew' in v. 29 seem to be an addition. The Hebrew has ותכתב אסתר המלכה בת־אביחיל ומרדכי היהודי; as Paton notes, the feminine singular agreeing with the nearest subject is possible, but is less usual than the plural.[28] The emendation mentioned by Brockington[29] and adopted by NEB, לְמָרְדְּכַי, 'to Mordecai', is far from convincing. The fact that Esther is called 'the queen' and also 'daughter of Abihail' whereas Mordecai is simply 'the Jew'—which does not distinguish him from Esther (gender apart!)—probably also suggests that the reference to Mordecai is secondary. What is more, it is evident that Esther is writing in order to support, or extend, the former letter of Mordecai; so it is perhaps less than natural that he should participate in this letter.[30]

In the second place, the phrase 'and Queen Esther' in v. 31 is also probably secondary. The verb here is, as in v. 29, in the singular, though on this occasion it is masculine, in agreement with the nearer subject, Mordecai. What is referred to is the letter(s) sent by Mordecai in vv. 20-23, in the composition and dispatch of which Esther took no part.[31]

In the third place, it is possible that the words 'this second' (הַזֹּאת הַשֵּׁנִית) in v. 29, modifying את־אגרת הפרים, 'the Purim letter', are a gloss[32] or perhaps a corruption.[33] For Esther's letter, which is itself the 'second' letter, can hardly have been written to 'confirm' or 'establish' itself (לקים את־אגרת הפרים הזאת השנית). It must be allowed, however, that it is possible to make sense of the Masoretic text if we ignore the force of the Masoretic punctuation; that is, by passing over the athnach under תקף, we could translate 'Esther wrote with full authority this second letter about Purim in order to make its observance obligatory'. That is to say, 'this second letter' would be the object of ותכתב, not of לקים.

However that may be, we are on reasonably firm ground in detecting secondary expansions in vv. 29-32. Our main point, nevertheless, is that vv. 29-32 are themselves secondary to vv. 20-28.

We may return now to consider the new aspect of the observance of Purim introduced by these verses. It is the element of 'matters of fasts and their (accompanying) lament(s)' (דברי הצמות וצעקתם). These words are syntactically awkward, so much so that several commentators regard them as totally unrelated to the rest of the verse and therefore secondary to vv. 29-32 as a whole.[34] We should perhaps, however, regard the 'matters of fasts and their lament(s)' as the object of קימו, 'they had established'; that is to say, whereas Mordecai had authorized the observance of the fourteenth and fifteenth of Adar as a celebration of Purim, the Jewish people themselves had instituted on their own initiative, 'for themselves and their descendants' (על־נפשם ועל־זרעם), a ritual of fasting and lamenting in commemoration of the danger.[35] Esther's letter then serves the double function of commending Mordecai's letter and of giving blessing to a custom that had grown up among her compatriots informally.[36] The addition of vv. 29-32, in other words, was made primarily to give official authorization to a popular Purim practice not envisaged by the scroll purporting to institute the festival of Purim. It may well be very much later than the previous verses, and certainly we are very far in time and intent from the original narrator of the Esther story.

6. Again we find that despite the note of pause upon which 9.32 ended the Masoretic book of Esther is not yet concluded. Various features of 10.1-3 mark it out as distinctive from everything that precedes it in the book, so that again we are entitled to raise the possibility of a separate origin.[37] Its distinctive features are:

a. The report of Ahasuerus's taxation is unmotivated and unlinked to the preceding material. It is difficult to see any purpose that is served by the sentence, which has the air of an introduction to a narrative that is summarily truncated.[38] From a narrative point of view, it is a false start. It certainly alludes to the power and wealth of the king, a theme with which the book began; but compared to the brilliance, colour, and irony of ch. 1, the inexplicitness of 10.1 is utterly lame, and in no way forms a suitable climax to a narrative so artfully begun.

Moore correctly remarks that many scholars have had difficulty in seeing the relevance of the imposition of a tax to the theme of Esther.[39] Those suggestions that have been made carry little

conviction. D. Daube thought that the levy was Mordecai's plan for
raising the 10,000 talents of revenue lost by the failure of Haman's
plan against the Jews (3.9)—a scheme moreover that would reap a
substantial annual benefit rather than a lump sum, however large.[40]
Ingenious though the suggestion is, it takes a lot for granted, and
comes to grief on the probability, which Daube admits (surprisingly),
that the narrative envisages that the money had actually been paid by
Haman. Thus, in 3.11 what we seem to read is a polite form of
acceptance of the money by the king; in 4.7 Mordecai informs Esther
of the 'exact sum of money that Haman had promised to pay' (no
hint of a refusal here); in 7.4 Esther's complaint is that 'we are *sold*';
and, to clinch it all, even if the 10,000 talents had not in fact already
been paid by Haman, in 8.1 the king had confiscated Haman's
property and had, by giving it to Esther, retained some sort of control
over it himself.

The more common view, that v. 1 serves simply to emphasize the
greatness of Ahasuerus's power and the well-nigh universal extent of
his rule, is more plausible an explanation, but an imposition of tax,
whether of tribute or labour (מם), was normally made either by way
of punishment of subjugated races (e.g. Jos. 16.10; 17.13; 1 Kings
9.20) or in order to achieve some royal project (e.g. 1 Kings 5.13). We
miss here any indication of a purpose in Ahasuerus's taxation.
Indeed, if we recall the only other passage in the book that may refer
to imperial taxation, we might well expect to read in 10.1 not of an
imposition of tax but of a *relaxation* of taxation. For in 2.18
Ahasuerus marked the joyful occasion of Esther's accession to the
throne with a הנחה for all the provinces—which may well have been a
remission of tax (so KB[3], RSV).[41] Might we not expect that the
installation of Mordecai as grand vizier (for the events of 8.15-17 are
surely in mind as a prelude to 10.2) should be accompanied by
another such act of royal benevolence? However that may be, we can
hardly count the book's failure to repeat that motif a narrative
weakness; the narrative weakness lies in the fact that the imposition
of taxation is given no logical motivation.

b. The reference to the 'Book of the Chronicles of the kings of
Media and Persia' (ספר דברי הימים למלכי מדי ופרס) appears to be
modelled upon the names of sources for *Hebrew* historiography—just
as the turn of phrase, 'And all the acts of *X*, are they not written in
Y?' is unmistakably reminiscent of the Old Testament historical
books (cf. 1 Kings 14.19, 24; 2 Chron. 25.26; 32.32). Have we not here

an author who is not content with the mere royal 'diary' (ספר דברי
הימים, 2.23) or 'memoranda' (ספר הזכרנות דברי הימים, 6.1), but must
introduce a new, more resounding, name for an evidently non-
existent work?[42]

A final, and rather decisive, indicator that these verses are the
work of an author other than the narrator of the main body of the
book is his use of the phrase 'Media and Persia' (מדי ופרס). Elsewhere
in Esther the names are in the reverse order: Persia and Media
(פרס ומדי) in 1.3, 14, 18, 19.[43] It is in Daniel that 'Media and Persia'
(מדי ופרס) appears (5.28; 6.9, 13, 16 [EVV 6.8, 12, 15]; 8.20)—and that
invariably.[44]

c. The last verse of the book is ineffably vague and general; it is so
inept a conclusion that it cannot be ascribed to the stylish narrator of
the main story. Are not the expressions 'great to the Jews' (גדול ליהודים),
'approved by the mass of his brothers' (רצוי לרב אחיו), 'seeking good
for his people' (דרש טוב לעמו), and 'speaking peace to all his offspring'
(דבר שלום לכל־זרעו) redolent of the sycophantic testimonial, the empty
rhetoric of the political speech?

We should compare some other conclusions to heroic tales, and
observe how the peroratory generalities are elsewhere always inter-
mingled with concrete details. The story of Judith, for example,
contains in its conclusion sentences like 'She was famous throughout
the whole country' (16.21) and 'Her fame continued to increase'
(16.23), and 'During her lifetime, and for long after her death, none
dared to threaten the Israelites' (16.25). But it also contains concrete
details such as 'She had many suitors', 'She lived until the age of one
hundred and five years', 'She gave her maid her liberty' (16.22f.). In 1
Maccabees 14, a summary statement about Simon includes generalities
such as 'He promoted his people's welfare' (14.4), 'His renown
reached the ends of the earth' (14.10), 'He rid the country of lawless
and wicked men' (14.14). But we also read that 'Among other notable
achievements he captured the port of Joppa' (14.5), 'He took Gazara
and Bethsura' (14.7), and 'He furnished the temple with many sacred
vessels' (14.15).

In summary, then, it may be argued that 10.1-3 forms an inelegant
and otiose conclusion to a book that already contained more than one
quite satisfactory conclusion. It is certainly not by the author of chs.
1–8; but it is impossible to tell, in view of its brevity and disjointedness,
whether it originally formed a piece with any of the matter of ch. 9 or
was yet another redactional supplement. Its concentration upon the

figure of Mordecai to the complete exclusion of Esther may give a clue to the purpose behind its creation. It may be that its author was unwilling that the book should conclude with the letter and command of Esther (9.32); but since we would not be wise to ascribe the alternation between Esther and Mordecai throughout ch. 9 to some imagined rivalry among their partisans, it may be better to confess that no satisfying explanation for the presence of 10.1-3 in the book suggests itself, apart perhaps from a desire to conclude the book with some grandiloquent phraseology that would match the self-esteem of a patriotic reader.

II

The most direct assault on the argument for the independence of 9.20–10.3 has recently been made by B.W. Jones in his paper on 'The So-Called Appendix to the Book of Esther',[45] who argues on a variety of literary and stylistic grounds that these verses are of a piece with the preceding narrative. The two primary features he notices are the use of 'approximate inclusio'[46] linking the beginning and end of the book, and a kind of finale effect called 'synthetic linear progression'.[47]

1. *Approximate inclusio*. This term indicates the repetition in the conclusion of motifs or terms present in the beginning of the story in the same or similar form. The instances given by Jones are the following:

(i) The one hundred and twenty-seven provinces of the Persian empire are mentioned both at 1.1 and at 9.30.

(ii) The king's wealth and power is described in some detail at the · beginning (1.1-4) and is referred to again at the end (10.1).

(iii) The empire of Ahasuerus is referred to as Persia and Media in 1.3, and as Media and Persia in 10.2 (the inversion of the names is called a 'chiastic inclusio').

(iv) The motif of eating and drinking is found both at 1.3, 5, 7ff. and at 9.17-19, 22, including the phrase עשה משתה, 'made a feast', three times in ch. 1 and three times in 9.17-19.

(v) The irreversibility of Persian law is referred to both at 1.19 and 9.27 (the phrase לא יעבור, 'it will not be altered / it will not fail', is used in both cases).

Grouping (i)-(iii) together under the rubric 'honour and greatness', we have *in toto* three 'themes' involved in the inclusio: honour and greatness, eating and drinking, irreversible law. In each case the language applied in ch. 1 to the Persians is applied in 9.20–10.3 to the Jews.

2. *Synthetic linear progression* refers to the recapitulation (synthesis) of key words that have appeared at earlier points of the book (not just at the beginning). The following eleven examples are referred to at various points in Jones's article:

(i) קִבֵּל: in 4.4 Mordecai refused to 'take' the clothes sent by Esther, in 9.23 the Jews 'undertake' to rejoice and in 9.27 'undertake' to observe the festival.

(ii) אָבֵל/אֵבֶל, 'mourning', has described the Jews' mourning in 4.3, Haman's mourning in 6.12, and the mourning that has been transformed into celebration in 9.22.

(iii) פַּרְשָׁה, 'exact accounting', in 4.7 refers to the exact sum Haman paid as a bribe for being allowed to kill the Jews, in 10.2 to the exact account of Mordecai recorded in the royal chronicles (the only two occurrences of the word in the book).

(iv) גְדוּלָה, 'greatness', is used in 1.4 of the greatness of the king, in 6.3 when the king asks what honour or dignity (גדולה) has been conferred on Mordecai, and in 10.2 of the honour to which Mordecai was ultimately advanced (cf. also the references to 'all the honours with which the king had honoured' Haman in 5.11 כל־אשר גדלו המלך).

(v) פוּר, the 'lot', is referred to in 3.7, and again in 9.24 (where the phrase הפיל פור הוא הגורל repeats that of 3.7 (הפיל פור הוא הגורל), and in 9.26 where the etymology is given. 'Without that ending, the first reference to the *pur* makes no sense and the book would have lost one of its reasons for being.'[48]

(vi) 'Fasts and their lamentation' (הַצֹּמוֹת וְזַעֲקָתָם) in 9.31 draws together elements from earlier places in the narrative: in 4.1 Mordecai utters a 'lament' (ויזעק זעקה גדלה), and in 4.3 and 16 the Jews 'fast' because of the decree and on Esther's behalf.

(vii) Haman is called in 9.24 'Haman the son of Hammedatha, the Agagite, the enemy of all the Jews', as in 3.10 and 9.10 (without 'all'). Four times he is 'Haman, the son of Hammedatha' (3.1, 10; 8.5; 9.10), four times 'Haman the Agagite' (3.1, 10; 8.3, 5), and three times 'the enemy of the Jews' (3.10; 8.1; 9.10). The first full description occurs at the crucial moment when Haman is given permission to slaughter the Jews (3.10), and it is only at this final mention of Haman in 9.24 that the full form appears again (with the addition of 'all' 'to avoid monotony' [Jones][49]).

(viii) Mordecai is called 'the Jew' three times in 9.20–10.3, making a total of seven times in the book as a whole, perhaps because 'seven often represents completeness'.[50]

(ix) The phrase 'to destroy, to kill, and to annihilate' (לְהַשְׁמִיד לַהֲרֹג וּלְאַבֵּד) has been used three times (3.13; 7.4; 8.11), at three crucial points in the narrative. In 9.24, 'to avoid monotony',[51] the author uses 'to annihilate them' and 'to crush and annihilate them' (לְאַבְּדָם, לְהֻמָּם וּלְאַבְּדָם).

(x) מַאֲמַר, 'commandment', is used three times, to call attention to the important shifts in power. In 1.15 it is the commandment of the king, which Vashti ignores; in 2.20 it is the commandment of Mordecai, which Esther obeys; in 9.32 it is the commandment of Queen Esther to observe the festival of Purim.

(xi) Esther is called 'daughter of Abihail' at 2.15 when she goes to the king, and again at 9.29 when she writes as queen to the Jews.

This accumulation of detail must of course be examined closely rather than simply weighed in order to determine its significance. Three observations suggest themselves:

(i) An important fact not given explicit recognition by Jones is that the author of 9.20–10.3, whether the same person as the narrator of chs. 1–8 or not, has deliberately included in the final verses of the book a recapitulation of its plot in the summary narrative of 9.24–25—a feature that very few narratives are likely to call for. It is therefore inevitable that many of the crucial motifs should be repeated, and likely that much of the vocabulary attached to important moments in the narrative should appear again. Given this circumstance, no argument about the identity of the author can be based upon the similarities. Jones does acknowledge this point in part when he writes:

> There is some significant similarity in vocabulary between 9.20–10.3 and the rest of the book ... This feature alone would not necessarily argue for the unity of the book since a later editor could have made use of the original vocabulary when adding his own ending.[52]

But he undercuts the force of this point by adding: 'However, we shall see that the repetition of certain words at the end of the story acts as a climax for the linear progression', not recognizing that even when the last in a series is truly climactic (and not just the last in a series) there is no reason why a 'later editor' rather than the original author should not have created the climax. In any case, criteria for determining that the last use of a word or phrase is truly climactic are very elusive.

(ii) Jones uses a double standard for accounting for similarity and dissimilarity between 9.20–10.3 and the rest of the book. When the language of 9.20–10.3 is identical to that of earlier chapters we have, in his view, an argument for unity; when it is dissimilar we still have an argument for unity since the difference is deliberately introduced by the one narrator in order to avoid monotony.

(iii) Jones does not give any consideration to differences in conception or story-line between 9.20–10.3 and the earlier chapters. He notes the observation of Paton[53] that several words, some of them quite rare in the Hebrew Bible, occur only in 9.20–10.3, but explains away their presence by the suggestion that 'the author is only dazzling us with a little fanfare in his finale'.[54] The more important issue of story-line is ignored in favour of this piece of special pleading on the relatively minor issue of vocabulary.[55]

I conclude that the observations of Jones, which are indeed observations of real data, signify no more than that the author of 9.20–10.3 was familiar with the preceding narrative of Esther (though in some respects he imperfectly grasped its essential narrative shape and some of its nuances) and set about to write a conclusion for it that would incorporate a recapitulation of its essential point.

At this point I have reached the end of my argument that the Esther scroll once ended at an earlier point than it does now in its Masoretic form. In succeeding chapters I will attempt to reconstruct earlier forms of the story and analyse what is distinctive about each of them.

Chapter 5

THE PROTO-MASORETIC STORY OF ESTHER

Almost all that has been said already in Chapter 2 about the literary art of the Masoretic story of Esther is true also of the proto-Masoretic story; for on the present hypothesis the proto-Masoretic story consisted of precisely chs. 1–8 of the Masoretic book. However, 8.15-17, as the ending of the postulated pre-Masoretic form of the story, must have held a more significant place in that earlier version of the story than it does in the Masoretic text, and therefore deserves a little further consideration.

I have suggested above, in Chapter 1, that 8.15-17 draws together the principal threads of the plot and in so doing gives every appearance of having been expressly designed as the conclusion to the tale.

If we examine first the most important twin threads of the danger to Mordecai and to the Jewish people we find them both neatly woven together and satisfyingly finished off in these verses.

The plot-element of the threat to Mordecai has been essentially located within the court: it has been the king's servants at the king's gate who in the first place noticed his insubordination to Haman (3.3), and it has been only at home with his wife and confidants that the fate of Mordecai has been discussed. An eunuch in attendance on the king has discovered that the pole in Haman's courtyard has been prepared for the impalement of Mordecai (7.9). But outside the world of the court, the people of Susa know Mordecai not as the Jew under threat of death but as 'the man whom the king delights to honour' (6.11). Both of these perceptions of Mordecai are brought together in the portrait of 8.15. The courtly threat to Mordecai's life has been entirely dissipated by the marks of his signal honouring by the court; and his anticipatory elevation (ch. 6) in the presence of the people in the open square of the city has now been regularized in a public display of his honour. Mordecai's royal robes, golden crown, and mantle of fine linen and purple signify both his own personal salvation from Haman's wrath, and, more than that, his public promotion to Haman's position. A plot of threat to the hero only requires his effectual deliverance from danger for it to be a worthy tale; if it can throw in for good measure the permanent undoing of the villain, and can have the hero promoted to higher status at the very moment of his escape from danger it is all the more rewarding. If it can on top of all that suggest that the hero gets by desert what the villain had got by stealth or chance it flavours the tale with a simple but pleasing irony.

The second of the primary threads, the danger to the Jewish people, is likewise woven into the paragraph. The king's edict brings to every province and every city the news, and not just the promise, of deliverance. The gladness and joy, the feast and holiday, signify that the matter is settled, not that their fate still hangs in the balance. So clear is it that the Jews are destined for life that pagans spontaneously attach themselves to the Jewish community. That act cannot mean that they now hope the Jews will successfully defend themselves in some civil disturbance still scheduled for the thirteenth of Adar; it does not even mean that it is safe to be a Jew—it means that it is desirable to be a Jew. There is a twofold reason for that: the 'fear' of the Jews and the position of Mordecai. The fear of the Jews cannot be fear of their military prowess or fear that they will exact terrible revenge upon non-Jews, for the royal edict does not envisage anything beyond their gathering to defend their lives against any armed force that might attack them (8.11). It must be old-fashioned religious awe, demythologized for the text of the story no doubt into merely a heightened form of respect, engendered by the remarkable— though unattributable—reversal of Jewish fortunes. Linked to this regard for the Jewish people is the pragmatic recognition that a Jew stands at the helm of government. Susa had shouted and rejoiced at the ceremonial exit of Mordecai from the palace, if only at first because every crowd loves a spectacle; but a deeper and more enduring rationalization spreads from Susa to the provinces, acknowledging the sudden wisdom of a definitely pro-Jewish stance. Again the plot, as in the case of its Mordecai strand, takes a step beyond what is needful for a safe homecoming. It would be enough for the resolution of the threat to the Jews if the danger should be averted; it is an unnecessary, though gratifying, conclusion if the process of averting the danger leads to greater long-term safety for the Jews by swelling their numbers with voluntary adherents.

Thus far we have noted now the primary threads of the plot are tied together and finished off in this final paragraph. We could also observe how many other plot-elements and motifs take their final curtain-call here.

1. The various conflicts that have formed the stuff of the plot have either been recently resolved or are here finally resolved. The conflict of Haman and Mordecai reached only its penultimate phase, we now see, with the execution of Haman; in its posthumous phase Haman is if anything even more convincingly marked out as the loser. For his dearest ambition, as we have noticed in 6.7-9, is intimacy with Persian royalty, even to the extent of wearing the king's clothing. Though he has his invitation to the royal dinner-parties (which gives him a frisson of delight, 5.12), he never gets to wearing royal garb—except perhaps the palace shroud[1] as he is escorted to execution (7.8). Mordecai, however, has not only had the royal treatment for a day (ch. 6) but now is pictured—in loving detail—as wearing all the emblems of royal, or at least near-royal, status: the royal robes of blue (or, violet) and white (תכלת וחור), conjuring up the décor of the imperial banquet scene in 1.6 with its fine cotton curtains in white (חור) and hangings in blue (תכלת);[2] the golden crown (עטרת), not perhaps itself the king's crown (כתר) we have encountered in 1.11, 2.17, and 6.5, but the next best thing to it, and the mantle of fine white linen (בוץ) and purple (ארגמן), again recalling the pavilion of 1.6 with its cords of fine white linen and purple (בוץ וארגמן). All this for a man who had earlier excluded himself from the court by his garb of sackcloth (4.2). The Agagite never has the opportunity of seeing how decisively in the Jew's favour the conflict is resolved, though the other courtiers have now definitively seen for themselves whether the cause of Mordecai will prevail or no (3.4).

2. The question of racial identity has now ceased to be a point of tension and has become a source of gratification. There are still 'Jews' as distinct from other peoples, but Gentile inhabitants of Susa selflessly join in rejoicing for Jewish good fortune, and Gentiles from the provinces throw in their lot with the Jews. There has not been any special reversal of attitude here, for the non-Jewish citizens had never been hostile to the Jews (3.15), but it is certainly an unexpected climax to the history of good racial relationships to witness an influx of sympathizers into the Jewish community.

3. The king's will has in the narrative preceding frequently led to disaster; the autocrat who must be 'pleased' has put his foot wrong on too many occasions. Now, at the climax of the story, his public relations image is clean again. No inhabitant of the empire has the slightest unhappiness about this latest 'command' (דבר־המלך, also in 4.3) of the king; he has managed to please all the people this time, even if the last time he was by no means so successful. It says something for the narrator's attitude to his own overlords (whoever they may be) that in the end the king emerges with some kind of credit as the signatory of the decree of deliverance—though we are not supposed to forget that the decree has not been written 'as it pleases the king' but under the rubric 'write as you [Mordecai and Esther] please' (כטוב בעיניכם, 8.8).

4. It comes as no surprise that the issue of legality should surface again in this closing paragraph. Only under the authorization of a binding 'law' (דת) can it be prudent for the Jews to celebrate their deliverance. But, as we have seen before (in Chapter 1, above), law, even law of the Persians and Medes, does not accomplish everything. The second decree is indispensable for Jewish survival, no question about it; but what makes this paragraph's narrative so climactic is not just the decree but Mordecai's elevation and the proselytism of the Gentiles—for which some nameless power other than the king must surely be held responsible. Law in the end is not undermined, but it is demoted to the infrastructure of the good life with its 'light' and 'gladness' (8.16).

5. What of irreversible law? Hitherto this element has functioned as black comedy (the monarch caught in the web of his own law) or as the intellectual puzzle of the plot (how will Mordecai subvert the law without contradicting it?). Now that the second decree has taken care of the first, law—and therewith its irreversibility—tends to fade into the background. Irreversible laws still stand unshaken, if anyone now cares to ask about them; but they can in fact be ignored, as if they had completely cancelled one another out. News of the second decree does not concentrate everyone's mind wonderfully on the forthcoming events of the thirteenth of Adar, but rather brings to the Jews in every province and every city gladness and a feast and a holiday. Irreversible law or no, their faces are now turned to a future that will be marked by 'honour' (their compatriot is the king's favourite now) and respect or 'awe' (many, seeing their star in the ascendant, join themselves to the Jewish people).

What I hope to have shown by this point is, in the previous two chapters, that chs. 9–10 are alien to the narrative of chs. 1–8 of Esther, and, in the present chapter, that the closing verses of ch. 8 form a highly successful conclusion to the earlier Hebrew story that I call the proto-Masoretic book.

Chapter 6

THE SEPTUAGINT ESTHER

The textual history of the book of Esther is, as is well known, quite complex. Beside the Masoretic text, there are two Greek texts, which may represent two additional Semitic forms of the text.

The Septuagint or B-text of the canonical portions of the book of Esther can be judged a literary, somewhat free and paraphrastic, somewhat concise version of a Hebrew text very like the Masoretic. Moore has noted that the Septuagint, as represented by LXX[B] (Vaticanus), has scarcely a verse without a minus of a word, phrase, or clause compared with the MT.[1] Almost everyone agrees, however, that no matter how free the Septuagint translator has been, it is essentially the Masoretic Hebrew text that was his *Vorlage*.

But more important for our purpose than the variants between the Hebrew and the Septuagint in wording is the presence of six substantial passages that are not to be found in the Hebrew at all. These Additions, which are now commonly known by the letters A-F,[2] are to be regarded as secondary to the Greek translation in which they are now embedded.[3] Though we do not know at what time or by what means they became incorporated in the text of Esther that is now commonly called the Septuagint, it is probable that four of the Additions (A, C, D, F) originally existed in a Semitic original, whereas the other two Additions (B, E) are patently Greek compositions.[4]

The contents of these six Additions were removed by Jerome—since they formed no part of the Hebrew—from their logical places in the Greek Esther narrative to the end of the book in his Latin version, though, not unreasonably, the concluding Addition was left in its place at the end of the 'canonical' Esther; this explains why the last of the Additions is now assigned the first verse numbers (10.4ff.) after the close of the 'canonical' Esther. The contents of these Additions are:

A. (vv. 1-17 = 11.2–12.6) A dream of Mordecai concerning coming destruction, and his discovery of the conspiracy of the eunuchs [A is prefixed to MT 1.1].

B. (vv. 1-7 = 13.1-7) The contents of the edict against the Jews sent out by Ahasuerus at Haman's instigation [B follows 3.13].

C. (vv. 1-30 = 13.8–14.19) The prayer of Mordecai and the prayer of Esther for deliverance [C follows 4.17].

D. (vv. 1-16 = 15.1-16; Vulg. 15.4-19⁵) An account of Esther's appearance before the king in anxiety for her own safety [D follows C, and forms an alternative to MT 5.1-2].

E. (vv. 1-24 = 16.1-24) The contents of the edict on behalf of the Jews sent out by Ahasuerus at Mordecai's instigation [E follows 8.12].

F. (vv. 1-10 = 10.4–11.1) The interpretation of Mordecai's dream as relating to the events of the narrative [F follows 10.3].[6]

The existence of these two additional layers, the Semitic Additions and the Greek Additions, to the original Septuagint translation attests a high degree of fluidity—or openness to alteration or adaptation—in the contents of the book of Esther. These Additions are not trivial alterations to the Esther story, but substantial reshapings of the material; in extent they together increase the 'canonical' (MT or 'original' LXX) Esther by more than two-thirds. I would argue that the Septuagint text, in bearing witness to at least two major extensions of the contents of the book by Semitic-speaking and Greek-speaking Jews, provides indirect support for the view advanced in Chapter 5 above that a significant extension to the story had already occurred in the composition of the Masoretic text. Putting it another way, we would be hard-pressed to say—on the basis of the Septuagint text-form and the MT—what precisely constituted the book of Esther prior to our earliest (fourth century AD) codices of the Septuagint. Nevertheless, despite this degree of fluidity, it cannot be denied that the Septuagint Esther agrees at least with the MT over the point at which the story should end: with the letters of Mordecai and Esther enjoining observance of Purim (9.20-32), and with the fame of Mordecai (10.1-3); the ending of the Septuagint Esther differs only in rounding off the book with an epilogue (Addition F in which Mordecai soliloquizes on the fulfilment of his initial premonitory dream (Addition A).

Chapter 7

THE A-TEXT ESTHER

I

Divergent though the LXX is from the MT in very many respects both major and minor, the most significant differences between the MT and a Greek Esther become apparent only when we turn to the so-called A-text (alpha-text; hereafter referred to as AT) of the book. This text has been printed a number of times; in its first edition, James Usher, Archbishop of Armagh, displayed the text of the miniscule ms 93 (Brooke–McLean: e₂) in columns parallel to that of the standard LXX text contained in the same manuscript; his edition, which appeared only a century and a half after the first printed editions of the Septuagint, was included in a volume entitled *De Graeca Septuaginta interpretum versione syntagma: cum libri Estherae editione Origenica, et vetere Graeca altera, ex Arundelliana bibliotheca nunc primum in lucem producta* (London, 1655). Being regarded by most scholars as a text inferior to the standard LXX text, the A-text has been largely ignored. But in 1848, O.F. Fritzsche published in Zürich a booklet entitled ΕΣΘΗΡ. *Duplicem libri textum ad optimos codices emendavit et cum selecta lectionis varietate edidit*, in which the LXX and AT were set out on facing pages; the same text, with minor alterations but similarly displayed, appeared in his *Libri Apocryphi Veteris Testamenti Graece* (Leipzig, 1871). P. de Lagarde, in his *Librorum Veteris Testamenti Canonicorum Pars Prior Graece* (Göttingen, 1883), published a critical text of the AT, giving the variant readings of manuscripts 19, 93, and 108—and printing his edition of the LXX text on facing pages. In the detailed but erratic commentary by A. Scholz, *Commentar über das Buch 'Esther' mit seinen 'Zusätzen' und über 'Susanna'* (Würzburg, 1892), an appendix presents the two texts of Lagarde in parallel columns, together with two further columns showing the text of Josephus's Esther story and of the MT in German translation. In the Larger Cambridge Septuagint, the AT of Esther appears as a separate book, with its own apparatus, following the LXX Esther: A.E. Brooke, N. McLean and H. StJ. Thackeray, *The Old Testament in Greek*, Vol. III, Part I (London, 1940), pp. 32-42. In the Göttingen edition, R. Hanhart has printed the AT in full, with its own apparatus, at the foot of the page beneath the LXX text and its apparatus: R. Hanhart, *Septuaginta. VT graecum auctoritate academiae scientiarum gottingensis editum*, VIII, 3 (Göttingen, 1966). The AT has never, I believe, been translated into any language in its entirety;[1] in view of its importance for the present study, and because of its absence from the standard hand-editions of the Septuagint by Swete and Rahlfs,[2] it is printed along with a translation at the end of this volume. The verse-numbering in the present study follows that of the Cambridge edition.

The importance of the A-text only begins to emerge when the long-standing opinion is rejected that it represents the Lucianic revision of the Septuagint, and is therefore of distinctly inferior significance to the Septuagint for the history of the Hebrew text. Though the A-text is contained in manuscripts which in other Old Testament books represent a Lucianic text (mss 19, 93, 108, 319; Brooke–McLean: b[1], e[2], b, y),[3] it has been universally agreed since Carey A. Moore's 1965 Johns Hopkins dissertation on *The Greek Text of Esther* and R. Hanhart's edition in the Göttingen Septuagint (1966)[4] that the A-text has nothing in common with any Lucianic type of text.[5] This means that, once a link with the relatively late Lucianic text has been severed, we can begin to see the A-text as potentially an independent witness to the wording and contents of the Hebrew book of Esther. Moore himself concluded that the A-text is 'a separate translation of the Hebrew', a Hebrew original (be it noted) 'at points quite different from the one presupposed by the LXX as well as from the one from which the MT descended'[6]—a conclusion with which this study will agree, but which it will not take for granted.

Superficially, of course, the AT seems to have more in common with the LXX than with the MT, principally because it contains the same major Additions as the LXX. But the textual character of those Additions in the AT (viz. the fact that they exhibit a text-type very much closer to the LXX's than AT usually has) make it more than probable that they are secondary to the original AT, just as they are secondary in the LXX as compared with the MT.[7] We are entitled therefore to consider the AT—*without* the Additions—as a text in its own right, which perhaps also witnesses to a Hebrew text other than the Masoretic.

Now the ending of the book of Esther—with which we are particularly concerned here—is in the AT very distinctive. In ten verses (AT 8.12-21) its narrative covers the following events that are spread over 34 verses in the MT (7.9–9.15):

1. The king orders Haman to be hanged on the gallows he has prepared for Mordecai (AT 8.12-13 = MT 7.9-10).
2. The king gives Haman's property to Mordecai (AT 8.15 = MT 8.1-2).
3. Mordecai (MT: Esther) requests that Haman's letter be revoked, and the king gives a general authorization (AT 8.16-17 = MT 8.3-8).
4. Esther requests permission to punish her enemies with death (MT: she requests a day's extension of the Jews' 'self-defence' in Susa), and to kill Haman's sons with their father (MT: to hang them, their father having already been hung); the king assents (AT 8.18-19 = MT 9.13-14).
5. Esther killed many of her enemies; the king gave permission to hang those in Susa (MT: the Jews slew 300 men in Susa [there is no mention of hanging]) (AT 8.20-21 = MT 9.15).

The book then continues with the 24 verses of the Greek Addition E, the letter of Ahasuerus to his provincial governors advising them to ignore the letter sent by Haman since he, a Macedonian plotting to usurp the Persian throne, has now been hanged at the gates of Susa. (In the LXX text, Addition E is inserted only after a report of the writing, dispatch, and contents of the letter—which is equivalent to 8.9-12 of the MT.[8]) There follow 20 verses (8.33-52) which selectively cover several events mentioned in the 32 verses between 8.8 and 9.22 of the MT, and which also introduce material not found in the MT, and repeat some material found in AT 8.12-21:

1. The king permits Mordecai to write whatever he likes (AT 8.33 [? = MT 8.8]).
2. Mordecai sends letters to the Jews, sealed with the king's ring, authorizing them to remain in their own place and celebrate a festival to God (AT 8.34, in part = MT 8.10-11).
3. The contents of Mordecai's letter: Haman's letter is to be ignored since Haman is now hanged, together with his household, at the gates of Susa (this passage must have

belonged to AT before the insertion of Addition E ascribing the letter of cancellation to the king) (AT 8.35-38, using material corresponding to MT 8.9-14 except that the contents of the letter are entirely different).

4. Mordecai goes out from the king's presence in royal robes, Susa rejoices, the Jews have light, drinking and a banquet. Many Jews (!) become circumcised (AT 8.39-41, roughly = MT 8.15-17).

5. All the imperial officials fear the Jews because the fear of Mordecai has fallen on them (AT 8.42 = MT 9.3).

6. The Jews in Susa kill 700 men and the 10 sons of Haman and plunder their goods (AT 8.44 = MT 9.6-10).

7. The king asks Esther how her compatriots in Susa and its surroundings have fared; she asks that the Jews be permitted to kill and plunder whomever they like. They slay 7100 men (AT 8.45-46, roughly = MT 9.12-15 [this material has already been used in part at AT 8.18-19]).

8. Mordecai records these things, and writes to Jews of the empire to observe the 14th and 15th of Adar as days for joy instead of grief. He sends portions to the poor. Hence these days are called 'Phourdaia' on account of the lots that fell out for these days for a remembrance (AT 8.47-49 = MT 9.20-22 and 9.26-28 much condensed).

9. The king writes of his might and wealth. Mordecai writes in the books of the Persians and Medes. Mordecai 'succeeded'[9] Xerxes, and remained popular with the Jews (AT 8.50-52 = MT 10.1-3).

The book concludes, as does the LXX Esther, with Addition F, the fulfilment of the dream of Mordecai.

II

The least that this sketch of the concluding contents of the A-text can do is to reinforce the impression gained from the LXX text, that there is considerable fluidity among our ancient witnesses to the shape of the end of the book. But a more impressive claim, nearer to the purpose of this study, was advanced by C.C. Torrey. He believed that the A-text represented a Semitic original different from that of the B-text (LXX) only in AT 2.1–8.21 (that is, more or less MT 1.1–8.8, plus some borrowing from 9.13-15),[10] and that its separate *Vorlage* ended at the original conclusion of the folktale of Esther, viz. with the execution of Haman and the annulment of his letter. His argument, however, was expressed rather loosely; he claimed that AT 2.1–8.13 contained the same material as in MT and LXX chs. 1–7, though they formed an independent translation from a 'slightly differing' Semitic *Vorlage*. The following verses in AT (8.14-17), narrating the king's gift of Haman's property to Mordecai and therewith permission to annul Haman's decree, were asserted by Torrey to be '*the* ending, precisely, which was intended by the author of this particular version'. The assertion was confirmed, for Torrey, by his conviction that following 8.17 the text of AT is no longer independent of the B-text but *derived from it*, vv. 18-21 being a transitional 'patch' between the two texts. The *purpose* of the extension of the A-text by the B-text was, according to Torrey, to link the story of Esther with the observance of Purim—which is of course completely absent from his 'original' A-text. It is unfortunate that Torrey did not attempt to demonstrate that AT 8.22 to the end is derived from the B-text, since simple recourse to what 'any careful reader of the Greek can see' is not the most convincing way to present one's case.[11]

The evidence is not lacking, however, even if the precise end of the AT should not be pinpointed exactly where Torrey did. A symbol of the propriety of Torrey's view may first be observed—rather unexpectedly—in the recent argument of E. Tov that the AT in general is 'closely connected with the LXX of Esth. and depends upon it'.[12] This argument, which at first sight militates against the general view being developed in this monograph, in fact hangs upon seven cases of apparent dependence of AT upon LXX, five of which are taken from the 20 (non-Additional) verses between AT 8.22 and the end of the book.[13] That is to say, the best evidence for dependence of the A-text upon the LXX comes from just those few verses which Torrey claimed were untypical of the A-text, being derived from the LXX.[14]

A much more concrete case, however, was provided by H.J. Cook[15] in his study of the A-text. His conclusion was that up to 8.5 (MT numbering) the Greek is 'in close touch' with its Hebrew original (which was not however, Cook thinks, our Masoretic text but a different recension of the Hebrew book).[16] After 8.5, however, the contacts are slight. Cook infers (i) that AT originally ended at MT 8.5; (ii) that the remainder of the book in our four mss that witness to the AT was an addition made in order to link the narrative to the Purim festival legend; (iii) that this addition to AT was derived either

from a longer Hebrew recension of the story or from a Greek version
with a text like that of Vaticanus (the LXX or B-text).

These conclusions support the general thesis here presented,
namely the existence of a pre-Masoretic Hebrew book of Esther
which ended somewhere in ch. 8 but which was at least fairly close to
the MT story (though not always its *wording*) throughout its extent.
Cook's conclusions do not indeed agree, in the form they are stated,
with my suggestion of the precise point at which the earlier Hebrew
Esther concluded; but a close examination of the grounds Cook gives
for his views will show his observations to be compatible with and
perhaps even supportive of my argument.

I begin my examination of Cook's position with the matter of the
point at which he claims the AT originally ended. It seems to me
difficult to believe that any narrative could have ended with 8.5 (MT
numbering)—as Cook says it did—since in that verse all that
happens is that Esther asks that the order dispatched by Haman
should be revoked (in AT, the equivalent verse, 8.16, has *Mordecai*
asking the king to repeal Haman's letter). It hardly seems possible
that any story could end on precisely such a note, without any kind of
further resolution. Only if the AT *accidentally* ended on such a note
could Cook's view be upheld, but I am convinced that he did not
mean that; he wrote '*A* [the A-text] *originally*[17] ended at 8_5',[18] and
no accidental end of a text can be original (except in the unlikely
event of the author not completing his work!).

We therefore must ask why Cook fixed on MT 8.5 as the point of
closure of the original form of the A-text and its *Vorlage*. Cook's
principal tools for analysing the character of AT were its 'omissions'
from and 'additions' to the Hebrew story (as attested by MT). Moore
had in his article on the AT given details of its 'omission' of
repetitions, of insignificant proper names, and of certain numbers
and dates.[19] Cook added another category of 'omissions': what he
designated 'irrational material'. It comprised:

1. 1.17b-18 [more appropriately 1.17-18] The fear of the Persian
    nobles that all women of the empire will disobey their
    husbands if they hear of Vashti's unpunished disobedience.
2. 1.20a, 22 The decree that wives should obey their husbands.
3. 2.3, 8a The gathering of the maidens by the officers of the
    king.
4. 2.10-11 Esther's silence about her race, and Mordecai's
    frequenting the court of the harem.

5.   2.19-20 Esther's obedience to Mordecai in not revealing her race.

6.   4.5-8a (AT 5.8) Mordecai informs Esther about the edict via the messenger Hathach.

7.   4.11-14 (AT 5.7-10) Mordecai's speech is somewhat abbreviated to 'If you overlook your race so as to give them no aid, but God will be their help and salvation, and you and your father's house will perish. And who knows whether you have come to the throne for this time?'

Cook then claimed that 'from 8_6 onwards the omissions . . . are not so clearly rational'.[20] By 'rational' he appears to mean: contributing to the reasonableness of the story as essentially a story of conflict between Mordecai and Haman, and as effectively concluding with the repeal of Haman's edict (MT 8.5 Esther: 'let an order be written to revoke the letters devised by Haman'; AT 8.16 Ahasuerus: 'What do you want?' and Mordecai: 'That you destroy the letter of Haman'). Cook's argument is here hard to follow, since he points out that after (MT) 8.5 AT omits 'the improbable decree encouraging Jews to kill Persians' and, at 8.17 (MT) the presumably 'improbable' 'mass conversion of Gentiles'—which are both quite *like* the earlier 'omissions' of AT. Cook does not appear to have made explicit his grounds for affirming that 'From 8_6 onwards the omissions and additions are not so clearly rational',[21] though it is true that after 8.6 (AT 8.16) the story sets off in a different direction from the main plot.

Cook's second tool for analysing the character of AT was the set of its 'additions' to MT. Without giving a full list of these pluses (as I prefer to call them), he characterized them as 'tend[ing] to improve the story, either adding to the reasonableness of the developments or heightening the dramatic effect'[22] (so additions at AT 2.6; 2.12; 4.3; 6.23; 7.4-6; 7.15-16; 8.2; 8.56 [= MT 1.6; 1.12; 3.3; 5.14; 6.2; 6.10-11; 7.2; 7.5 respectively]). Furthermore, Cook observed that all these 'additions' 'are effected by the addition of clauses interspersed in the story of the Masoretic text'. After 8.6 (AT 8.16) there are no more additions of this character, but rather the remainder of the book is a highly *summarized* account of a certain amount of the material presented in MT. There can be little doubt that Cook has made out his case on this point, the significance of the AT pluses vis-à-vis the MT: they indicate that the ending of the AT has a different relationship to the MT from that of the main body of the narrative.

I conclude therefore that although his presentation was brief and not entirely convincing, especially in regard to AT minuses vis-à-vis the MT, Cook has made two correct observations of importance: 1. that AT presents a coherent narrative of a plot that is slimmer than the MT; and 2. that after MT 8.5 (AT 8.16) there is something quite different about the texture of the story, a 'change in the character of the *A* text'.[23]

III

I would now extend and further ground these observations made by Cook.

(i) If we consider the AT (minus the Additions, which we must regard as secondary) as a story in its own right, we would best describe its plot as at base the story of a conflict between two courtiers which precipitates a threat to the Jewish people.[24] In the AT there is no explanation of why Mordecai does not bow before Haman (beyond perhaps Haman's elevation over him) nor of why Haman extends his fury to Mordecai's people (contrast MT 3.6). There is no unalterable law of the Medes and Persians in AT (contrast MT 1.19; 8.8), so that when Haman is unmasked there is no reason why his decree should not be promptly rescinded, as Mordecai indeed asks (AT 8.16). Esther is not required by Mordecai (in the AT) to keep her ethnic origins a secret, and we must suppose that the king knows that she is Jewish. He does not know, of course, that Haman's decree is against the Jews; but he does know, at least after the chronicles have been read to him, that Mordecai is a Jew (AT 7.12 = MT 6.10), and he explicitly recognizes that Mordecai is of the same race as Esther (AT 8.14).

These differences between AT and MT are not enormous, but they are not trifling either. The two story-lines are distinct. What is particularly significant is that AT's deviations from the plot of MT are self-consistent, and therefore not likely to have resulted from a mass of small-scale alterations to the text of MT.

(ii) What happens to the narrative of AT after MT 8.5 (AT 8.16) is not to be described in terms of omissions (or additions), though it is true that AT is shorter than MT or LXX. Rather, the narrative logic, which in preceding chapters was remarkably consistent throughout a narrative differing at several significant points from MT, falls apart in the verses following 8.16 (AT). In the following pages I will note sixteen oddities in the text of AT from 8.17^{25} to 8.52, that is in the remainder of the book that corresponds to MT, excluding Addition E (AT 8.22-32) and Addition F (AT 8.53-59). The conclusion I will draw from these observations is that these final 25 verses formed no part of the AT as it must have once existed, and that Cook was more or less correct in asserting that '*A* originally ended at [MT] 8_5'[26] — the precise point of closure being the only matter of my disagreement.

1. In 8.17, after Mordecai has asked the king to abolish Haman's decree, AT says merely, 'And the king put into his hand the affairs of the kingdom'. This fails to say the crucial thing: namely, that Haman's edict was actually revoked; but it casts a generalizing haze over the concrete situation. It is true that in the MT also the king himself takes no action to revoke or nullify Haman's decree, but the narrative there shows how the story ought to proceed: the king gives Mordecai permission to write to the Jews as he pleases, in the king's name (v. 8), and the letter is actually written (v. 9) and dispatched (v. 10) and its contents are given in summary form (vv. 11-12). This narrative segment as presented in MT could unquestionably be much abbreviated and still make sense, but AT's v. 17 evaporates the concrete detail which must be left as a residue in any foreshortening of the narrative. The fault lies not much in what v. 17 contains, since it has the makings of a very reasonable conclusion to the tale, but in what it omits.

2. The next verse (AT 8.18) reads 'And Esther said to the king next, Grant me to punish my enemies with slaughter'. 'Next' (τῇ ἑξῆς) is a feeble and suspicious narrative link. And Esther's request is poorly motivated, since it is Mordecai and not Esther who has been asked, 'What do you want? I will do it' (v. 16). After all the fuss about the difficulty of approaching the king with a request, it is astonishing that Esther can intervene in Mordecai's audience with an imperious Δός μοι, 'Give me', without any by your leave, any conventional 'if it pleases the king'. (In MT, by contrast, Esther only speaks when she is spoken to.) The logic also is strange, since it is not apparent why if Mordecai has been entrusted with the business of the kingdom (τὰ κατὰ τὴν βασιλείαν, v. 17) Esther should have to make such a request of the king. Moreover, it is not clear at this point who Esther's enemies are, nor in fact will it ever be divulged.

3. In v. 19 we appear to be confronted with a *separate* conversation of Esther with the king: 'And Esther the queen took counsel with the king also against the sons of Haman as well, so that they also should

die together with their father. And the king said, So be it.' Presumably the sons of Haman could satisfactorily be numbered among Esther's enemies, so why are they not covered by the permission of the previous verse? And Haman is already dead, so how can they die μετὰ τοῦ πατρός, with their father? And if the king has given official permission for their execution, why do we find in AT 8.44 that 'the Jews in Susa killed . . . the ten sons of Haman'? Where is Persian efficiency now? (In MT, of course, the Jews slay the sons of Haman in the course of the massacre they carry out on Adar 13; and there Esther's request to the king is only that—after their death—Haman's sons should be impaled, and so, presumably, meet the same fate as their father already has.)

4. There is an awkward juxtaposition in v. 19 of Esther's request in indirect speech (ἐνέτυχε ἡ βασίλισσα . . . ὅπως, 'the queen conversed . . . so that') and the king's reply in direct speech (καὶ εἶπεν ὁ βασιλεὺς γινέσθω, 'And the king said, So be it.').

5. Verse 20 is strangely vague, even to the extent that the subject of the verb is not clear. It reads: 'And he/she smote the enemies in great numbers'. The nearest antecedent for ἐπάταξε is the king, but he can hardly *both* say 'Let it be so' *and* make it so himself. If Esther is meant to be the subject, it is strange that her name does not appear, that we do not find τοὺς ἐχθροὺς αὐτῆς, corresponding to τοὺς ἐχθρούς μου in v. 18. τοὺς ἐχθρούς without further definition is itself strange.

6. In v. 21 we have: 'And in Susa the king made an agreement with the queen to slay men, and he said, Behold, I give [them] to you to hang. And it was so.' This appears to be a meaningless repetition of the matter of vv. 18, 20; perhaps it is an *alternative* version of vv. 18-20. 'In Susa' is quite unnecessary, since there is no doubt that the conversation is set in Susa; and even if the phrase was meant to refer to the place where the slaughter took place, it makes little sense to stress Susa unless slaughter in other parts of the empire is being compared (as in MT 9.11f.). 'To kill men' (ἀποκτανθῆναι ἄνδρας) is very odd without any qualification of ἄνδρας.

7. If we omit from the AT's narrative Addition E which follows AT 8.21, the next verses, 8.33-38, include the contents of a letter from Mordecai. It runs:

> [36]Haman has sent to you letters as follows: Hasten with all speed to send to destruction on my behalf the disobedient race of the

Jews. [37]But I, Mordecai, advise you that the man who did this has been hung at the gates of Susa, and his family has been slain. [38]For he planned to kill us on the thirteenth day of the month which is Adar.

This material, peculiar to AT, displays some oddities.[27] The substance of it shows that it is fairly clearly addressed to provincial governors (like the letter of Mordecai mentioned in MT 8.9, and like Addition E, the letter of Ahasuerus, which also informs governors and satraps that Haman has been hanged at the gates of Susa [AT 8.28]); but in its present place in AT it is introduced by a clause that suggests it is envisaged as addressed to the Jews: 'And Mordecai sent orders in writing, and sealed them with the king's signet ring, that his people should remain each in his own place and should keep festival to God' (... μένειν τὸ ἔθνος αὐτοῦ κατὰ χώρας ἕκαστον αὐτῶν καὶ ἑορτάζειν τῷ θεῷ) (v. 34). In addition to this lack of clarity is the inconclusive nature of the letter, which fails to make the one pressing point, namely, that Haman's decree is now annulled. That information could no doubt be guessed at fairly easily, but is strange that Mordecai's letter does not reach that point, especially when MT and Addition E feel the need for some such statement. Thus MT, in reporting (rather than reproducing) the letter, explicitly says: 'The king permitted the Jews ... to gather and defend themselves'. And Addition E explicitly says, 'You will do well if you disregard the letters sent by Haman' (LXX 8.17; AT 8.28 'Do well by disregarding ...'). Finally, this letter of Mordecai is at odds with the body of the narrative in claiming that Haman's body has been hung at the gates of Susa (AT 8.37), since according to AT 8.12f. (MT 7.9f.) Haman had been hung on the gallows in his own courtyard.[28]

8. Following this letter of Mordecai we have AT 8.39 'And Mordecai went out clothed in royal garments ...' and 8.40 'And when those in Susa saw [him] they rejoiced. And the Jews had light, a feast (πότος) and a goblet (κώθων)', corresponding to the narrative (though not the exact wording) of MT 8.15-16. We then read in v. 41 'And many of the Jews circumcised themselves, and no one opposed them; for they feared them'. MT 8.17 has many from the 'peoples of the land' (עמי הארץ) declaring themselves Jews, or, making themselves Jews (מתיהדים), which is not unreasonably represented by LXX as circumcising themselves (πολλοὶ τῶν ἐθνῶν περιετέμοντο). AT is absurd, having the Jews circumcise themselves[29] without resistance[30] (πολλοὶ τῶν Ἰουδαίων περιετέμνοντο [περιετέμοντο ye₂], καὶ οὐδεὶς

ἐπανέστη αὐτοῖς); evidently material corresponding to MT 8.17 *and* 9.2 has been combined rather unthinkingly.

9. Verse 43 is virtually unintelligible: 'And it came about that in Susa Haman was mentioned by name and in all the kingdom those who were opposed' (καὶ προσέπεσεν ἐν Σούσοις ὀνομασθῆναι Αμαν καὶ τοὺς ἀντικειμένους ἐν πάσῃ βασιλείᾳ). It may perhaps signify that the enemies of the Jews were mentioned by name in Mordecai's letter—which may in turn explain why certain persons (other than the ten sons of Haman) are named in AT 8.44, and may further form the background to Esther's request in 8.46 for an extension of the purge to any whom the Jews in general would like to see slain. But if all that is the significance of AT 8.43 it is very cryptically expressed.

10. Verse 44 displays an inner-Greek corruption, as noted by Tov.[31] Whereas LXX 9.7 has, in the list of Haman's sons, the names Φαρσανvνεσταιν καὶ Δελφων corresponding to MT את פרשנדתא ואת דלפון, AT has Φαρσαν καὶ τὸν ἀδελφὸν αὐτοῦ. AT further understands the proper names (five in all, as against MT ten) as the names of men who were slain *in addition to* the ten unnamed sons of Haman (. . . καὶ τοὺς δέκα υἱοὺς Αμαν).

11. In v. 45 the king says to Esther, 'How have your people here and in the countryside fared (or, behaved)?' (Πῶς σοι οἱ ἐνταῦθα καὶ οἱ ἐν τῇ περιχώρῳ κέχρηνται;). The question is poorly motivated, since the narrative has given no reason for the king to suspect that the Jews were in any danger, or were behaving in any noteworthy way (contrast MT 9.11 where the massacre by the Jews is reported to the king).

12. Esther's response in v. 46 is, even so, much more poorly motivated. She replies, 'Let permission be given to the Jews to slay and plunder whomever they wish' (Δοθήτω τοῖς Ιουδαίοις οὓς ἐὰν θέλωσιν ἀνελεῖν καὶ διαρπάζειν). Such a request comes naturally only after an invitation to make a request, such as we find in MT (and LXX) at 9.12, and certainly not after a question that seeks information such as we have just read in v. 45.

13. In v. 47, following the report of v. 46 that the Jews slew 70,100 men,[32] Mordecai writes these matters in a book which he sends to Jews throughout the empire so that they should 'keep (στῆσαι) these days (τὰς ἡμέρας ταύτας) for hymns and rejoicings in the place of pain and grief—the fourteenth and the fifteenth'. 'These days' refers to nothing in the preceding narrative. We had learned at AT 4.7 (MT

3.7) that Haman had cast lots for the thirteenth of 'Adar Nisan',[33] and—in a passage peculiar to AT—we have recently been reminded that Haman had planned to kill the Jews on the thirteenth of Adar (v. 38). But this is only one day, and it is not the fourteenth or fifteenth. It is true that those days are mentioned at the end of the verse, but in such a position as to raise the suspicion that they are a gloss. Whether or not they are, no explicit explanation is given for keeping them as days for hymns and rejoicing (as, for example, MT 9.18, which says it was because they *rested* on that day), and no explanation is hinted at for the observance of *two* days. The AT here seems to be a rather unintelligent abbreviation of a longer account of the institution of the festival.

14. In v. 48 the narrative recounting Mordecai's recording the events and dispatch of his letter (ἔγραψε . . . καὶ ἐξαπέστειλε, v. 47) is continued by *Mordecai's* sending (καὶ ἀπέστειλε)[34] portions to the poor, which they accepted. This is nothing like a report of or prescription for a regularly recurring festival custom, such as we find in MT 9.19. We seem to be reading an author who is unfamiliar with the observance of Purim.

15. Similar misapprehension is revealed by v. 49: 'Wherefore these days were called Phourdaia [or, Phourmaia (b); Phourdia (e₂); Pharaia (y)] on account of the lots which fell out for these days for a memorial' (διὰ τοῦτο ἐκλήθησαν αἱ ἡμέραι αὗται φουρδαια διὰ τοὺς κλήρους τοὺς πεσόντας εἰς τὰς ἡμέρας εἰς μνημόσυνον.) The lots in question here do not appear to be the lots cast by Haman but lots cast to establish the days that are to be observed as a memorial. MT and LXX are very clear, in their own different ways, that Purim derives from Haman's lot-casting: MT 9.24, 26 says: 'Haman had cast Pur, that is the lot, to destroy them . . . therefore they called these days Purim, after the term lot'; and LXX 9.23, 24, 26 has: 'The Jews accepted what Mordecai had written to them, how Haman . . . had fought against them, how he had cast a vote and a lot to annihilate them . . . On this account these days were called Phrourai on account of the lots, because in their language they are called Phrourai.' The AT does not appear to relate the lots cast for the festival to Haman's casting of lots. It had indeed mentioned Haman's casting of lots (AT 4.7), but *after* his conversation with the king, rather than *before* it (as in MT 3.7), and in a form that suggests this element is not an integral part of the AT.

16. In v. 52 Mordecai is said to have 'succeeded to'[35] (διεδέχετο)

King *Xerxes*.[36] Elsewhere in AT the king is always Ahasuerus (Ασσυῆρος) (2.1, 2; 3.1; 4.1). (It may be significant that in the Additions in the AT, Ασσυῆρος is also used consistently[37] even though LXX has Αρταξέρξης throughout.) This is the final piece of evidence which, I believe, clinches the argument that the ending of Esther in AT is not of a piece with the body of the story in AT.

Not all of the above-mentioned features are to be laid to the charge of the author or translator of the AT ending; at least one item (no. 10) above may be solely the responsibility of the copyists of AT. But the conclusion we have reached is that the character of AT does indeed alter quite radically after 8.16 (= MT 8.5). The concluding verses, 8.17-21, 33-52,[38] are a poorly written narrative, almost unintelligible at places, that cannot be attributed to the same author or level of redaction as the principal part of the book, and can only be regarded as secondary to it. Apparently the original form of AT ended at the point in the narrative reached by the time of 8.17 (whether or not 8.17 was itself the original conclusion). Why then was a distinctly inferior narrative tacked on to the end of the story? It can hardly have been for the sake of linking the story more closely to a (Purim) festival, since festival celebrations play only a marginal role in v. 47, and the name Purim is not known. Since the ending has no obvious *Tendenz*, it is most probable that it owes its origin to what was felt to be a *narrative* deficiency. However clumsily the story was supplemented, the narrative without supplementation must have been perceived as ending too summarily, too pacifically or too undramatically.

We have now established, on the intrinsic evidence of AT, that its narrative concluded at a very similar point to that of our proto-Masoretic Hebrew story. Due allowance being made for the major plot difference between the two narratives (Haman's decree can be *annulled* in AT but only *balanced* in the proto-MT story), the AT in its earlier form ('the proto-AT') becomes supporting evidence for the existence of a Hebrew story without the material of MT ch. 9. The diagram at the beginning of Chapter 10 will outline the relationship of these varying Esther texts.

Where we should now turn is to examine the relationship between the proto-MT and the proto-AT stories of Esther (Chapter 8), but first we must take stock of the status of the AT as a whole.

IV

So far we have considered principally the ending of the AT. It is desirable now to form some general impression of the nature of the essential AT (viz. up to AT 8.17, i.e. without its Appendix, and, of course, excluding the Additions)—which is what I call the proto-AT—before considering in some detail how its text witnesses to a pre-Masoretic Hebrew text (the task of Chapter 8).

The principal issue is the AT's relation to the LXX. I have cited at the beginning of this chapter the conclusion of C.A. Moore that the AT is 'a separate translation of the Hebrew', a Hebrew original 'at points quite different from the one presupposed by the LXX'.[39] This seems to me to be undeniable, but it has not been the common view in the history of Septuagintal scholarship,[40] and it is implicitly opposed by the most recent paper on the subject, that of E. Tov. So some justification of the view here adopted is required.

The question of the relation of the AT to the LXX has often been discussed in terms of whether it is a 'recension' of the LXX or not. Paton, for example, maintained that it 'is a recension, not a version; nevertheless, it is the most widely variant recension that is found in the whole Greek OT'.[41] As against such judgments, it must be stated quite categorically that all discussion of this question that does not distinguish between the Additions and the Appendix (the ending, AT 8.17-21, 33-52) on the one side and the remainder of the AT on the other is obsolete and insufficiently discriminating. Even the carefully nuanced position of R. Hanhart, that the AT is not a recension of the LXX but a re-working (*Neugestaltung*) of the Greek Esther-tradition, with heavy dependence on the LXX text,[42] can be faulted in this respect. For once the distinction between different materials in the book is made, it becomes apparent that the text of the Additions in AT can best be regarded as a *recension* of the LXX text (that is, when they *are* dependent on the LXX), while the text of the core of the book is quite unrelated to the LXX (except for occasional examples of contamination of AT-type manuscripts by the LXX text-form[43]), and so forms a distinct *version* of a Hebrew *Vorlage* distinct from the MT.

It is noteworthy that evidence advanced in favour of the dependence of AT upon LXX is very largely drawn from the Additions. Hanhart, for example, points to three such cases.

(i) He regards AT 5.27[44] (C 28) as the clearest example of such dependence. LXX has (at 14.17 = C 28) οὐκ ἔφαγεν ἡ δούλη σου τράπεζαν Ἀμάν, 'thy handmaid has not eaten Haman's food', whereas AT has οὐκ ἔφαγεν ἡ δούλη σου ἐπὶ τῶν τραπεζῶν αὐτῶν ἅμα, 'thy handmaid has not eaten at their tables together with them'—where the adverb ἅμα seems clearly out of place and must, Hanhart thinks, be explained as resulting from a reinterpretation of the LXX, a reinterpretation in which the pronoun αὐτῶν was introduced at the same time as ἅμα was substituted for Αμαν.[45]

(ii) Hanhart's next example is from AT 5.23 (= LXX C 22, Vulg. 14.11), where AT μισοῦσί σε, 'give not your sceptre to [your] enemies *who hate you*', seems secondary to LXX μὴ οὖσιν, 'give not your sceptre to those *who are not*'.[46]

(iii) His final example is from AT 8.24 (= LXX E 7, Vulg. 16.7), where AT ἀξίως seeems secondary to LXX ἀνάξια.[47] All three cases are, of course, from the Additions, so they can prove nothing about the dependence or otherwise of the core of AT upon LXX. It is really very misleading to use the material of the Additions as evidence of the character of the AT's text.

The *core* of AT or the 'original' AT, 'proto-AT', viz. AT without the Additions and without its Appendix or secondary ending (AT 8.17-21, 33-52), is the principal matter when the question of the relation of AT to LXX is to be raised. For this reason most of the examples adduced by E. Tov to demonstrate the dependence of AT upon LXX are irrelevant to the 'original' AT, since they are drawn from those secondary ending verses. He mentions three cases from these verses of renderings common to AT and LXX (I use the text as cited by him):

(i)   9.3 (AT 8.42)   מנשאים את־היהודים
        LXX, AT   ἐτίμων τοὺς Ιουδαίους

(ii)   9.3 (AT 8.42)   עשי מלאכה אשר למלך
        LXX, AT   οἱ βασιλικοὶ γραμματεῖς

(iii)   10.3 (AT 8.52)   כי מרדכי היהודי משנה למלך אחשורוש
        LXX, AT   ὁ δὲ Μαρδοχαῖος διεδέχετο τὸν βασιλέα
                         Αρταξέρξην (AT Ασσυῆρον)

He also notes two cases where a corruption in AT shows itself to be secondary to LXX:

(i)   9.7-10   ואת־פרשנדתא דלפון . . . עשרת בני המן
        (AT 8.44)
        LXX   τόν τε Φαρσανννεσταιν καὶ Δελφωὶν . . .
                         τοὺς δέκα υἱοὺς Ἀμάν

AT   καὶ τὸν Φαρσαν καὶ τὸν ἀδελφὸν αὐτοῦ . . .
       καὶ τοὺς δέκα υἱοὺς Αμαν

Here the corruption of Δελφών to τὸν ἀδελφόν has brought in its train the addition of αὐτοῦ and the addition of καί before τοὺς δέκα υἱούς.

(ii)   8.17 (AT 8.41) ורבים מעמי הארץ מתיהדים
       LXX   καὶ πολλοὶ τῶν ἐθνῶν περιετέμοντο
       AT   καὶ πολλοὶ τῶν Ιουδαίων περιετέμνοντο

Here, the verb περιετέμ(ν)οντο appears to relate AT to LXX, while AT's τῶν Ιουδαίων is presumably an erroneous second rendering of מתיהדים.

There is no reason to dispute the relationship between the AT and the LXX evidenced by these readings; and certainly if the reading of the AT mss at 9.7-10 (AT 8.44) is an authentic AT reading there is no reason to doubt that the direction of influence is from LXX to AT.[48]

What Tov does not give, nor any other scholar who has discussed the relation of LXX and AT (Langen, Jacob, Hanhart), is examples of cases in the 'original' core of AT where dependence of AT on LXX is *contra-indicated*. These are cases where AT is divergent from LXX for none of the reasons that are generally advanced to explain divergence (the dependent text expands, or abbreviates, or misunderstands, or corrects, or conforms to a different *Vorlage*, or improves the style). They are cases where the divergence of AT from LXX is inexplicable except on the assumption that it had no knowledge of the LXX and was not dependent on it in any way.[49] An abundant collection of examples could be made, far more extensive than those in any category presupposing relationship with LXX. Here are some examples:

(i)   2.2 (AT 3.2)   ויאמרו נערי המלך משרתיו יבקשו למלך נערות
                        בתולות טובות מראה

       LXX   καὶ εἶπαν οἱ διάκονοι τοῦ βασιλέως Ζητη-
                θήτω τῷ βασιλεῖ κοράσια ἄφθορα καλὰ
                τῷ εἴδει.

       AT   καὶ εἶπον οἱ λειτουργοὶ τοῦ βασιλέως
                Ζητήσωμεν παρθένους καλὰς τῷ εἴδει

(ii)   2.4 (AT 3.4)   והנערה אשר תיטב בעיני המלך תמלך תחת ושתי
                        וייטב הדבר בעיני המלך ויעש כן

LXX   καὶ ἡ γυνὴ ἣ ἂν ἀρέσῃ τῷ βασιλεῖ βασι-
λεύσει ἀντὶ Αστίν. καὶ ἤρεσεν τῷ βασιλεῖ
τὸ πρόσταγμα, καὶ ἐποίησεν οὕτως.

AT   καὶ ἡ παῖς ἣ ἐὰν ἀρέσῃ τῷ βασιλεῖ, κατα-
σταθήσεται ἀντὶ Ουαστιν. καὶ ἐποίησαν
ἑτοίμως κατὰ ταῦτα.

(iii)   3.1 (AT 4.1)   אחר הדברים האלה גדל המלך אחשורוש את־המן
בן־המדתא האגגי וינשאהו

LXX   μετὰ δὲ ταῦτα ἐδόξασεν ὁ βασιλεὺς Ἀρτα-
ξέρξης Ἀμὰν Ἀμαδάθου Βουγαῖον καὶ
ὕψωσεν αὐτόν

AT   καὶ ἐγένετο μετὰ τοὺς λόγους τούτους,
ἐμεγάλυνεν ὁ βασιλεὺς Ασσυῆρος Αμαν
Αμαδάθου Βουγαῖον, καὶ ἐπῆρεν αὐτόν

(iv)   3.8 (AT 4.8)   ויאמר... ישנו עם־אחד מפזר ומפרד בין העמים
בכל מדינות מלכותך

LXX   καὶ ἐλάλησεν... λέγων Ὑπάρχει ἔθνος
διεσπαρμένον ἐν τοῖς ἔθνεσιν ἐν πάσῃ τῇ
βασιλείᾳ σου

AT   ἐλάλει... λέγων Ἔστι λαὸς διεσπαρμένος
ἐν πάσαις ταῖς βασιλείαις

(v)   4.1 (AT 5.1-2) ומרדכי ידע את־כל־אשר נעשה ויקרע מרדכי
את־בגדיו וילבש שק ואפר

LXX   ὁ δὲ Μαρδοχαῖος ἐπιγνοὺς τὸ συντελού-
μενον διέρρηξεν τὰ ἱμάτια ἑαυτοῦ, καὶ
ἐνεδύσατο σάκκον καὶ κατεπάσατο σποδόν

AT   ὁ δὲ Μορδοχαῖος ἐπέγνω πάντα τὰ γεγονότα... περιείλετο τὰ ἱμάτια αὐτοῦ καὶ
περιεβάλετο σάκκον, καὶ σποδωθεὶς...

(vi)   4.2 (AT 5.2)   כי אין לבוא אל־השער המלך בלבוש שק

LXX   οὐ γὰρ ἦν ἐξὸν αὐτῷ εἰσελθεῖν εἰς τὴν
αὐλὴν σάκκον ἔχοντι

AT   οὐ γὰρ ἠδύνατο εἰσελθεῖν εἰς τὰ βασίλεια
ἐν σάκκῳ

(vii)   7.9 (AT 8.12f.)   ויאמר הרבונה אחד מן־הסריסים לפני המלך גם
הנה־העץ אשר־עשה המן למרדכי אשר דבר־טוב
על־המלך עמד בבית המן גבה חמשים אמה
ויאמר המלך תלהו עליו

LXX   εἶπεν δὲ Βουγαθὰν εἷς τῶν εὐνούχων πρὸς
τὸν βασιλέα Ἰδοὺ καὶ ξύλον ἡτοίμασεν
Ἀμὰν Μαρδοχαίῳ τῷ λαλήσαντι περὶ τοῦ
βασιλέως, καὶ ὤρθωται ἐν τοῖς Ἀμὰν ξύλον
πηχῶν πεντήκοντα. εἶπεν δὲ ὁ βασιλεὺς
Σταυρωθήτω ἐπ' αὐτοῦ.

AT   καὶ εἶπεν Αγαθας εἷς τῶν παίδων αὐτοῦ
Ἰδοὺ ξύλον ἐν τῇ αὐλῇ αὐτοῦ πηχῶν
πεντήκοντα, ὃ ἔκοψεν Αμαν ἵνα κρεμάσῃ
τὸν Μαρδοχαῖον τὸν λαλήσαντα ἀγαθὰ
περὶ τοῦ βασιλέως... καὶ εἶπεν ὁ βασιλεὺς
κρεμασθήτω ἐπ' αὐτῷ.

This last example is particularly impressive since with one minor
exception (the omission of טוב after דבר in the LXX's *Vorlage*) it
appears that LXX and AT had before them exactly the same Hebrew
text but handled it quite differently syntactically, as well as semantically
(note the translations of עשה, בית, and תלה) without any evident
tendency that could be called typical of either text. All seven cases
that I have just cited confirm the impression that with AT and LXX we
are speaking of *different translations* (indeed translations of *Vorlagen*
that often diverged from one another) and furthermore, of different
and unrelated translations even when they are translating identical
Vorlagen.

Now if the *independence* of AT and LXX is accepted as the
fundamental datum about their relationship, it follows that other

categories of relationship analysed by previous scholars must be redefined. Thus readings which AT and LXX have in common can form no argument for a relationship of dependence in either direction but are the unremarkable result of both texts being translations from an identically or similarly worded Hebrew original. A reading that stands closer to a Hebrew original is not a matter of 'correction towards' the Hebrew, since each translator was only translating and not at the same time reworking another Greek translation. And 'expansions' or 'abbreviations' on the part of the AT (better, pluses or minuses vis-à-vis LXX) are not expansions or abbreviations of the LXX, but probably pluses or minuses of the AT's *Vorlage* vis-à-vis the MT (they could of course also be expansions or abbreviations by the AT translator of his original, but I think we can never tell if that is ever the case).

We are now in a position to examine the two cases adduced by Tov that are taken from the 'original' or 'proto-'AT as *prima facie* evidence of the AT's dependence on the LXX.

Tov's general position concerning the AT (he uses the siglum L) is that it is closely connected with LXX and depends upon it (p. 4), but also that it reflects some type of *revision* of the LXX (p. 7). Since it is clear that the AT is often closer to the Hebrew than is the LXX, the AT must, he argues, have had independent access to a Hebrew *Vorlage*; and that Hebrew sometimes differed from the MT (p. 10). Now because he regards the AT as having *both* Hebrew and Greek *Vorlagen* he has to explain its relationship to each of its *Vorlagen*: it is that AT is a 'revision' of the LXX 'towards' the MT (p. 10)—and presumably his concluding summary, that it is a 'translation' which is 'based' on the LXX but 'corrects it towards' a Hebrew *Vorlage* (p. 25) means the same thing.[50]

The two cases from canonical Esther prior to AT 8.17 which he refers to as evidence of AT's dependence on LXX deserve serious examination. They are 1.20 (AT 2.20) and 4.8 (AT 5.4).

(i)	MT	למנדול ועד־קטן
	LXX	ἀπὸ πτωχοῦ ἕως πλουσίου
	AT	ἀπὸ πτωχῶν ἕως πλουσίων

Prima facie, it must be allowed, LXX and AT at this point are related, though such evidence of relationship in itself shows nothing about the direction of *dependence* (for Tov of course it is part of a larger argument for the dependence of the AT on the LXX). But the significance of this item for the question of the relationship of AT and LXX becomes less clear when we consider another case of the identical phrase in the MT (1.5 = AT 2.5):

MT	למגדול ועד־קטן
LXX	*om.*
AT	ἀπὸ μεγάλου ἕως μικροῦ

For the record, we should note that one corrector of Sinaiticus (S[c.a]) and three uncials (fkz = 583, 58, 93) have ἀπὸ μεγάλου καὶ (– καί fk) ἕως μικροῦ; but fkz are known to contain Hexaplaric readings[51] and this particular reading has no claim to be a genuine Septuagintal reading. If we now compare 1.20 with 1.5, we find the evidence of 1.20 that AT follows LXX is counterbalanced by the evidence of 1.5. To be sure, 1.5 in AT *may* be an instance of correction of LXX in the direction of MT, but—if we allow that—we are compelled to view 1.20 in AT as an instance of *non*-correction of LXX in the direction of MT. We are not likely to argue that the identity of the AT's reading at 1.5 with that of the corrector of Sinaiticus and manuscripts fkz evidences any relationship between them; must we, however, suppose that the identity of the AT and LXX at 1.20 shows *their* relationship? Do we *know* that they each had the same Hebrew *Vorlage*, itself identical with the MT? It turns out that so many questions raise themselves that it is difficult to see that any general statement about the nature of AT and its relationship to LXX can be safely drawn from the readings displayed above.

The second passage is particularly interesting:

(ii)	LXX +	διότι Ἀμὰν ὁ δευτερεύων τῷ βασιλεῖ ἐλάλησεν
	AT +	ὅτι Αμαν ὁ δευτερεύων λελάληκε τῷ βασιλεῖ

Tov comments that 'The separation between the translation of the two elements of the phrase משנה המלך ... in L is clearly secondary'[52]— i.e. that the more natural reading is that of LXX, where the words ὁ δευτερεύων τῷ βασιλεῖ are to be taken together, as a translation of the Hebrew phrase משנה המלך. (The MT has nothing corresponding to this phrase at this point, nor, unfortunately, have LXX or AT anything corresponding to משנה המלך where it does occur in MT, at 10.3.) Now it is true that משנה המלך, 'the second to the king', is an attested phrase, not only at 10.3 but also at 2 Chronicles 28.7. However, משנה can also be used absolutely (1 Chron. 5.12; 16.5; 2 Chron. 31.12; Neh. 11.9, 17; cf. 1 Sam. 23.17 אהיה לך למשנה). If we

suppose the Hebrew *Vorlage* of AT to have been כי אמר המן המשנה למלך,
both LXX and AT represent possible independent translations of the
same Hebrew: either 'because Haman the second to the king has
spoken' (so LXX) or 'because Haman the second has spoken to the
king' (so AT). Thus, even if we allow that the AT's translation is
inferior to the LXX's at this point, it is not at all the case that AT is
'clearly secondary' to LXX, as Tov maintains.

This chapter may be concluded with a repetition of what the
tendency of its argument has been. The AT of Esther, in its essential
core (i.e. up to AT 8.17 and excluding the Additions), is a translation
of a Semitic original that was different from the MT. The LXX, on the
other hand, is a translation of an original that was in all important
respects and probably in most details identical with the MT. Any
affinity between AT and LXX in the core of the story arises solely from
the similarity of their respective *Vorlagen* (a few minor exceptions
from this rule, viz. apparent contaminations of AT by a LXX-type text,
and the curious case of the 'religious' contaminations, will be
examined in the next chapter).

Chapter 8

THE PRE-MASORETIC STORY OF ESTHER

The argument developed in the previous chapter is that the proto-AT (AT 2.1–8.16) was translated from a Hebrew text similar to, but not identical with, the text of the proto-Masoretic book. In this chapter I shall be arguing that the *Vorlage* presupposed by the proto-AT text is *older* than the proto-Masoretic book. AT is thus the witness to a *pre-*Masoretic Hebrew story of Esther, itself the ancestor of the *proto-*Masoretic story that now forms the core of our canonical Hebrew book (see the diagram at the beginning of Chapter 10). The pluses of (proto-)MT compared with (proto-)AT are on this theory expansions of that pre-Masoretic text; the primary expansions are due to two major extensions of the plot (the second decree, the conspiracy of the eunuchs). The minuses of (proto-)MT, which concern the wording rather than the plot, have no evident rationale, except perhaps for one group of nine minuses (relating to divine activity and religious behaviour).

The position nearest to the theory that will be developed here is that of H.J. Cook, who argued that:

> The Hebrew story of Mordecai and Haman, consisting of our Hebrew book 1–8$_5$, in a recension differing considerably from our Masoretic text, was translated into Greek to form the text we call *A*.[1]

This statement differs from my view in that Cook regards the *Vorlage* of proto-AT as a variant *recension* of proto-MT, whereas I regard that *Vorlage* as the *ancestor* of proto-MT. Cook, in fact, in speaking of AT's 'additions' and 'omissions' vis-à-vis the MT, tends to regard MT as the ancestor of AT. I regard AT's pluses and minuses vis-à-vis MT as omissions and additions respectively on the part of MT (or, to be more precise, proto-MT).

Any closer relationship between AT and MT than between LXX and MT I explain as due to AT and LXX being independent translations of a Hebrew text which went through three phases: (i) pre-MT, from which proto-AT was translated; (ii) proto-MT; (iii) MT, from which 'proto-LXX' (i.e. the LXX without the Additions) was translated. I do not agree with Tov that AT is based on the LXX and corrects it in the direction of a Hebrew recension variant from MT.[2]

If we compare the (proto-)AT with the (proto-)MT we note several groupings of pluses and minuses. Two of these are especially significant, and will be examined in sections I and II of this chapter. The third of such groupings (of 'religious' pluses) needs special examination (section III). Some concluding observations form section IV.

I

The Masoretic text's most important plus from a narrative point of view is the element of the unalterability of the royal decree against the Jews. For it is the unalterability of the decree that projects the tension of the story far beyond the conflict of Mordecai and Haman, so that the danger to the Jewish people has by no means been averted even when Haman has been put to death. In the plot of the MT the overcoming of the Persian decree is as much a difficulty as the overcoming of Haman himself. The earlier Hebrew story (proto-MT) comes to an end at precisely the moment of the resolution of that second problem.

The conflict between the decrees is so valuable a source of narrative tension that it is difficult to imagine any reviser of the story writing it out of the record. It is true, as I have argued above, that the author of MT 9.1-19 did not properly appreciate the irony of the conflict between the two decrees, and composed his supplement to the narrative as if the second decree (misunderstood by him as permission to kill those who 'hate' as much as those who 'attack') had completely overturned the first. But he did not eliminate the evidence in chs. 1-8 that a real conflict existed! Nor is it probable that the AT translator would have deliberately excised from his text reference to the unalterable law if his *Vorlage* was the full MT containing an explanation both of how the force of Haman's edict was averted *and* of how the Jews managed, under cover of the second edict, to slaughter several myriads of their enemies.

The only persuasive explanation for the AT's minus on this crucial element of the story is that at the time of AT's Hebrew *Vorlage* this element did not exist in the Hebrew narrative. The story AT tells is coherent enough and, utterly reasonably, concludes with the destruction of Haman and his decree. It is not hard to make an intelligent guess as to where the development of the story originated. The tradition of Persian law's unalterability plays a decisive part in the tale of Daniel in the lions' den (Dan. 6), where the movement of the story of the imperial officials' putsch against Daniel hangs entirely on this factor, which is explicitly played upon (vv. 8, 12, 15). It is not important that elsewhere in the tales of Daniel the king's command is overturned (by Daniel [cf. 2.12 and 24] or God [3.28]), or can be asserted without recourse to the doctrine of its immutability (3.4-6, 10, 15, 19). Once that doctrine is introduced into the Esther story—whether derived from Daniel itself or from some other narrative stuff—a new dimension to the decree of Haman which is sealed with the king's ring is brought into being. In the expansion of the story from its *pre*-Masoretic form to its *proto*-Masoretic form, three narrative expansions were required to accommodate the new twist given to the story by the introduction of the motif of the unalterability of Persian law.

(i) It becomes important, in the first place, to give greater weight to the reversal of Haman's decree. So long as there is no problem about overturning a Persian decree, Mordecai can simply say, '[My request is] that you repeal (ἀνέλῃς) Haman's letter' (AT 8.16), and the king can adequately respond by putting into Mordecai's charge imperial affairs (AT 8.17³). But once it is not just a problem, but a sheer impossibility, to overturn the decree, the ingenious device of a second decree that does not contradict the first but promises to nullify its effect can be introduced. The Jewish spokesperson (Esther in MT, not Mordecai as in AT) still asks that an order be given to 'overturn' (להשיב)⁴ the letters sent by Haman (MT 8.5),⁵ but the king must point out that, however sympathetic he is to her request, matters are not so simple—'an edict written in the name of the king and sealed with the king's ring cannot be overturned' (אין להשיב) (MT 8.8)—and Esther and Mordecai will have to manage as best they can within the framework of that unalterability.⁶

(ii) In the second place,⁶ once the conception of a second decree pitted against the first is developed, it becomes necessary to elaborate the contents and dispatch of that decree. Some mere generalizing statement such as AT's 8.17, 'He [the king] put into [Mordecai's]

hands the affairs of the kingdom', will not suffice, and neither will the
mere permission to issue a decree, such as we have in MT 8.8. What is
required is an elaboration, with much the same narrative weight as
had earlier been given to the dispatch of Haman's decree. The
narrator of the proto-MT had no doubt about where to turn for his
model for this elaboration: the narrative of 4.12-14. So we read in 8.9-
14, just as in ch. 4, of the summoning of the scribes, the date of their
summoning, the edict written according to the vizier's command
(Mordecai, of course, not Haman now), its destination to satraps,
governors and princes, its various editions in all languages of the
empire, its being written in the king's name and sealed with the
king's seal, its dispatch by couriers, its command to 'destroy, slay,
and annihilate', and to plunder the goods of the slain, on a specified
date, its issuance as a written order and as an oral proclamation
throughout the empire, its departure with the couriers, its authoritative
issuance in Susa. But in addition to this highly formal repetition from
ch. 4, some new material was inserted: 1. The extent of the empire,
'from India to Ethiopia, a hundred and twenty-seven provinces' (8.9),
a phrase borrowed from 1.1 to stress how widespread the Jewish
dispersion was and how numerous therefore the Jewish population of
the empire. 2. The decree is addressed 'also to the Jews in their script
and in their language' (v. 9), an addition that is strictly speaking
otiose, since the Jews must be included in the previous phrase, 'to
every province in its own script and to every people in its own
language'; but the Jews are the principal subject of the decree and are
therefore conceived of as specifically addressed. 3. The detail of the
courier system, 'mounted couriers of the various post-stations'[7] (or
however הרצים רכבי הרכש האחשתרנים, v. 8, is to be translated) is now
elaborate—by contrast to the bald reference to הרצים, 'the couriers',
in 3.13. It is not a matter of a more rapid postal service being
employed by Mordecai than by Haman, but rather that the speed of
the imperial post is worth stressing when it is being used in the
service of Jewish survival.

(iii) In the third place, now that the second decree has been
speedily issued throughout the empire 'to all peoples' (v. 13) and not
just the Jews—so that there will be no surprise for anyone on Adar 13
and all the citizens of the empire will have plenty of opportunity to
decide where their loyalties lie—it remains only for the narrative of
the proto-Masoretic text to be finally concluded. The two dangers—
Haman and his decree—have now been thoroughly dealt with, and

the narrative needs only to move out from the palace into a longer focus for the closing scene (as indeed it did when, earlier, it ended at AT 8.16-17 or would when, later, in the final Masoretic version, it ended at MT 10.3). The material for the closing scene was largely borrowed from earlier parts of the story: (a) The notice that Mordecai 'went out' (יצא) into the city in royal robes perhaps recalls 4.1 where he 'went out' (יצא) into the city with rent clothes and in sackcloth and ashes. (b) The phrase 'royal robes' (לבוש מלכות) comes from the לבוש מלכות which Haman designated for Mordecai in 6.8. (c) 'Blue and white' (תכלת וחור) are the imperial colours of the hangings we saw in 1.6. (d) The 'great golden crown' (עטרת) is perhaps not the king's or queen's own crown (כתר) of 1.11; 2.17; 6.8,[8] but the idea of the splendid headdress has obviously figured in the story already. (e) The 'fine linen' (בוץ) and 'purple' (ארגמן) have already occurred as the material of the cords of the hangings of the imperial marquee (1.6). (f) The city of Susa shouts and rejoices, in contrast to its being in consternation in 3.15. (g) The fourfold depiction of the Jews' joy, with four abstract terms (light, gladness, joy, honour) is obviously modelled on the depiction of their gloom at 4.3, where we also have four nouns (mourning, fasting, weeping, lamenting). Perhaps also the fourfold formula concerning the Jews throughout the empire (gladness, joy, festival, holiday) is modelled on the same phrase.[9] (h) The wording, 'And in every province and in every city, wherever the king's command and his edict came' ובכל-מדינה ומדינה ובכל-עיר ועיר מקום אשר דבר-המלך ודתו מגיע), is mostly repetition of 4.3 (only ובכל- עיר ועיר is added here).

In short, the proto-MT narrator creatively adapted earlier material and added two significant items of his own in order to round off the tale in an elegant and satisfying manner. From earlier Israelite traditions he borrowed the motif of religious awe falling upon the heathen (e.g. Jos. 2.9; Exod. 15.16; Ps. 105.38), and, removing the name of God from the usual phrase, transformed it into 'the fear of the Jews'. Finally, he added his own novelty, a clause which perhaps gives some clue to the historical ambience in which he worked: many Gentiles made themselves Jews (became proselytes).

All of this new conclusion to the story was tastefully and stylishly executed in the manner of the earlier, pre-Masoretic, story of Esther. The formal and elaborate account of the dispatch of the second decree carries just the right amount of authoritative conviction, while the final paragraph ends the story with a burst of colour, a spray of synonyms and a show-stopping punchline of mass spontaneous proselytism. Even the focussing technique, as the picture pans from the close-up of Mordecai stepping out from the palace, to the cheering crowds in Susa, to the Jews throughout the empire, to—at the broadest extent—the inhabitants of the empire generally, bears the mark of a skilled narrative craftsman.

Nevertheless, at one point the reworking of the earlier (pre-MT) story has left a visible seam. It is not unsightly but it has attracted the notice of some sharp-eyed critics—though they, not recognizing it as a seam, have thought it a flaw in the cloth. I refer to MT 8.2f., where the king has just given his ring to Mordecai and where Esther thereupon 'spoke again' (ותוסף אסתר ותדבר) to the king, requesting him to revoke Haman's decree, and had the golden sceptre held out to her. Paton, who speaks for many, imagines that we have here the depiction of another audience of Esther's with the king, and wonders at the narrative logic. 'From v. ⁴', he says, 'it appears that Esther once more risked her life in going to the King unsummoned (*cf.* 5¹). It is hard to see why this was necessary, now that Mordecai was grand vizier . . . It is also hard to see why Esther should run this risk when the day for slaughtering the Jews was set nearly a year later . . .'[10] Bardtke likewise believes that 8.3 introduces a new scene, later than the events of 8.1-2 and set in a different locale, the royal throne-room.[11] This is not an unnatural assumption to make. It is, I think, not what is intended, and Moore is right in firmly rejecting that interpretation, observing that the text says, not that Esther *came* again but that she *spoke* again. The same continuing royal audience as is pictured in vv. 1-2 would then be the occasion for Esther's falling at the king's feet, not in an act of obeisance but as a supplicant (neither כרע nor השתחוה, the more technical terms for prostration [cf. 3.2, 3], is used, but the more general term נפל). Unlike Haman, who also has 'fallen' (נפל) in supplication in 7.8, she is begging not for her own life, but for her people's (v. 4), and to her the king extends the sceptre not as a sign of clemency but as a token of encouragement. The earlier scene of 5.1-3 is replayed with a rather different tonality; and we may permit a sensitive author to adapt his material as creatively as this. But the slight hitch or uncertainty of continuity between v. 2 and v. 3 (which indeed persuaded the Masoretes to mark v. 2 as an open *parashah*) may suggest that some revision has been slightly imperfectly executed.

To learn how the revision of the earlier story by the proto-

Masoretic author was effected we shall have to pay close attention to the AT. In AT we find a translation of what I suppose to have been the pre-Masoretic text at this point. At AT 8.13 the king removes the ring from his hand, thus 'sealing' Haman's life (καὶ ἐσφραγίσθη ἐν αὐτῷ ὁ βίος αὐτοῦ). Though he is not explicitly said to give the ring to Mordecai (as he does in MT 8.2), he calls Mordecai and gives (ἐχαρίσατο) to him everything that was Haman's (in MT the house of Haman is first given to Esther, who then sets Mordecai over it, vv. 1-2). The king then (AT 8.16) says to *Mordecai*, 'What do you want? I will do it', and Mordecai replies, 'That you should revoke Haman's letter', whereupon the king puts into his hand all the affairs of the kingdom. The scene in the king's presence is, in AT, an unmistakable unity with the scene of the banquet at which Haman is unmasked. The pace of events is even more rapid than in the MT, with the king moving from 'Let [Haman] be hung' in v. 13 to 'What do you want?' to Mordecai in v. 16, with only a brief pause to exclaim in astonishment to Esther, 'And did he plan as well [i.e. as well as massacring your people] to hang Mordecai who saved me from the eunuchs? Did he not know that Esther was his kinswoman?' (ὅτι πατρῷον αὐτοῦ γένος ἐστὶν ἡ Εσθηρ). Mordecai's appearance at the private dinner party is well motivated and explicitly narrated in the AT. The attendant Agathas (MT Harbona) mentions the pole on which Haman has intended to hang Mordecai—which speech serves both to decide Haman's fate *and* to give the king a new piece of knowledge, that Mordecai has been in immediate danger from Haman. The king thereupon summons (ἐκάλεσεν) Mordecai into the dining room in order to induct him into Haman's office and give him a boon of Mordecai's own devising.

This well-constructed but rather breathlessly narrated chain of events has been broken up and slowed down by the second narrator, the author of the proto-Masoretic story. His purpose is transparent: in order to give appropriate weight to the removal of the second danger to the Jews, the unalterable decree which still stands as the law of the Medes and Persians even after Haman has been dispatched, he must close off the scene in which Haman's fate is sealed and begin a new scene in which the question of the decree will be settled. We observe the following alterations he made to the earlier story:

1. The king's command to hang/impale Haman on his own gallows/stake (AT 8.13; MT 7.10) is now followed by a report: 'So they impaled Haman on the pole which he had prepared for Mordecai'.

2. 'Then the anger of the king abated' (MT 8.10) (וחמת המלך שככה)
closes off the episode with a clause borrowed from 2.1, 'When the
anger of the king had abated' (כשך חמת המלך), where it introduces a
new episode and links it to the preceding.

3. The new episode of the nullifying of the second decree is
introduced with a time notation, 'On that day', which links back to
'on the second day' at 7.1, itself connecting with 'on that night' of 6.1,
'on that day' of 5.9 (cf. 'tomorrow', 5.12), 'this day' of 5.4 (cf.
'tomorrow', 5.8). This notation both affects a disjunction of the
scenes of chs. 7 and 8 and links them as two halves of one whole
action by explicitly setting them on the same day.

4. The king gives his signet ring to Mordecai (MT 8.2), meaning
thereby that Mordecai is now promoted to Haman's position, not
indeed in view of anything that Mordecai has done but because of his
relationship to Esther. For she has just now told the king 'what he
was to her' (8.1). Perhaps the giving of the signet ring is also meant to
echo the previous giving of the ring, to Haman in 3.10, authorizing
the murderous edict against the Jews; here the narrator may be
faintly foreshadowing the eventual outcome of the ensuing interview,
the authorization of the second edict, which is similarly sealed with
the king's ring (8.8).

It was all rather different in the AT: in it and, presumably, in its
Vorlage, the king's ring had been given to Haman (AT 4.10) only for
the purpose of sealing the original edict; at AT 8.13 (MT 7.10) the ring
is back in the king's possession, where it has unobtrusively been for
most of the action, and he takes it off his own finger in order to
authorize persons unspecified to execute Haman. Later, in the
appendix to AT, Mordecai will use the king's ring to certify *his* letter
to the Jews (AT 8.34). Neither Haman nor Mordecai *wears* the king's
ring in AT, but the MT narrator envisages both Haman and Mordecai
as wearing it in their capacity as vizier, and so must explain to us—as
AT did not need to—that the king has taken his ring back from
Haman (8.2).

5. The 'house' of Haman is given to Esther; in AT's *Vorlage* all that
was Haman's (AT 8.15 πάντα τὰ τοῦ Αμαν) was given to *Mordecai*.
In MT it is to Esther rather than Mordecai because the dynamics of
the now extended plot require another scene for Esther. That is to
say, now that the unalterable decree has to be dealt with, the Jewish
cause has another battle to fight with Persian officialdom; Esther is
brought out of retirement by the proto-MT narrator in order to

present that Jewish case for the repeal of Haman's edict. Of course she cannot go through the same routine of dangerous entry to the king's presence as in ch. 5—that card has already been played—and in any case the psychology of the story leads us to expect pro-Jewish sentiment on the part of the king now that the enemy of the queen's people has been caught in an act of treason against the king personally (7.8). So Esther simply appears—without ceremony—in the royal presence (v. 1), and soon will fall at the king's feet with the chief matter in her mouth (v. 3). Mordecai could not have played this scene—he is not *sympathique* enough; in AT he could gruffly respond to the king's Τί θέλεις ('What do you want?') with his direct Ὅπως ἀνέλῃς τὴν ἐπιστολὴν τοῦ Αμαν ('For you to revoke Haman's letter') (AT 8.16), but it needs Esther to turn on the charm. Turn it on she does, with her collapse at the king's feet, her tears, her emotional language (the 'evil design' of Haman [את־רעת המן] and the 'plot he hatched' [מחשבתו אשר חשב] are surely her words, though they are not directly reported[12]).

6. But it is more than charm: it is also the skilful rhetoric (8.5-6) that is fully worthy of her guardian Mordecai who we recall 'brought her up' (2.7, 19)—in courtier's style, no doubt. (We have noted earlier good evidence of his own persuasive skills displayed in ch. 4.[13]) Aware of the delicacy of her request to rescind (להשיב) a decree issued in the king's name, she prefaces it with four conditional clauses, the first two familiar as forms of courtly politeness, the second two, however, being freshly minted for the occasion. We have heard courtiers, or Esther herself, often enough saying, 'if it please the king' (אם על־המלך טוב) (1.19; 3.9 [Haman!]; 5.4 [Esther!]; 5.8; 7.3)[14] or 'if I have found favour in his sight' (אם־מצאתי חן לפניו) (5.8, אם־מצאתי חן; 7.3, אם־מצאתי חן בעיניך; cf. also 2.15, 17; 5.2). But the third clause, 'and [if] the thing is right (כשר) in the eyes of the king' is a novelty: she means that she realizes how improper it is to suggest that a royal (or, royally authorized) decree should be tampered with.[15] The fourth clause, 'and [if] I am pleasing in his eyes' (וטובה אני בעיניו), is new too: it is her own play upon the everyday phrase 'if *it* is pleasing to the king' (אם על־המלך טוב). Her conditions for having her request heard have unobtrusively become reasons why her request should be heard; the last of them, her own beauty, though the least relevant (logically speaking) to her cause, is the reason which she may reasonably expect to linger most efficaciously in the king's mind.

7. With these conditional clauses, however, her speech is barely begun. In v. 5 she is moving in a touchy area to ask for the decree to be rescinded: she can hardly call it a decree 'written in the name of King Ahasuerus and sealed with the king's ring' as the narrator has certified it (3.12), and some non-committal phrase like 'letters devised by Haman the Agagite [viz. non-Persian]' will serve her well enough and still stay within the bounds of truth (not the whole truth, we must allow). But if she is making out that the infamous letter was just personal hate-mail from Haman's desk and not the official correspondence of the chancellery it hardly comes within the ambit of irrevocable law of the Medes and Persians. So will the old words 'recall, rescind, revoke' (השיב, העביר; AT ἀνέλῃς) do? She takes the gamble. The king does not demur; he can hardly insist, now that the conversation has taken this turn, on processing appeal against it under the rubric of an irreversible law by which his queen and newly appointed prime minister are sentenced to death. But he will signal, at the end of his response (v. 8), that he has not been taken in by Esther's little ploy: he has chosen to let it pass. The principle of the law's irreversibility stands unshaken.

8. Esther's final word is a little masterpiece of psychology and rhetoric: 'How can I endure to see the calamity that is coming to my people? . . . ' (v. 6). This is a trifle disingenuous on Esther's part, for as things stand, with Haman's decree still in force, it is not just her people but she herself who is threatened with 'calamity' and 'destruction'. When Mordecai had predicted that if she kept silence at such a time, she and her father's house would perish (4.14), he did not predict that if she spoke up the danger would be averted; there was no guarantee of that, and to this point Haman's decree still threatens her and her father's house. But how can she imply, having now received so many tokens of the king's good will, that she still feels under a personal threat? Much wiser to suggest that it is not her own fate but that of her people that moves her—selflessly—to entreat the king's favour. Wise, too, to write off all arguments about ethics, decency, or honour, and to play solely upon the king's regard for her feelings—which she can now fairly take for granted, having had the sceptre of clemency extended to her in her tearful prostration before him (vv. 3-4): 'how can *I* endure . . . how can *I* endure?' (איככה אוכל). She is her own trump card, and she plays it gallantly.

This whole scene, so patient of probing in its narratival, psychological, and dramatic dimensions, reveals itself as the writing of a superior talent. The narrator of the proto-MT, though in one sense he did no more than plump out the thinner story-line of his predecessor, in another quite transformed his *Vorlage* with a fresh, ingenious dramatic twist (the need for a second decree), and in yet another amply maintained the stylish standards of the original story.

I have already referred to one point where the second narrator's reworking of the brief conclusion of the earlier story has left a seam (at 8.3; see p. 98 above). I list now some minor points at which the narrative of the proto-MT in these concluding verses has not entirely smoothed over the shape of the earlier story (the pre-MT).

(i) In MT 8.1, Mordecai 'came before the king, because Esther had told what he was to her' (ומרדכי בא לפני המלך כי־הגידה אסתר מה הוא־לה). The sentence is perspicacious, if a little inelegant; but it omits a *tertium quid*. Surely something must intervene between Esther's revealing her relation to Mordecai and Mordecai's entering the king's presence, viz. the king's sending for Mordecai. This is just what AT has: καὶ ἐκάλεσεν ὁ βασιλεὺς τὸν Μαρδοχαῖον (8.15). But the proto-MT did not show the king as already aware that Mordecai and Esther were related (as did AT 8.14), and so, in order to get Mordecai a slice of the action, the most important thing was to explain how the king had come to connect Esther and Mordecai. That explanation (... כי) supplanted the smoother narrative link that in the AT had Mordecai summoned by the king. This little narrative omission, which is no real fault, is, like so many other details, readily explained on the supposition of an AT-like *Vorlage* of the MT.

(ii) The sequence 'Ahasuerus gave to Esther the house of Haman' (v. 1), 'the king gave his ring to Mordecai' (v. 2), 'Esther set Mordecai over Haman's house' (v. 2), 'Esther spoke to the king' (v. 3), 'the king said to Esther and Mordecai' (v. 7), 'I have given Esther the house of Haman' (v. 7), is ever so slightly vertiginous. The focus shifts a little too fast for comfort, though the sequence of events is all quite explicable. Esther must play the leading role, since she has all the charm, and the king desperately needs to be charmed into a creative attitude to Persian law. At the same time Mordecai must be brought to centre stage, for it is he who will have to be authorized to write to satraps and governors (cf. v. 9). It was all so much simpler in AT where (with its proper conclusion at AT 8.17) Esther yielded the limelight entirely to Mordecai. But more ingenious means more complicated, and the complication is a small price to pay for the delightfully intriguing invention of the proto-Masoretic narrator.

(iii) Why does Esther 'set Mordecai over the house of Haman' (v. 2)? Nothing comes of it, and the king still believes that it is Esther to whom he has given the house of Haman.[16] The sentence in the MT is gratuitous, though nothing worse than that. Does it not owe its existence to the pre-Masoretic *Vorlage* where first the king gives Mordecai 'all that is Haman's' (AT 8.15) and then commits into his hand 'the affairs of the kingdom' (AT 8.17)? In MT the first gift— which is after all the important one—is the king's signet ring, and the second the house of Haman, which had been given to Esther at the beginning of v. 1 mainly because she was the only one around to whom the gift, which was crying out to be made, could be given.[17] In AT, on the other hand, Mordecai was first given Haman's house by way of recognition of him as the king's saviour who had been unjustly plotted against by Haman (AT 8.14-15).

So far the implications for the proto-Masoretic story of introducing into the plot the motif of the irrevocability of Persian law, in particular Haman's decree.

II

In the story of Mordecai's discovery of the conspiracy of the eunuchs (2.21-23; 6.1-3 [AT 7.1-4]) AT has an important plus *and* minus vis-à-vis MT. While it has nothing corresponding to MT 2.21-23, the story of the discovery, at its appropriate chronological place, it has a plus at MT 6.1-3. AT reads:

> [2] . . . and the book of the chronicles was read to him. [3]And there was a conspiracy of the eunuchs and a benefit which Mordecai had rendered the king. [4]And the king paid close attention, saying, Mordecai is a faithful man for protecting my life. Since he has kept me alive until now, and I sit today on my throne, and I have done nothing for him, I have not acted rightly. [5]And the king said to his servants, What shall we do for Mordecai, the saviour of affairs[?] (τῷ σωτῆρι τῶν λόγων)?[18] And when they considered [it], the servants envied him; for the fear of Haman fell upon their bowels. [6]And the king pondered[?].[19] Now morning dawned (ἐγένετο ὄρθρος).

Now the reference to *a* conspiracy (there is no article before ὑπόθεσις) and *a* benefit Mordecai had done (καὶ ὃ ἐποίησε Μαρδοχαῖος εὐεργέτημα, 'what Mordecai had done by way of benefit') does not presuppose a previous recounting of the events.

And AT does not in fact have any such previous recounting. It is obvious, however, that the allusion cries out for expansion, the kind of expansion provided by MT in its 2.21-23. The narrative of MT is a little masterpiece (see next paragraph), which it is hard to imagine being deliberately omitted by any later recension. Its absence from AT is best explained as due to the priority of AT's *Vorlage* to MT.

The story of the conspiracy at MT 2.21-23 has several important functions in the narrative as a whole: (i) On the surface it establishes Mordecai's loyalty to the king—which is worth knowing before we read in 3.3 of Mordecai's transgressing the king's command in not doing obeisance to Haman. (ii) Below the surface, 2.21-23 is preparing for the narrative of the king's sleepless night in 6.1-3. That is to say, the segment 2.21-23 is self-contained and satisfactorily closed off by the notice of the recording of the events in the royal chronicles; no further reference to the affair is called for. The reprise in ch. 6 is thus a pleasingly dramatic turn, in which we will learn for the first time that something was missing from the narrative of 2.21-23: there was no record of a reward for Mordecai. And that omission, which we had not noticed to be an omission, will prove a springboard for the further development of the plot in ch. 6: just because of the omission Haman will have to parade Mordecai through the streets and so receive symbolic notification of his own impending downfall. (iii) At the same time the narrator of 2.21-23 uses the episode to reinforce the hand-in-glove character of the relationship between Mordecai and Esther: '[Mordecai] told it to Queen Esther, and Esther told the king in the name of Mordecai' (v. 22)—which corresponds to what we have only a moment ago read, that 'Esther obeyed Mordecai just as when she was brought up by him' (v. 20). Their relationship as depicted here will be the indispensable background to the depiction of the tension between them in ch. 4.

It is noteworthy that H.J. Cook does not mention 2.21-23 among the 'omissions' of AT, presumably because in no way can it be categorized as 'irrational material'. E. Tov, allowing that in MT the episode is of major importance, is compelled to argue that its omission from AT was because it was narrated *in Addition A* (1.11-16), and Tov insists on regarding the Additions in AT plus the canonical extent as forming an 'organic whole'.[20] While it is true that patches have been made between the Additions and the canonical sections (e.g. at AT 2.1; perhaps AT 5.16[21]), AT is not significantly different from LXX in this respect and it cannot be argued that the two Greek versions have by any means systematically integrated the Additions into their text. Tov's view of the AT as an 'organic whole', and therewith his explanation of its minus at this point, is therefore open to criticism—all the more so because he does not consider those places where AT does *not* harmonize with the Additions.

As for the plus in AT 7.3-6, which has been quoted above, it cannot be regarded—in the Greek at least—as one of the most successful episodes in the narrative. Peculiarities in the narrative suggest at first sight a contamination of the text of vv. 4-5: (i) No one answers the king's question, 'What shall we do for Mordecai?'. (ii) There is no apparent reason why the courtiers should be *envious* (διεφθόνουν) of Mordecai; for even though it looks as if he will soon be greatly honoured they can hardly doubt that he deserves to be. (iii) There is no reason why their fear of Haman should make them *envious* of Mordecai.

But if we suppose that διεφθόνουν translated a form of קנא which was intended in its Hebrew original to mean 'was angry' rather than 'was jealous' and that ἐνενόησεν means that the king *noticed* that the courtiers were angry (a reaction they could have been expected—as courtiers—to conceal) the narrative hangs together far better— except at one point: the king gets no answer to his question, Τί ποιήσομεν τῷ Μαρδοχαίῳ, 'What shall we do for Mordecai?' The Hebrew original of ποιήσομεν was doubtless נעשה, which the trans- lator of AT has read as נַעֲשֶׂה; that is the same consonantal text as MT נַעֲשָׂה, '[What] has been done?', to which the answer is given, 'Nothing has been done for him' (לא־נעשה עמו דבר, MT 6.3). But if the first [מה־]נעשה is read as future, 'What shall we do?', any following לא־נעשה דבר can hardly give an acceptable sense ('We shall do nothing'[!]). Let us therefore suppose that the translator of AT simply omitted a clause that seemed to him implausibly bold on the part of the courtiers, and we have restored integrity to the pre-Masoretic Hebrew *Vorlage* of AT. But the translator of AT, having embarked upon the interpretation of נעשה as 'we shall do', saw nothing in his text that developed the crucial narrative point that no reward had *already* been given to Mordecai. To move from the reading of the chronicles in vv. 2f. to the king's decision to do something for Mordecai in v. 5 required some account of the king's recognition of the omission; the translator of AT therefore composed v. 4 in which it is the king who is immediately aware that nothing has been done for Mordecai, and does not need to check it out with his courtiers that such is the implication of the chronicles (as he does in MT 6.3). Furthermore, if the courtiers do not answer the king, some explanation for their behaviour needs to be given: it can only be because they are afraid to take Mordecai's part by recommending a reward for him, and it can only be Haman that they are afraid of. Hence the origin of the clause ἐνέκειτο γὰρ φόβος Αμαν ἐν τοῖς σπλάγχνοις αὐτῶν (AT 7.5). It needs only to be added that the AT interpretation of נעשה was not very probable, since the king in Esther does not use the royal plural, and since the king's admission in AT 7.4, 'I have not done right', seems entirely out of character for this monarch and all the more likely to derive from a less skilled author than the original storyteller. The plus in AT 7.4-6 is thus to be ascribed principally to the translator of the AT, and not to his *Vorlage*, the pre-Masoretic story.

III

There is one group of pluses in AT which are unlike the previous two groupings in that they are not connected through some element of the story-line; but a single explanation might be thought desirable since they have something in common: the name of God or reference to religious practices. These are the following nine passages:

(i) At AT 4.7 (MT 3.7) 'Haman went to his gods to learn the day of their death [viz. of the Jews]'. This sentence is absent from MT.

(ii) At AT 5.5 Mordecai urges Esther to enter the king's presence and 'after calling upon God speak to the king concerning us, and deliver us from death'. MT has no direct speech at this point but reported speech: Mordecai gave the eunuch instructions 'to charge her to go to the king to make supplication to him and entreat him for her people' (4.8).[22] Here and at AT 7.1, 22 the AT and LXX have similar 'religious' pluses (see [vi] and [viii] below).

(iii) At AT 5.9 Mordecai replies to Esther, 'If you neglect your people so that you do not help them, God will be their helper and salvation, but you and your father's house will perish'. MT 4.14 has 'relief and deliverance will rise for the Jews from another quarter'.

(iv) At AT 5.11 Esther responds: 'Announce an assembly (θεραπεία)[23] and pray earnestly to God (δεήθητε τοῦ θεοῦ ἐκτενῶς), and I and my maidens will do likewise'. MT has 'Go, gather all the Jews to be found in Susa, and hold a fast on my behalf, and neither eat nor drink for three days, night or day. I and my maids will also fast as you do'

(4.16). In this case, if we had only MT and AT without any knowledge of their relationship, we should suppose AT to be prior, since a fast is a religious occasion, and the 'gathering' of Jews implies a religious ceremony; MT looks distinctly coy about the religious implications of what it describes.

(v) At AT 6.23 Haman's wife says: 'He is of the race of the Jews; since the king has agreed with you to destroy the Jews, and the gods have given you a day of destruction for taking revenge on them, let a tree of fifty cubits be cut down . . . ' In MT 5.14 she says only, 'Let a gallows fifty cubits high be made . . . '

(vi) At AT 7.1 'The Almighty took away the king's sleep that night, and he was wakeful' (ὁ δὲ δυνατὸς ἀπέστησε τὸν ὕπνον τοῦ βασιλέως τὴν νύκτα ἐκείνην, καὶ ἦν ἀγρυπνῶν). MT has simply 'On that night the king's sleep fled' (בלילה ההוא נדדה שנת המלך), a sentence on which Paton, for example, could comment: 'The author goes out of his way to avoid mentioning God'.[24] The LXX and Old Latin attribute the sleeplessness to God. LXX has Ὁ δὲ κύριος ἀπέστησεν τὸν ὕπνον ἀπὸ τοῦ βασιλέως τὴν νύκτα ἐκείνην, καὶ εἶπεν . . . (6.1).

(vii) At AT 7.15-17, when Haman is about to parade Mordecai through the streets he tells him to take off his sackcloth, which frightens Mordecai into thinking he is about to be executed. But he takes off his sackcloth and puts on the garments of glory (τὰ ἱμάτια δόξης). 'And Mordecai thought that he saw a miracle, and his heart was toward the Lord; and he was speechless' (καὶ ἐδόκει Μαρδοχαῖος τέρας θεωρεῖν, καὶ ἡ καρδία αὐτοῦ πρὸς τὸν κύριον. καὶ ἐξίστατο ἐν ἀφασίᾳ) (v. 17). In MT 6.11 we learn only that 'Haman took the robes and the horse, and arrayed Mordecai . . . '

(viii) When Haman returns home, his wife and wise men say, 'From the time that you spoke evil about him, evil has been coming upon you; be quiet (ἡσύχαζε), for God is among them' (ὅτι ὁ θεὸς ἐν αὐτοῖς, AT 7.22). There is no reference to God in MT, of course, but LXX 6.13 has ὅτι θεὸς ζῶν μετ' αὐτοῦ, 'because God dwells with him'. Similarly also the Old Latin.

(ix) At the second banquet, when the king asks Esther what her request is, AT 8.2 has 'And Esther was anxious as she replied because her enemy was before her eyes, but God gave her courage when she called upon him'. The silent prayer of Nehemiah in the king's presence at a critical moment (Neh. 2.4) comes to mind as a parallel.

These nine pluses in AT vis-à-vis MT which have some explicit religious content invite a single explanation. So long as AT is regarded as representing a text later than the Masoretic text it is easy enough to suppose that these pluses are attempts to inject a religious dimension into the overly secular story as told by the MT. But the argument of this monograph runs counter to that admittedly fairly natural explanation, since AT is here viewed as a translation of a Hebrew text earlier than the MT. Some more complex explanation of the religious pluses of the MT has therefore to be offered.

To begin with, we should note that the content of the pluses is not in all cases of the same type. While in five cases (AT 5.5, 9, 11; 7.15; 8.2) some action of the Lord towards the Jews (whether for punishment or deliverance) is the subject, in three cases the religious language is in a pagan context (4.7, where Haman goes to his gods; 6.23, where Haman's wife refers to his gods having given him a day of vengeance against the Jews; and 7.22, where Haman's family and friends decide that God is 'among' the Jews). If we were to regard these pluses as *additions* to a Masoretic-type text made by AT or its *Vorlage* we should have to explain why both types of religious material were inserted. It is noteworthy that the Additions to the LXX, which undeniably represent a deliberate attempt to add an explicitly religious dimension to the story as found in the MT, contain no religious references at all from a pagan perspective (the only reference to foreign gods is from Esther's perspective, in a traditionally-shaped anti-idolatry passage [14.7, 8, 10]). It would indeed be simpler to suppose that the MT represents a deliberate excision of *all* religious langauge, from whatever perspective, than to suppose a supplementer who added not only the references to God's activity from a Jewish perspective but also such passages as 4.7 and 6.23 from a pagan perspective.

As it turns out, however, no one redactional activity seems to be responsible for the group of AT's religious pluses. The textual affinities and diction of the pluses indicate for them a rather diverse parentage.

The most interesting case is that of AT 5.4-5 (MT 4.8), numbered (ii) above, where an unusually close correspondence of AT with LXX arouses our suspicions. In the LXX, as in MT, Mordecai informs Esther through a messenger of the decree that stands written against the Jews, and bids her go to the king and make supplication on behalf of her people. AT tells the same segment of the narrative in direct speech (rather than the indirect speech of LXX) and—as is its wont— in quite different language. Thus:

AT

εἶπεν [ὁ Μαρδοχαῖος] Οὕτως
ἐρεῖτε αὐτῇ
Μὴ ἀποστρέψῃς τοῦ εἰσελθεῖν
πρὸς τὸν βασιλέα
καὶ κολακεῦσαι τὸ πρόσωπον
αὐτοῦ
ὑπὲρ ἐμοῦ καὶ τοῦ λαοῦ.

[Mordecai] said, Thus
you shall say to her,
Do not refuse to enter
to the king
and to charm him
on behalf of me and the people.

LXX

εἶπεν αὐτῷ ['Αχραθαίῳ]
ἐντείλασθαι αὐτῇ
εἰσελθούσῃ
παραιτήσασθαι τὸν βασιλέα
καὶ ἀξιῶσαι αὐτὸν

περὶ τοῦ λαοῦ.

He said to him [Hathrachaios],
to charge her,
having entered,
to request the king
and to ask him
concerning the people.

But in the next clauses the two texts converge in a manner not
paralleled, as far as I can see, outside the Additions (where we know
the two texts to be directly related):

μνησθεῖσα ἡμερῶν
ταπεινώσεώς σου
ὧν ἐτράφης ἐν τῇ χειρί μου
ὅτι Αμαν ὁ δευτερεύων
λελάληκε τῷ βασιλεῖ
καθ' ἡμῶν εἰς θάνατον.
ἐπικαλεσαμένη οὖν τὸν θεὸν
λάλησον
περὶ ἡμῶν τῷ βασιλεῖ,
καὶ ῥῦσαι ἡμᾶς ἐκ θανάτου.

... remembering the days of
your humility,
when you were brought up by
me,
because Haman the 'second'
has spoken to the king
against us for death.
So, having called upon God,
speak
concerning us to the king,
and deliver us from death.

μνησθεῖσα ἡμερῶν
ταπεινώσεώς σου
ὡς ἐτράφης ἐν χειρί μου,
διότι 'Αμαν ὁ δευτερεύων
τῷ βασιλεῖ ἐλάλησεν
καθ' ἡμῶν εἰς θάνατον,
ἐπικάλεσαι τὸν κύριον
καὶ λάλησον
τῷ βασιλεῖ περὶ ἡμῶν
καὶ ῥῦσαι ἡμᾶς ἐκ θανάτου.

... remembering the days of
your humility,
how you were brought up by
me,
because Haman the 'second'
to the king has spoken
against us for death.
Call upon the Lord,
and speak
to the king concerning us,
and deliver us from death.

These two texts, in these clauses, are related to one another as *recensions* and not—as is elsewhere the case in the proto-AT—independent translations of variant Hebrew texts. Only in the Additions, where dependence of the AT upon the LXX is generally acknowledged, do we encounter such close correspondence. The most natural assumption at this point is that the AT text has here been contaminated by the LXX text. The AT's plus vis-à-vis MT is then not an authentic AT reading, and therefore can contribute nothing to a theory about the AT's explicit religious language. It will be recalled that this passage is one of the very few cited by E. Tov from the body of the AT to prove its dependence on LXX; he is right in discerning very close correspondences between LXX and AT at this point, but, although the direction of dependence cannot be conclusively proved, the passage certainly reflects contamination of the two text-types of a kind that is quite untypical of the book as a whole.

The second case requiring examination is AT 7.1 (MT 6.1), numbered (vi) above. The curious feature here is the presence of the term ὁ δυνατός, 'the Almighty', as a name for God. This term as a title for God occurs elsewhere in the Greek version of the Old Testament (according to the testimony of Hatch and Redpath) only at Zephaniah 3.17, translating גבור, and then only in some manuscripts (it is just δυνατός in Rahlfs's edition). This is a poetic text, however, and it is strange to find the term in a prose context, in which הגבור is far from expected. Rather surprisingly, however, the term occurs also in the first Addition to the AT, at 1.9, where however the LXX has instead ὁ θεός. The only other occurrence of the term as a name for God known to me is at Luke 1.49, another poetic text with a Semitic background. It is a reasonable assumption that this very rare piece of Greek prose diction does not represent a translation of the AT's Hebrew *Vorlage* but comes from the same redactional influence that introduced ὁ δυνατός into 1.9. When we add to the implications of the diction the fact that at this point the LXX also introduces a reference to divine activity, in the same words (ὁ δυνατός apart), we become entitled to judge that this passage also is not original to the AT.

In the third case, numbered (viii) above, AT shares with LXX one more 'religious' plus vis-à-vis the MT. There are no special indications here that the AT reading may be secondary, though ὁ θεὸς ἐν αὐτοῖς can hardly be a literal rendering from Hebrew (אלהים בהם is, I believe, not paralleled, though אלהים בתוכם could perhaps be postulated as a Hebrew *Vorlage*). It may be an indication that the text has suffered some interference that there is no plural antecedent for AT's αὐτοῖς; it has been *Mordecai* of which the sentence has otherwise spoken (περὶ αὐτοῦ). In the LXX, we may observe, the singular—in reference to Mordecai—is used throughout the verse. Once again, the existence of an AT 'religious' plus at this point may perhaps be best explained as contamination of the genuine AT text.

In the fourth case, numbered (iii) above, there is no clear-cut case for the originality of the one text or the other, but the candid reader is invited to judge whether 'relief will rise for the Jews from another quarter' (MT) has a strong claim to be more original than 'God will be their helper and salvation' (AT).

Likewise in the fifth case, numbered (iv) above, it may plausibly be argued that a 'gathering' of Jews at which prayer is to be offered (AT) may be more original than one at which no religious activity is mentioned (MT). But we can hardly be sure.

In the remaining four cases, numbered (i), (v), (vii) and (ix) above, there is nothing to indicate whether AT expands the MT or MT abbreviates the AT (or rather, its *Vorlage*).[25] The general view propounded in this monograph, that the AT's *Vorlage* is older than the MT, can adequately cope with these data of the last six examples. For the allusions to prayer (AT 5.11; 7.17; 8.2), to divine help (AT 5.9; 8.2), and to Haman's gods (AT 4.7; 6.23) are not made much of and are mentioned only in passing; by way of contrast to these occasional notices we may note the lengths to which a conscious decision to develop the religious element in the story has led in a phase we know to be later than MT, viz. the Additions: not only to the insertion of two lengthy prayers (Addition C), but also to the framing of the whole story by a divinely-sent dream (Addition A) whose fulfilment gives rise to a kind of speech in praise of God (Addition F). And in the end, I would argue, the pluses of the AT can more readily be explained by supposing that MT represents a systematic attempt to remove religious language than by supposing AT to represent a systematic attempt to introduce religious language. For at no point is the religious language of the AT at all unnatural or forced, whereas the absence of such language from the MT has very frequently seemed to commentators unnatural or at least due to a deliberate avoidance of usual Hebrew manners of speech.

IV

All other pluses and minuses of (proto-)AT vis-à-vis (proto-)MT are of minor significance, and, not surprisingly, reasons for their existence cannot often be pinpointed. We must recall that what is here envisaged is a relatively free reworking by a creative and talented storyteller of an earlier but equally sophisticated tale (i.e. a reworking by proto-MT of the *Vorlage* of proto-AT); hence divergences of (proto-) AT from (proto-)MT may really be the result of proto-MT's adaptation of his *Vorlage*, the 'pre-MT' story.

One AT plus which can explain an oddity in MT only if AT is regarded as representing a prior form of the story to MT should be mentioned. At MT 7.5 the Hebrew has ויאמר המלך אחשורוש ויאמר לאסתר, 'And King Ahasuerus said, and he said to Esther'. Paton bluntly remarks, 'The verse has two beginnings, due doubtless to a combination of alternate readings'.[26] Gerleman thinks the repetition a simple oversight,[27] but Bardtke comments 'Das zweimalige ויאמר stilistisch hart, aber wohl Absicht',[28] which intention he explains as developing a tension over the person whom the king will address.[29] Others emend the text, changing the first ויאמר to וימהר 'and King Ahasuerus hastened to speak',[30] or deleting the second ויאמר.[31] The Second Targum and bMegillah 16a attempted to make sense of the two verbs by interposing an interpreter: 'And King Ahasuerus said to an interpreter, and *he* said to Queen Esther' (unfortunate that an interpreter should need to be called in only at this most highly charged moment!).

All these explanations are rendered otiose if AT is read as the background to MT. In the corresponding passage (AT 8.7) *two* speeches by the king are implied, though they are narrated in indirect speech: 'And the king adjured her to tell him who had dared to do this, and with an oath he undertook to do whatever she wanted' (καὶ ὤμοσεν ὁ βασιλεὺς τοῦ ἀπαγγεῖλαι αὐτὴν αὐτῷ τὸν ὑπερηφανευσάμενον τοῦ ποιῆσαι τοῦτο, καὶ μετὰ ὅρκου ὑπέσχετο ποιῆσαι αὐτῇ ὃ ἂν βούληται). MT may be supposed to preserve a small slip on the part of the proto-MT narrator, who had two verbs of speaking before him in his *Vorlage*, but wished to preserve only the first speech in his narrative. In this case, AT can explain MT, but MT cannot explain AT, since AT is not evidently an attempt to smooth out the MT text.[32]

I should not fail to comment on an important point of method: I have assumed throughout this chapter that AT is a faithful version of the Hebrew text it translated (the 'pre-Masoretic' text). This may seem to be an unwise assumption, since it is inevitable that differences in wording, major or minor, will have been made by the translator. Indeed, if the LXX translation is anything to go by (and if the *Vorlage* that *it* followed was really the MT), there may well have been alterations in practically every verse. But we cannot know what is *echt* translation and what deviation, so I believe that we are obliged to treat the AT as if it *were* the pre-Masoretic story, since it is our only witness to it. If my theory of the priority of AT's *Vorlage* to the MT could be established only by dint of brushing aside the AT whenever it did not square with my theory and hypothesizing that at the particular point in question it deviated from its *Vorlage* I would be engaging in special pleading. In fact, I think it a strength of my theory that it is comfortably supported by the AT *without recourse to the fact that the AT is only a translation of the text which the theory concerns.* (I have noted just one case, at AT 7.5, where I believe it can be proved that AT has misunderstood its *Vorlage*.) Of course I realize that it is not the AT itself that is prior to the (proto-)Masoretic story. And I am, thankfully, not obliged to explain how in every particular case the wording of AT could be prior to the (proto-)Masoretic text, since at any particular point AT does not necessarily represent the pre-Masoretic text, and in many individual cases the AT may well be a free or poor translation. This is the reason why the investigation of the relationship of the texts of Esther can be most profitably conducted on the basis of their various story-lines, rather than by restricting the examination to the wording of individual verses—as has perhaps too frequently been done in the past.[33]

Chapter 9

THE QUESTION OF SOURCES FOR THE ESTHER SCROLL

Our investigation of the origins of the Hebrew Esther scroll has yet to be supplemented by a study of the possibility that still older sources or traditions lay behind the Masoretic text. I will first outline the view of H. Cazelles, whose study provides the most thorough analysis of an 'Esther' and a 'Mordecai' source for the Masoretic narrative (section I below). Then I will propose some modifications to Cazelles's analysis (section II) and show how such a theory can be integrated with my postulation of a 'pre-Masoretic' form of the text (section III). In the light of the position there advanced, I will review other scholars' ideas about variant sources or traditions for the Esther scroll (section IV), and attempt to state some conclusions (section V).

I

In his article, 'Note sur la composition du rouleau d'Esther',[1] H. Cazelles finds in the Masoretic Esther a 'deliberate fusion of two texts', one liturgical in character, centred on Esther and primarily concerned (*préoccupé*) with the provinces, and the other more political or administrative, centred on Susa and Mordecai's victory over Haman.[2] Inconsistencies in the text and the occurrence of doublets are the evidence for the existence of the two sources. Cazelles makes the following observations:

(i) In ch. 9 there are two accounts of a Jewish massacre of their enemies. In one the sons of Haman are *slain* along with *five* hundred men in Susa (v. 10), the massacre takes place in the *provinces* (v. 2) under *Mordecai's* aegis (vv. 3-4), and the date is the *thirteenth* of Adar (vv. 1, 16, 17a). In the other the sons of Haman are *hung* (vv. 13-14) and the massacre of *three* hundred men takes place in *Susa* (v. 15) in accord with *Esther's* request (vv. 12-13), and the date is the *fourteenth* of Adar (v. 15).[3]

(ii) The two letters in ch. 9 may likewise be attributed to the Mordecai and Esther sources respectively, the first letter being an *administrative* decree from Mordecai (presumably as Persian official, since he is not here called 'the Jew'), the second evidently a *liturgical* decree (cf. especially references to fasting and laments in v. 31).

(iii) In 3.1-4a Mordecai is portrayed as the enemy of Haman. In vv. 4b-6, however, it is the Jews throughout the empire who are portrayed as the enemy of Haman; and it is in this connection that Esther will play her part. Though Cazelles does not say so explicitly, he apparently assigns 3.4b-6 to the Esther source.

(iv) In 8.3 Esther requests the revocation of Haman's edict, as if the imperial authority had not already been granted to Mordecai (v. 2) and as if Esther had not already made her successful petition on behalf of her people (7.3). The narrative of 8.3-14a belongs to the Esther passages in which the interest of the provinces is most prominent (cf. v. 5); it is not clear, however, whether Cazelles regards 7.3 (or ch. 7 as a whole) as forming part of the Esther texts. Certainly the centre of interest shifts in 8.14b-15 to Mordecai, his reception by the people of Susa being a natural sequel to his promotion in v. 2; so in v. 2 and vv. 14b-15 the Mordecai source would be visible.

(v) There are two banquets of Esther's, of course, in ch. 5 and ch. 7. It is not clear whether Cazelles would assign them to different sources. His chief remark on this point is that between the two banquets is narrated the exaltation of Mordecai (ch. 6), which has a very different character and is moreover over-full with events. This arrangement of events is not, says Cazelles, 'métaphysiquement impossible',[4] but the interposition of the Mordecai scene between two banquets 'makes another solution more probable'—but he does not specify this alternative solution. Bardtke surmises that he means that the multiplicity of events in ch. 6 argues for the derivation of the material of that chapter from two sources;[5] but it is hard to see how any of ch. 6 could be appropriately incorporated in the Esther source, or how the 'doublet' of the banquet scenes could be explained by the hypothesis of two sources. Cazelles's point is not clear.

(vi) There are two banquets in ch. 1, the former for the officials of the one hundred and twenty-seven provinces, the latter for the citizens of Susa. Presumably the former comes from the Esther source, the second from the Mordecai source.

(vii) The list of the seven eunuchs in 1.10 has a doublet in 1.14 in the list of the seven counsellors—if J. Duchesne-Guillemin is correct in seeing in the second list the same names (with one exception) as in v. 10, but in reverse order.[6] The advice of the counsellors concerns the provinces (v. 16)—hence it is from the Esther source; the eunuchs, on the other hand, are concerned only with Susa (Mordecai source).

(viii) In 2.7 Esther is introduced as cousin of Mordecai and is forbidden to reveal her race (presumably Mordecai source); in 2.15 she is again introduced, this time with her father's name being mentioned, and again is forbidden to reveal her race (presumably Esther source).

(ix) In 2.8 we hear of a harem supervised by Hegai; in 2.14 of 'the second harem' supervised by Shaashgaz. Presumably Cazelles means us to ascribe 2.8 to the Mordecai source, 2.14 to the Esther source.

(x) The further doublet of the gathering of the maidens in 2.8 and 'a second time' in 2.19 is presumably to be explained similarly.

(xi) In 2.22-23 Esther tells the king of the plot discovered by Mordecai (Esther source, as in (viii) to (x) above). 6.3 (? Mordecai source—see (v) above) is out of harmony with 2.22-23 in representing Mordecai as unrewarded by the king.

(xii) In ch. 4 we have the Esther source (note the reference to fasting; cf. 9.31)—except for v. 3 which interrupts the narrative and conflicts with v. 16 (Esther can hardly need to enjoin fasting if the Jews are already fasting). Mordecai in 4.1-2, 4, deliberately excluding himself from his post at the palace in order to participate in lamentations that are 'singulièrement moins efficaces', is not quite the same Mordecai at the court officials' post at the king's gate (3.3).

We may deduce that for Cazelles each of the two sources, 'Mordecai' and 'Esther', told essentially the same story. Mordecai and Esther each figure in the alternate source, Haman figures in both sources, each source begins with a royal banquet, continues with an episode in which seven Persians play a part, then moves into a story of Esther's entry into the palace and the king's presence. Both sources know of the conspiracy of the eunuchs and of Mordecai's detection of their plot, both attest Haman's enmity and a Jewish response of fasting. Both have a scene of a banquet of Esther's to which Haman is invited, both record the triumph of a Jewish protagonist over Haman, both recount a massacre by the Jews of their enemies, both contain a letter from a Jewish dignitary at the Persian court enjoining observance of the Purim festival.

CAZELLES'S SOURCE ANALYSIS

Esther source	*[unassigned]*	*Mordecai source*
1.1-4 banquet for provincial chiefs		
		1.5-8 banquet for citizens of Susa
	[1.9-22 Vashti's refusal]	
	[2.1-4 search for a bride]	
		2.5-11 Mordecai's ward Esther is taken to the court
2.12-18 Esther becomes queen		
2.19-23 Esther reports eunuchs' conspiracy		
		3.1-5 Mordecai's rivalry with Haman
3.6-15 Haman plots to destroy the Jews		
4.1-17 Esther learns of the plot from Mordecai (except 4.3)		
	[4.3 mourning everywhere]	
		5.1-14 Esther's banquet with Haman and the king; Haman plots to kill Mordecai
		6.1-13 Mordecai is honoured, Haman humbled
6.14-7.10 Esther unmasks Haman as enemy of the Jews		
		8.1-2 Mordecai appointed to Haman's position
8.3-14 Esther requests a countermanding of Haman's plot		
		8.15-16 Mordecai is esteemed in Susa
8.17 Jews everywhere rejoice		
		9.1-10 Jews' massacre in the provinces [Susa is of second importance]
9.11-15 Jews' massacre in Susa		
	[9.16-19 differing Jewish practice reconciled]	
		9.20-28 Mordecai's letter
9.29-32 Esther's letter		
		10.1-3 Mordecai's greatness

The major narrative difference between the Esther and Mordecai sources is in Cazelles's theory the fact that Mordecai is involved in a purely personal contention with Haman, whereas Esther knows Haman as the enemy of the Jewish people in general. Though Cazelles did not himself say precisely what material he regarded as derived from one source or the other, the table on the opposite page is an attempt to represent his position fairly.

A number of difficulties in Cazelles's view can be noted:

(i) The distinction between the sources on the ground of their orientation either to Susa or to the provinces is not entirely convincing. For at the very point where Cazelles begins his analysis, in ch. 9, where he finds the 'most striking anomaly' in the narrative,[7] Mordecai is associated with the *provinces* and Esther with *Susa*. The fear of Mordecai falls upon 'all the princes of the provinces' (9.3), and his fame spreads 'throughout all the provinces' (9.4), while Esther is concerned only with a second day of fighting in Susa (9.13), even rejecting the king's invitation (as Cazelles sees it) to extend her interest to the provinces.[8] Cazelles himself writes of ch. 9 that 'there is a conscious fusion of two texts, one in which the massacre is first carried out in the provinces under authorization given by Mordecai . . . In the other text the emphasis is on the massacre in Susa . . . requested by Esther.'[9]

This discrepancy between the geographical orientations of the Esther and Mordecai sources would not matter so much if it were not that the orientation becomes the primary criterion for assigning certain blocks of material to one source or to the other. This is the case in the observations labelled (iii), (iv), (vi), and (vii) above. If indeed the provinces are more Mordecai's sphere than Esther's, it becomes difficult to explain why in ch. 8 (see point (iv) above) Esther should figure most prominently in passages concerned with the provinces, and Mordecai in passages concerned with Susa.

When we further consider that both the letter of Mordecai and the letter of Esther are directed to the provinces we are entitled to doubt whether the distinction between two geographical orientations is valid. And finally, if we spare a thought for the exigencies of the narrative (the narrative of either presumed source or of the present text) it becomes evident that Mordecai's sphere prior to his promotion to the viziership must be Susa and thereafter must be the whole of the empire, while Esther has a potential significance to the Jewish people as a whole from the moment she becomes the Persian queen.

It appears from the inconsistency with which the criterion of orientation must be applied and from its inherent implausibility that a major ground advanced by Cazelles for distinguishing an Esther source from a Mordecai source lacks cogency.

(ii) Certain narrative difficulties arise if we consider the coherence of the sources as reconstructed by Cazelles.

We may first note that the narrative of the discovery of the eunuch's conspiracy (2.19-23) makes no sense in the Esther source, since nothing depends upon it. It is in the Mordecai source that the king finds that Mordecai has not been rewarded (6.2-3). Cazelles explicitly finds a lack of harmony between the two passages—but on the unconvincing grounds that Persian kings were not in the habit of failing to reward benefactors and that the LXX has already represented Mordecai as having been rewarded (ἐπέταξεν ὁ βασιλεὺς Μαρδοχαίῳ θεραπεύειν ἐν τῇ αὐλῇ, καὶ ἔδωκεν αὐτῷ δόματα περὶ τούτων, 12.6 = A16). We must surely leave the LXX Addition out of account when discussing the origins of the Masoretic text, and allow that the usual custom of Persian kings (which is not, in any case, a datum of the book) has, by the testimony of MT 6.3, evidently been breached—regardless of whether the narrative of the uncovering of the conspiracy had previously been told or not. The 'lack of harmony' having evaporated, 2.19-23 could preferably be assigned to the Mordecai source. This conclusion, of course, is only a suggestion for improving the analysis, and in no way an argument in principle in favour of the analysis of sources.

(iii) A more serious problem may arise over the matter of the two banquets. Cazelles apparently sees in the 'doublet' some kind of evidence for two sources, though his comment is somewhat cryptic: 'The *two banquets* given by Esther to Ahasuerus and Haman are not without their surprise, especially since the first is barely described and since the offer made again by Ahasuerus in 8.1 will recur again in 9.12'.[10]

Assuming that Cazelles means that the banquet narratives come from different sources, I have provisionally assigned ch. 5 to the *Mordecai* source in Cazelles's scheme for the following reasons: (a) The second half of ch. 5 (vv. 9-14) must belong to the Mordecai source since it depicts Haman's wrath against Mordecai, and puts forward the idea that Mordecai should be impaled by Haman; and these verses are necessarily preceded by some account of a banquet given by Esther. (b) Chapter 7 must belong to the Esther source, not only because Mordecai is never mentioned, but also because the issue at the second banquet is the threat facing the Jewish people.

The difficulty with assigning the narratives of the two banquets to different sources is that the first banquet demands the second—not only in the wording (5.18), which could no doubt be attributed to a harmonistic redactor, but in its story line, since nothing at all appears to happen at the first banquet.

I conclude that Cazelles's analysis as it stands is not wholly convincing but I suspect that it is worth development and modification.

II

The elements in Cazelles's analysis that could with advantage be drastically modified are these:

(i) It is necessary to abandon the distinction between differing geographical orientations of the Esther and Mordecai sources, and therewith the assignment of 1.1-4; 1.5-8; 1.10; and 1.14.

(ii) It would be well also to mistrust the detection of 'doublets' as a clue to the existence of sources; thus, for example, the narrative of the conspiracy of the eunuchs (2.19-23) is better understood as belonging to the same source as the reference to the conspiracy in 6.2-3 (on the narratives of the two banquets see (v) below).

(iii) It is furthermore of no special advantage to a theory of two sources (Mordecai and Esther) to attempt to assign the material of ch. 1 to either source—or to both; for it is more likely that the Vashti story was in origin separate from either major source.

(iv) And in the light of what has been argued above (in Chapters 3 and 4) about the secondary character of ch. 9, it would not be necessary to assign the material of that chapter to the two sources, tempting though it may be to do so in view of the two letters of Mordecai and Esther.

(v) In the case of the two banquet scenes, it would be preferable to assign the first (5.1-8) as well as the second to the Esther source. It would follow naturally from Esther's resolve to enter the king's presence (4.16), and it would lead into the second banquet scene in ch. 7; the issue throughout would be the safety of the Jewish people.

But what of the Haman scene in 5.9-14? Verse 9a would have to be designated a redactional link verse; but that is no problem. Verse 9b would follow 3.5 very naturally as a recapitulation: 'When Haman saw that Mordecai did not bow down nor do obeisance to him,

Haman was filled with fury' (וירא המן כי־אין מרדכי כרע ומשתחוה לו
וימלא המן חמה) (3.5), leading to 'When Haman saw that Mordecai in
the king's gate did not rise[11] or tremble before him, he was filled with
fury at Mordecai' (וכראות המן את־מרדכי בשער המלך ולא־קם ולא־זע ממנו
וימלא המן על־מרדכי חמה) (5.9). Verse 12 would also have to be redactional, since *ex hypothesi* there has been no preceding banquet scene;
but this is no problem either, since v. 13 follows easily upon v. 11.
And the reference to the second banquet in v. 14 ('Go merrily with
the king to the banquet') would also have to be excised. The Haman
scene of 5.9-14 would then merge well into the following scene in ch.
6 in which Haman visits the palace early only to find himself detailed
to honour Mordecai. The final verse of ch. 6 (6.14) could also be a
redactional link between the Mordecai source in ch. 6 and the Esther
source in ch. 7.

The only difficulty with this reconstruction arises when we
reconsider the Esther source. It would have moved directly from the
first banquet (5.8) to the second banquet—which may strike many
readers as problematic. For if nothing intervened between the two
banquets, we may wonder what narrative purpose lay behind the
twofold banquet. As things stand, the events of 5.9–6.13 tantalizingly
delay Esther's expression of her request and at the same time
stylishly foreshadow the impending fall of the house of Haman.
Nevertheless, I have already shown, in Chapter 2 above, that Esther
achieves significant progress at the first banquet: she there commits
the king to 'grant [her] petition and fulfil [her] request'—which is to
be made at the second banquet—before he has even heard what it
will be. So it is not at all improbable that in an Esther source the
narrative of the second banquet should have followed immediately.
upon that of the first.

Of the remaining chapters, only ch. 2 now requires analysis. I have
argued that 2.19-23 must be from the Mordecai source, if from any. It
is the only place in the Mordecai source where Esther would be
referred to, and her function here is not crucial (the same events can
be told in 6.2 without any reference to Esther); it would not be
unreasonable to suggest that Esther did not originally figure in this
episode. 2.5-11, it is true, seems to be told from Mordecai's perspective,
but it tells us nothing germane to the Mordecai story, and so should
best be assigned to the Esther source. As for 2.12-18, we would most
naturally attribute this account of the régime of the harem and of
Esther's installation as queen to the Esther source.

We are now in a position to offer a revision of Cazelles's source analysis, taking as our analytic criteria the differing focus on Esther and Mordecai and the differing focus of Haman's anger—against the Jews in general or against Mordecai. The following table can then be drawn up:

Esther source	Mordecai source
(?) 2.2-4 search for a bride	
2.5-11 Mordecai's ward Esther is taken to the court	
2.12-18 Esther becomes queen	
	2.19-23 Mordecai uncovers eunuchs' conspiracy
	3.1-5 Mordecai's rivalry with Haman
3.6b-15 Haman plots to destroy the Jews	
4.1-17 Esther learns of the plot from Mordecai, and is persuaded to see the king	
5.1-8 Esther's first banquet	
	5.9b-14 Haman decides to kill Mordecai
	6.1-13 Mordecai is honoured, Haman humbled
7.1-8 Esther's second banquet	
	7.9-10 Haman is hanged
	8.1-2 Mordecai is appointed to Haman's position
8.3-14 Esther requests a countermanding of Haman's plot	
	8.15-16 Mordecai's fame throughout the empire
8.17 The Jews rejoice because the plot is revoked	

The fact that such an analysis *can* be made is of course no argument that it *should* be made. The usual argument in favour of a source analysis—that it explains discrepancies, repetitions and unevennesses—can hardly be advanced in the case of the Masoretic Esther chs. 2–8. For there are no serious discrepancies or unevennesses in the present narrative, and the major repetitions (the two banquets; the two references to the eunuchs' conspiracy) have been shown to be from the same source. Minor unevennesses like the 'second' gathering of the maidens (2.19) or the double 'and he said' in 7.5 cannot be explained by the hypothesis of sources. The best argument in favour of the hypothesis is that it is coherent—which is at least a *necessary* condition of its truth, if not a *sufficient* one.

The coherence of the theory can be demonstrated by outlining the profiles of the sources as reconstructed by this analysis. In the Esther source, Esther, who is the adopted daughter of the Jew Mordecai, is taken into the Persian harem along with many other beautiful girls from the empire. She pleases the king and becomes his queen. At the court, however, is a certain official, Haman, who for some reason undivulged has taken upon himself to destroy the Jewish people— unaware, of course, that the queen is a member of that race. The king, who knows Esther's racial origins, has signed the decree against the Jews in ignorance of the specific object of Haman's plot. When Mordecai, a private citizen, learns of the fate Haman has prepared for the Jews, he persuades Esther to use her influence with the king, dangerous though it is to enter his presence unbidden, in order to plead for the life of the Jewish people. On receiving the sign of the king's favour, Esther invites him and his courtier Haman to a banquet, at which she further reinforces her position by gaining the king's consent in advance to a request which she will make at a second banquet the next day. At that banquet, with Haman in attendance, Esther pleads for the life of her people, and reveals to the king that it is against the Jews that Haman has plotted. Haman is summarily executed[12] and, at Esther's prompting, the king gives permission for a decree to be written revoking the plans of Haman.

In the Mordecai source, Mordecai, who is an official at the Persian court, and is perhaps also a Jew by race, discovers a plot against the life of the king and reveals his knowledge. Subsequently Mordecai falls foul of a certain Haman when the latter is promoted above him. Mordecai refuses the customary obeisance, apparently out of pique. Haman is furious, and on returning home complains to his family that his promotion is soured by the spectacle of Mordecai's insubordination. They advise him to prepare a gallows for Mordecai and seek the king's permission to hang Mordecai. That very night, however, the king, being unable to sleep, is reminded from the chronicles of Mordecai's deed, and determines to honour Mordecai. Haman, early at the palace, is the first high-ranking official available to carry out the king's command. Haman's family interprets his involuntary honouring of Mordecai as a symbol of Haman's impending doom. That doom comes quickly when a courtier informs the king that Haman has planned to execute the king's benefactor. The king has Haman hanged on his own gallows, and promotes Mordecai to Haman's position. Mordecai goes out from the presence of the king in royal robes, to the acclaim of the citizens of Susa.

Both narratives know of three of the four principal characters, Mordecai, Haman, and Ahasuerus. In the one there is a plot of Haman's against a courtier who is perhaps a Jew, in the other a plot of Haman's against the Jews as a people. But the latter story is a story of deliverance of the Jewish people through the courage and charm of a Jewish girl, Esther. The former story, of the (Jewish ?) courtier who is ultimately rewarded with the highest office in the Persian empire is more fundamentally a success story—in which indeed a deliverance from a deadly plot is narrowly averted, by chance—than a deliverance story as such.

It must be admitted that certain material apparently lying within the source documents must be argued to be redactional if this analysis is to stand. The following is, I believe, a reasonably complete list: (i) Mordecai's telling the courtiers he is a Jew (2.5) may be redactional, as indeed the whole of v. 5 may well be (see (v) below). (ii) Haman's extension of his wrath from Mordecai to the Jewish people ('he disdained to lay hands on Mordecai alone', 2.6) would be due to the combining of the Esther and Mordecai stories. (iii) In the Esther story, Mordecai is unlikely to know of the sum paid by Haman for the Jews (4.7). (iv) 5.9a 'Haman went out that day joyful and glad of heart' must be a link verse, since in the Mordecai source 5.9b (Haman sees Mordecai) must have followed 2.5 (perhaps 2.4 was not in the Mordecai source, and the failure to bow down was the event of one day only, the same day as is envisaged in 5.9).[13] (v) 5.12 is redactional, since the banquets are only in the Esther source. (vi) 6.14 is a redactional link verse. (vii) In 7.10 the last sentence ('The king's anger abated') must be redactional, because the king is not angry in the Mordecai source. (viii) 8.1-2 is a redactional interweaving of material from the two sources.—An opponent of source analysis could use these eight cases of postulated redactional activity against the whole theory, but I submit that *if* two narratives *were* combined, it is reasonable to envisage something like this amount of redaction being required.

The modifications I have proposed to Cazelles's analysis make it, I suppose, more plausible, especially because they eliminate the more

questionable argumentation and because they do not attempt to
account for the origins of ch. 1 and ch. 9 in the same theory as that
devoted to the origins of chs. 2–8. In this respect the modified
analysis is consistent with the view I had earlier put forward, that ch.
9 in its entirety is secondary to the main Esther story.

III

The analysis of sources by Cazelles naturally worked on the
assumption that the sources lay immediately behind the redaction of
the Masoretic text. And in my modification of his analysis (section II
above) I also have proceeded on that basis. But earlier, in Chapter 8, I
concluded that the Masoretic text of Esther 1–8 existed previously in
a form (the 'pre-Masoretic' Esther) attested by its translation into the
Greek A-text. So now I must investigate whether the analysis of
sources holds good for the pre-Masoretic Esther; for, on my reasoning,
any sources must lie behind—not the Masoretic text, or even the
proto-Masoretic text, but—the *pre*-Masoretic text, since of course the
material of *both* the Esther *and* the Mordecai sources is represented
in that pre-Masoretic text.

Naturally, it is only at those places where the pre-Masoretic story
differs from the Masoretic story of chs. 2–8 that we must check how
the pre-Masoretic story aligns with the analysis of sources. The
following points require observation:

(i) The narrative of the eunuchs' conspiracy at 2.19-23 is absent
from AT and was also absent from the pre-Masoretic story, as I have
argued above in Chapter 8 (section II)—though the episode was
alluded to at MT 6.2 (= AT 7.3). There is no difficulty in assuming
that such was also the case in a Mordecai source, especially because
the narrative at 2.19-23 is not linked at all to the immediately
subsequent narrative of Haman's preferment.

(ii) At 3.4, where the MT has the king's servants speaking to
Mordecai 'day after day' (in imitation of Potiphar's wife in Gen.
39.10[14]), AT has nothing. The story-line is that on the day of
Haman's appointment Mordecai did not join in the universal acclaim;
whereupon the other courtiers told Haman of Mordecai's refusal of
obeisance, and Haman became angry with Mordecai (ὡς δὲ ἤκουσεν
Αμαν, ἐθυμώθη τῷ Μαρδοχαίῳ, AT 3.5; contrast MT 3.5 'When
Haman *saw* that Mordecai did not bow down . . . Haman was filled
with fury'). The AT continues: 'And anger burned within him, and he

sought to destroy Mordecai' (καὶ ὀργὴ ἐξεκαύθη ἐν αὐτῷ, καὶ ἐζήτει ἀνελεῖν τὸν Μαρδοχαῖον)—which plan to destroy Mordecai is not explicitly stated in the MT. If we assume that AT represents the pre-MT text faithfully here—which is our normal presupposition—the narrative would suit the Mordecai source well. For the report of the courtiers to Haman would have led directly to Haman's decision, on the same day, to destroy Mordecai—and to Haman's complaint, on the same day, to his wife and friends that his promotion does not satisfy him so long as there is one person (Mordecai) who does not pay him homage (MT 5.13; AT 6.22).

(iii) If we move ahead now to the scene in Haman's house (MT 5.10-14), we find a real difficulty for the theory. For AT has Haman's boast that he alone is invited to the banquet (AT 6.21 = MT 5.12), but not his recounting of his promotion which MT has in v. 11. The invitation to the banquet is of course a reference to Esther source material—and that is redactional (see section II above[15]). The boasting about his promotion seems a necessary part of the Mordecai source, for what else could 'all this does me no good' (v. 13) refer to if not to the news of his promotion? The problem is that the boasting about the promotion cannot be in the Mordecai source *and* in the MT without also being in the pre-MT—and it is *not* in the AT, which is our testimony to that pre-Masoretic text. For the MT author can hardly have invented a sentence which he did not find in his *Vorlage* (the pre-MT) but which happened to have been in the Mordecai source—which the MT author had not seen.

The only possible solution in favour of the source analysis *and* the text-history I am proposing—short of special pleading that the AT here misrepresented its *Vorlage*—is that the Mordecai source did not have the equivalent of MT 5.11. This initially unattractive possibility becomes more interesting when we observe that the AT (and thus also the pre-MT, *ex hypothesi*) does not say 'all this does me no good' (MT 5.13), referring back to a previous boast. It has 'only this grieves me: when I see Mordecai the Jew in the king's court, and he does not prostrate himself before me' (τοῦτο δὲ λυπεῖ με μόνον . . .)—where 'this' refers forward to Mordecai's disrespect. This wording would argue that the Mordecai source did not proceed simply according to the letter of MT v. 11 + v. 12, and that v. 11 as well as v. 12 is redactional. It must be allowed, however, that *something* must have intervened in the Mordecai source between 'Haman went home and gathered his friends and his sons and his wife Zosara' (AT 6.20) and

'Only this grieves me . . . ' (v. 22). The evidence of AT at 6.21-22 is thus by no means fatal to the analysis of a Mordecai and an Esther source behind the pre-Masoretic story, but it does require a modification at this point.

(iv) Reverting now to the scene of Haman's fury at Mordecai's insubordination at AT 3.5 (MT 3.6), we note an interesting difference between MT and AT at the point of juncture of the Mordecai and Esther sources. The Mordecai source, it will be recalled, has *ex hypothesi* Haman angry against Mordecai alone, and plotting only Mordecai's downfall; whereas the Esther source has the Jewish people in their entirety as the object of Haman's anger and plot. We may suppose that the simplest way of combining these two represent-ations is to say that Haman became angry with Mordecai *and* his people, the Jews—which is what the AT has. Such a statement, however, does not present a fully adequate motivation for Haman's extending his animosity against Mordecai—which is not unreason-able—to a hatred of the Jewish people as a whole—which *is* unreasonable. To be sure, Haman knows that Mordecai is a Jew (the courtiers have presumably told Haman, AT 3.4), but the conflict is not presented as primarily a racial one but as one essentially between two rival courtiers. The MT offers an evidently expansionist reading intended to satisfy the question of motivation: 'he disdained to lay hands on Mordecai alone' (ויבז בעיניו לשלח יד במרדכי לברו). The more one thinks about it the less of an explanation this becomes (it is something like: the reason why he extended his hatred to the Jewish people is because he did not confine it to Mordecai); but it does conjure up some irrational disproportionateness in Haman's personality that will suffice as an explanation for his behaviour. The other MT expansion in 3.6, 'for they had told him the people of Mordecai' (כי־הגידו לו את־עם מרדכי), fills another tiny narrative gap: it has up to this point not been certain, either in AT or MT, whether the courtiers have told Haman of Mordecai's race or only of his disrespectfulness. The MT account, as the more thoughtful, not to say subtle, of the two, is well explained as a reworking of the earlier pre-Masoretic narrative as attested by AT.

Of course, on the present hypothesis, the author of MT did not know that he was working with a redacted *Vorlage*; his only concerns were for the flow of the story, the smoothness of the narrative logic, and the opportunities the *Vorlage* gave him for improving on the story.

(v) The second speech of Haman's wife Zeresh, at MT 6.13, refers to the Jewish people—which is probably not to be expected in material from the Mordecai source: 'If Mordecai, before whom you have begun to fall, is of the Jewish people (מזרע היהודים), you will not prevail against him'. It may be significant that in the AT, which we presume to be closer to the Mordecai source than is the MT, there is no equivalent reference to the Jewish people; Haman's wife says only that 'Since the time that you spoke evil against him, evil has come upon you' (ἀφ' ὅτε λαλεῖς περὶ αὐτοῦ κακά, προσπορεύεταί σοι τὰ κακά, AT 7.22). It must be admitted, however, that in the following words of the AT there is an allusion to the Jewish people: 'Keep silence, for God is among them' (ἡσύχαζε, ὅτι ὁ θεὸς ἐν αὐτοῖς)—though there is no expressed antecedent for 'them' (αὐτοῖς). It is curious that in the LXX, despite its close attachment to the MT wording, 'If Mordecai is of the Jewish race' (ἐκ γένους Ἰουδαίων), the concluding clauses are: 'you will not be able to ward him off, because God dwells with *him*' (ὅτι θεὸς ζῶν μετ' αὐτοῦ).

(vi) I have earlier (section II above) voiced the suspicion that at MT 7.8 the Esther source gave some account of Haman's end—which has now been supplanted by the much more fitting punishment of impalement on the very pole that he had destined for Mordecai. The MT of 7.8 is far from clear, but the AT does give a hint of a more explicit account of Haman's end. After exclaiming 'Does he also rape my wife before my eyes?', in the AT (8.11f.) the king commands, 'Let Haman be taken away, and let him not seek (? mercy)' (ἀπαχθήτω Αμαν, καὶ μὴ ζήτω)—to which is added, 'And so he was led away' (καὶ οὕτως ἀπήγετο).

(vii) The AT continues with a passage (8.12-17) that may be straight from the Mordecai source. The courtier Agathas (MT Harbona) mentions the gallows in Haman's house, and counsels the king to hang Haman on that; to which the king agrees, takes the ring from his finger (his own, not Haman's, who has already been led away), and 'his life (Haman's) was sealed with it' (ἐσφραγίσθη ἐν αὐτῷ ὁ βίος αὐτοῦ, AT 8.13). In the next sentence (v. 14) the king says to Esther, 'Did he plan to hang even Mordecai, who saved me from the hand of the eunuchs? Did he not know that Esther was his kinswoman?' (οὐκ ᾔδει ὅτι πατρῷον αὐτοῦ γένος ἐστὶν ἡ Εσθηρ, AT 8.14). This is a purely rhetorical and reflective question, which does not advance the action and merely serves to emphasize the twin flaws in Haman's plan: it was directed against the king's benefactor *and* the king's protégée. The point of the question is already obvious to the attentive reader, and perhaps for that reason the sentence was abandoned by the Masoretic author—who indeed preferred to round off the scene with his own trademark, 'the king's anger abated' (MT 7.10, as in 2.1, also the MT author's own). In the AT, on the other hand, the decision about Haman's fate merges with a brief statement of Mordecai's elevation to Haman's position: 'The king called Mordecai, and bestowed on him everything that was Haman's. And he said to him, "What do you want? I will do it for you." And Mordecai said, "That you will revoke Haman's letter." And the king entrusted to him the affairs of the kingdom' (AT 8.15-17). With some such words the Mordecai source may reasonably be thought to have concluded. I have shown above (Chapter 8) how the MT (more precisely, the proto-Masoretic author) adapted the pre-Masoretic text of this passage.

I conclude that the theory of two sources for the Hebrew Esther story, containing the material I have assigned to each in section II of this chapter, is consonant with the theory of the priority of the pre-Masoretic narrative as attested by the AT. This conclusion does not amount to much of an argument in favour of the source analysis, but it certainly permits it, making two adjustments in the Mordecai source necessary (at MT 2.19-23 [see (i) above]; and at MT 5.11 [see (iii) above]), and further defining the profile of the sources.

IV

Having now established what I believe must have been the lineaments of the Mordecai and Esther sources—if there were such sources—I can now review the opinions of other scholars who have expressed themselves upon this subject. For the most part they content themselves with speaking of 'traditions'—rather than 'sources'— which lay behind the book of Esther. It is hard to know whether this is because they have some aversion, a hangover perhaps from the excesses of Pentateuchal source criticism, to 'mechanistic' theories of composition,[16] or because the notion of the author as artist seems to jibe badly with close dependence on written sources, or because they are unwilling to enquire too deeply into the matter. It does not matter too much, fortunately, whether we call the narrator's material 'sources' or 'traditions'; any storyteller who could weave together two such stories as we have delineated above (section II) and create a strongly unified tale is a writer of distinct talent. And as for 'traditions', they are in this case just another name for 'sources' considered from the point of view of their story-line rather than their wording.

(i) H. Bardtke, in his commentary, begins his discussion of the source question by separating off a Vashti-tradition—reasonably enough, since as he says the story would not have been so very different if ch. 1 had been missing altogether. The Mordecai tradition told of a conflict between the Persian official Haman and the Jew Mordecai. The conflict is precipitated by Mordecai's refusal to honour Haman, but is resolved when the king remembers Mordecai's loyal deeds. The upshot of the story is that Mordecai resumes his place at the palace door.[17]—This appears a rather tame story; though Haman endeavours to do away with (*vernichten*) Mordecai, and Mordecai is saved (*gerettet*) by the intervention of the king, Bardtke does not apparently envisage a gallows scene in the story, nor any grisly end for Haman. And a story of deliverance that concluded with the hero in precisely the same position he was in when the tale began would be remarkable for its insipidity; was the parade on royal horseback no more than a flash in the pan for the man who saved the king by his word? And must Mordecai return to the king's gate (6.12) only to be overlooked once again in the promotion stakes? Bardtke does not grasp firmly the nettle of the beginning and end of the story: the first question must be, Why does Mordecai refuse Haman the honour prescribed for him by the king?; and the second must be, What happens to Mordecai—and Haman—finally?

As for the Esther source, Bardtke depicts it as the tale of a Jewish girl at the Persian court, who uses her influence to plead for her people when they are threatened by persecution. Apparently Haman did not figure in the Esther story—but without Haman, or his deed, it is difficult to envisage what a persecution of the Jews might constitute, or how it could be quashed. Bardtke infers the existence of an Esther source from certain difficulties in the present text, among which he mentions the problems of how Esther's racial origin could have remained unknown and why Esther prepares two banquets when at the first she has the opportunity to unmask Haman. The former is a very insubstantial difficulty,[18] since it is hardly to be supposed that an oriental despot should be greatly concerned with the racial origins of the women of his seraglio[19]—and in any case the supposition of two sources is not a natural way of handling what difficulty there may be. On the issue of the two banquets, our demonstration above that the two occasions are constructively employed by Esther does not quieten the suspicion that a source-critical reason may lie behind their existence; Bardtke opines that the author in blending his two traditions had to create an interval of time during which the rewarding of Mordecai could occur.[20] But since the tale could presumably have had Mordecai honoured *before* Esther's one and only banquet, there is no reason to suppose that because it has Mordecai's reward *between* banquets one and two the narrator was hard pressed to accommodate his variant traditions. Since, if sources are to be identified, it seems quite satisfactory to assign both banquet scenes to the Esther source (as I have proposed in section II above), Bardtke's reasoning carries little conviction.

Bardtke asks finally what motivated, or permitted, the conflation of the two stories, and finds his answer in the circumstance that in both tales Mordecai has a young female ward (variously named). Much more probable is the argument previously presented, that the two tales had three of their four principal *dramatis personae* in common and that the persecution of the race of the *Jews* by Haman mirrored the harassment of the singular *Jew* by Haman.

(ii) The view of H. Ringgren[21] is very similar to that of Bardtke. While affirming that the book is undoubtedly a unity (with the possible exception of the two accounts of the institution of Purim in ch. 9), he believes that from the point of view of its traditions and motifs (*überlieferungs- und motivgeschichtlich*) its material is of very diverse origins. He distinguishes the Vashti, the Esther, and the Mordecai–Haman traditions. The Esther tradition stems ultimately from legends and tales connected with the Persian new year.[22] The Mordecai tradition, on the other hand, probably has a Babylonian background.

Ringgren makes little of the hypothesis of sources in the course of his commentary. On the section 5.9–8.2 he remarks that the Mordecai and Esther material cannot be completely separated, since they are linked by the banquet scene. This is only the case, however, if it is thought that Haman belongs exclusively to the Mordecai source; I have argued the contrary, since it is hard to envisage what the Esther story could have been about if not the overturning of a plot by an enemy of the Jews. Ringgren clearly thinks, however, that the narrative in this section is basically derived from a Mordecai source, since he remarks that the focus is Mordecai and not the Jewish people as a whole (with the exception of 7.3f., in the second banquet scene). Again it can be replied that there is no need to connect the downfall of Haman vis-à-vis Mordecai with the banquet scenes—which are surely Esther's scenes—especially if 7.9-10 is read as the sequel to the premonition of Haman's fate in 6.12-13.

The only other places where, so far as I can see, Ringgren refers to the Esther and Mordecai sources are at 3.13, where the question of the long delay between the dispatch of Haman's decree and its execution is accounted for as possibly because of the difficulty of reconciling the Haman–Mordecai story with the date fixed by the institution of Purim, and at 2.19 where 'the second time' is thought to be perhaps the result of an incomplete fusion of the two sources. These are of course minor matters, and in general it appears that Ringgren did not set himself the task of systematically examining the sources and their contents.

(iii) A much more thorough study was made by E. Bickerman in his chapter on Esther in his *Four Strange Books of the Bible*.[23] He plainly says at the very beginning: '[The book] has two heroes because it has two plots'[24]—two tales combined by the author 'with extraordinary skill', though some stitches are apparent.

The Mordecai story, according to Bickerman, was a traditional court tale (like that of Ahiqar or the tales of Daniel 3 and 6). Usually such tales were of an upstart who acquires royal favour by luck, or of an accused minister who saves himself by his own cleverness. Mordecai's trump card is his detection of the eunuch's conspiracy. His mischance is that the arrival of girls for the royal harem distracts the king from his proper business of rewarding his benefactor (an amusing explanation which suffers from the difficulty that the king appears from 2.8-12 to have been kept in the dark about new arrivals until their lengthy period of preparation was complete). Mordecai, passed over for promotion by the king's neglect, fights for his honour. His Jewishness (3.4) is an insertion by the compiler to link the Mordecai and Esther plots.[25] The story then follows a course such as I have outlined in section II above, Bickerman noting that the means by which Haman is destroyed—which must have been narrated in the original story of Mordecai—has now been omitted.[26] He wonders whether it told of Haman's being involved in the conspiracy of the eunuchs, remarking that Addition A (v. 17) in the Greek actually says that Haman sought to destroy Mordecai because of the two eunuchs.[27] However that may be, Bickerman's profile of the Mordecai source agrees substantially with that set out in section II above.

The Esther tale, according to Bickerman, was a story of conflict between a royal lady and a vizier—not an accidental conflict as it is in the present book of Esther, but a deliberate conflict engineered by Esther. In the original story, she was no queen, but a concubine, who plotted the courtier's death in revenge for some crime committed by him against a relative of hers. Such a background would explain both her hatred for the vizier and her concealment of her kinship. Oriental court tales, as Bickerman notes, contain many examples of conflicts between royal ministers and royal ladies, to the consistent disadvantage of the former.

This reconstruction of the tale is of course much further from the profile of the Esther source as I have earlier defined it than is that of the Mordecai tale. If such a story did lie behind the Biblical Esther narrative, it has been very considerably transformed. For in the tale we now have the Esther-oriented elements of the story consistently represent her as *defending* the Jewish *people* from an *impending* disaster rather than (in Bickerman's story) *revenging* a *relative* who has suffered a *past* punishment. At this point we wonder how far a story may be transformed and still be the same story; or, to put it the other way around, in our quest for antecedents for the Biblical story how different may the 'original' be from the final version and still be justifiably regarded as the original? Intriguing though Bickerman's 'original' Esther story is, the supposition of an Esther source along the lines I have suggested earlier still seems to me to be more probable.

Finally, Bickerman very properly offers an account of how the two stories came to be combined, or 'contaminated', as he puts it. He writes: 'Having heard two parallel tales about a Jewish courtier and a Jewish queen who struggled with and overthrew the evil minister of their sovereign, the author of the Book of Esther thought that the stories represented two complementary versions of the same events and accordingly combined them'.[28] This statement, however, is hard to square with what he has said previously about the two originals. For he doubted that the hero of the Mordecai story was originally a Jew (p. 181), and he said nothing of what the racial origin of the heroine of the Esther story might have been but affirmed that she certainly was only a concubine (p. 184). So at what point did the two protagonists become Jewish? Furthermore, the Mordecai story, whether in its original form or as it stands within the Esther scroll, is hardly a story of how Mordecai struggled with and overthrew his opponent; he resisted him, to be sure, but the overthrow of Haman had really nothing to do with Mordecai at all. The two stories in reality have very little to do with one another—and it is very hard to account for their combination—unless we suppose, as I have done above, that each had the same villain, and/or that there was something in common between the threats posed in the two tales. Haman is firmly rooted, in my opinion, in both tales, and a threat against the *Jews* and against a *Jew* would be just the common link that could account for a conflation of the two tales—and such threats I would find in the sources as I have delineated them.

(iv) A different tack is taken by W. Lee Humphreys, who, recognizing the force of the arguments of Cazelles and others for distinguishing between an Esther and a Mordecai source, nevertheless argued that 'there was once an independent Jewish tale of the adventures of Esther and Mordecai, which was not yet linked to Purim, and which had the form of a court tale'.[29] In this tale both Esther and Mordecai feature, two distinct figures who are 'so closely bound in situation and purpose that they act in the wider sense as one (Esth 2.7, 10-11, 19-22; 4.1-17)'. Humphreys sees the story as essentially 'a tale of conflict between courtiers for position and power'.[30] This personal conflict indeed eventually 'becomes the basis for the endangering of the whole Jewish community',[31] but in the end Humphreys wants to make the role of Mordecai the central issue. For him, what happens at the resolution of the story is that 'one courtier is destroyed and his opponent elevated to the highest position ... Specifically, the tale tells of the remarkable rise of a Jewish courtier in the service of a foreign monarch.'[32] And the serious function of the narrative is that it expresses (essentially in the figure of Mordecai) a 'life-style for diaspora', which is: 'the possibility of a rewarding and creative life in a foreign court' *and* at the same time 'the possibility of service and devoted loyalty to one's people and religious identity'.[33]

As against Humphreys, nevertheless, it should be remarked that however true it is that a plot of rivalry between courtiers runs through the book, and that a wider issue addressed by the narrative is the question of loyalty to the state and to one's people, no account of the plot or the stance of the book can be persuasive if it downplays the threat to the Jewish *people*. This element makes the book of

Esther quite different from the Daniel stories—with which Humphreys
is comparing it—for the survival of the Jewish people is never in
question in Daniel 1–6. Almost inevitably, if the national dimension
of the Esther narrative is understated an unbalanced view of the
book's origins will result; and Humphreys's view, which effectively
subsumes Esther and her concerns for the people as a whole under
the issues confronting Mordecai, is open to such criticism.

Where I find Humphreys's proposal congenial is not so much in
his decision that the Esther and Mordecai material cannot be
separated as in his clear recognition that the tale of Esther and
Mordecai—for practical purposes we may say chs. 2–8 of the present
book—could stand independently of any connection with Purim.
Whether the incorporation of the tale into the context of the Purim
festival radically altered the thrust of the story, doing violence to its
basic emphasis is another question, to which we must return in
Chapter 10.

(v) A different, and very independent, approach is taken by J.C.H.
Lebram.[34] Emphasizing that he is speaking of *traditions* rather than
sources,[35] he argues that the original Esther story was expanded by a
(Palestinian) Mordecai story and legislation about the observance of
Purim. The expansion entailed several redactional additions, since
Esther did not figure in the Mordecai tradition nor Mordecai in the
Esther tradition. The Mordecai tradition begins with 2.21-23 (the
discovery of the plot), continues with 3.1-6 (Mordecai's insubordination
to Haman), 5.9-14 (Haman's decision to build a gallows for Mordecai),
and 6.1-13 (Mordecai's elevation). This is an independent narrative,
Lebram says, though he goes on to assign 7.7-10 (Haman begs for his
life, but is executed) to the Mordecai narrative.[36] All other reference
to Mordecai within the Esther material is secondary: so 2.10 (Esther
conceals her race, as Mordecai has bidden her), 2.19-20 (Mordecai is
at the king's gate; further reference to Mordecai's instruction about
her race), 2.5-7 (Mordecai's origins and relation to Esther), 2.15
(Esther's relation to Mordecai). At all these points the figure of
Mordecai is only loosely integrated into the Esther narrative. In ch. 4
indeed it is closely integrated; but that chapter, he argues, is an
element dispensable from the Esther narrative (and it is not in
complete harmony with it since the rest of the story does not know of
the hindrances to approaching the king stressed by 4.11, 16). It is a
secondary psychologizing of Esther's behaviour—which arose from
the insertion of the Mordecai material. Further redactional material

is 7.5-6 (Ahasuerus asks who the enemy is and Esther names him)—
redactional because in the Esther story the king knows Haman's plan
and does not need to ask, and because in the Mordecai story there is
no plot against the Jewish people.

As for the figure of Haman, it too appears in the Esther narrative
only in transitional, redacted, passages. To be sure, there was an
enemy of the Jews against whom Esther's wit was pitted, but he was
some unknown courtier. It is his name that enters the story of ch. 7
(at v. 6), as a replacement for some other name because 3.1-5 has now
linked Haman, the enemy of Mordecai, with the Esther narrative. In
3.7-11 as well Haman was not the original perpetrator of the plot
against the Jews; indeed in all probability 3.7 originally had the king
as the one who cast lots, so that it was the king himself who
determined the fateful day for the Jews, without knowing of course
that he was consigning his queen also to disaster.

This is all very ingenious, but the price is too high to pay. For to
exclude Mordecai and Haman entirely from the original Esther story
requires virtual elimination of two of the finest scenes in the book,
ch. 4 and ch. 7. As for ch. 4, it is 'dispensable' from an Esther story
only at the cost of removing the major point of tension from the
whole narrative. If there is no danger in entering the king's presence,
and if Haman is unknown to the narrator, Esther has only to hear of
the decree against the Jews (presumably in the same way as any
citizen of Susa; cf. 3.15), to invite the king to a cosy dinner party for
two, and casually mention over the liqueurs (7.2) that she would be
greatly obliged if he could rectify an unfortunate bureaucratic error.
It is true that the rest of the Esther narrative does not know of the
danger in approaching the king that is emphasized by 4.11, 16—but
how could it? For the only danger lies in approaching the king
unbidden, and once Esther has made the first daring move, every
subsequent entry to the king's permission is with prior royal approval.
As for ch. 7, the absence of Haman from the banquet robs this
climactic narrative of its essential three-way tension, and denies the
crucial question 'Who is he and where is he?' to either of the sources
on grounds that are far from cogent. For it is not the case that the
king does not need to ask who the 'enemy' is, for *ex hypothesi* he has
not associated Esther with the decree against the Jews; when she
protests, therefore, that she and her people are 'sold to be slain' (7.4)
it is self-evident to the king that the fault lies in the arrangement with
the Haman-figure. The king may well wonder what a nice Jewish girl

is doing in his palace when her people is a race 'scattered abroad and dispersed among the peoples in all the provinces' (3.8).

What Lebram's argument demonstrates, to me at least, is that it is impossible to remove Mordecai from the Esther tradition (or source), or Haman (or a Haman-figure; the name is not important) from either tradition (source). For the result of so doing is to hypothesize a run-of-the-mill court tale for the Mordecai source and an unbelievably banal domestic story for the Esther source, and to attribute to the redactor of the present text (who by Lebram's theory had his hands quite full enough reconciling Palestinian and Babylonian Jewry over calendrical differences) not only the skill to integrate the stories pretty smoothly but also the imagination to create at the same time an original and exciting story, penetrating in its psychology and adroit in its dramatic structure, out of two quite feeble source-traditions.

V

The foregoing survey of other opinions concerning sources or traditions behind the present Esther story has tended, I think, to reinforce my argument that if sources are to be identified they are likely to have had something like the shape of the Esther and Mordecai sources I outlined in section II, with some small modification in section III. If it is possible to reconstruct coherent sources without excessive appeal to missing elements or to redactional activity— which is what I hope to have done—then it is probably preferable to envisage written sources than more loosely conceived 'traditions'.

A key issue has still not been settled, however. I said earlier that our ability to reconstruct sources does not really amount to evidence that sources existed. There remain moreover the two questions whether such sources are likely to have existed, and whether any author is likely to have combined them. I cannot say with any conviction that I believe that the existence of the two stories, of Mordecai and Esther—so alike in many ways but so fundamentally different—is very probable. Nor do I feel confident that the relatively straightforward fusion of the two tales would have resulted in the literary unity and work of artistic achievement that we have now in chapters 1–8 of the Masoretic story of Esther. But I would still argue that *if* sources lie behind the Esther scroll—or rather, to be more exact, behind the pre-Masoretic form of the Esther scroll—they are likely to have had the profiles I have described in this chapter.

Chapter 10

FIVE ESTHER STORIES AND THEIR MEANING

In this final chapter I will attempt to show how the development of
the Esther tale through the stages I have identified modified the
meaning of the Esther story. The five stages are:

1. the Esther (and Mordecai) stories, hypothetical sources for
2. the pre-Masoretic story, witnessed to by the Greek AT, and
   expanded into
3. the proto-Masoretic story, itself expanded by various appendices
   to form
4. the Masoretic story, translated and supplemented by major
   Semitic and Greek Additions to form
5. the Septuagint story.

The ways in which these various Esther texts are related is illustrated
in the Table overleaf.

I. *The Esther (and Mordecai) Stories*

As I have said in the preceding chapter, the evidence for the
existence of distinct Esther and Mordecai sources is not very
compelling; but it is strong enough for us to include such stories
within the present discussion. At the very least, the isolation of the
Esther and Mordecai stories may alert us to elements that create
meaning within later phases of the unified story.

The Mordecai story is the simpler, so we shall begin there. It is a
tale of the conflict of two courtiers that revolves about the question of
their relative rank and issues in a dramatic reversal of their standing
at the Persian court.[1] But it is also a deliverance story, for the
conflict exposes to death that protagonist who will ultimately be
successful. Whatever Mordecai's reason for refusing homage to
Haman, the plain fact is that he does not acknowledge Haman's

The Growth of the Esther Story

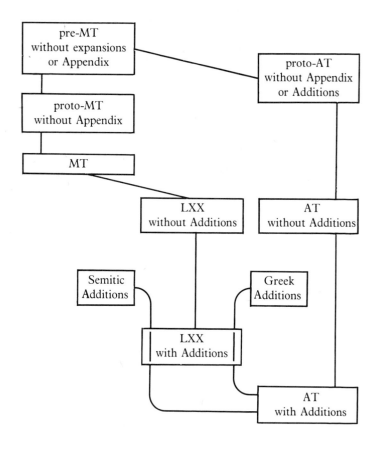

elevation in the customary way, and so initiates the kind of conflict that is characteristic of courtly life and courtly literature. The original Mordecai tale did not, so far as we can tell, suggest that Mordecai had a better claim to the promotion than did Haman. If we could be certain that the story of the eunuchs' conspiracy formed part of an original Mordecai story, we could speculate that such a story told how Mordecai, who had recently saved the king from falling victim to a palace plot, was thoughtlessly and unjustly passed over by his monarch in favour of Haman. That would indeed make a more satisfying story, but even more attractive would be the supposition that Haman was himself implicated in the conspiracy of the eunuchs which Mordecai uncovered, as is suggested by both the Greek versions (12.6 = Addition A18; AT 1.18).[2] This latter supposition, however, we know to be anachronistic because of the relative date of the Addition in the Greek versions, and the former supposition has against it the argument developed above (Chapter 8, section II) that the pre-Masoretic story as attested by the AT did not have any account of the eunuchs' conspiracy at this point. So we are left with the simple fact that the reason for Mordecai's disdain of Haman was not apparently spelled out; and we reflect that of course it does not need to be, since it is the conflict itself, and not the reasons for it, that is the all-important thing.

Once aroused, Haman's anger cannot be pacified except by the complete elimination of Mordecai. One refusal of proskynesis may well have been enough to rouse Haman's wrath, and indeed in what appears to be the oldest form of the story (as represented by AT 4.3-6) no repeated refusal such as we find in MT ('they spoke to him day after day', 3.4) seems to be envisaged. One act of dishonour will cost Mordecai his life, since it costs Haman his enjoyment of his status (MT 5.13).

The peripeteia in this story of courtly conflict comes with the king's discovery that Mordecai has saved his life, and, moreover, has never been appropriately rewarded. The honour bestowed on Mordecai, the parade through the square of the city, may seem to us nugatory and transient enough, but we reflect that it is the very dignity wished for by Haman the chief vizier (MT 6.6b-9), so it cannot be a trivial matter. Haman is humiliated by having to honour his inferior, and his family lose no time in interpreting for him the ominous symbolic meaning of the day's events. If MT 7.9-10 (AT 8.12-13), which is the next surviving element that can be attributed to the

Mordecai tale, immediately followed (and there is little reason to doubt it), even while Haman's family is predicting his downfall his fate is being decided at court. A eunuch reveals to the king that Haman has been preparing to impale Mordecai on a pole in his courtyard.[3] Such a crime against the man who 'spoke good concerning the king' (AT 8.12) can only be correctly punished by the principle of talion. So Haman is impaled, and Mordecai is installed in Haman's place (AT 8.15; MT 8.2); perhaps also some more formal installation of Mordecai as vizier, such as we have in MT 8.15, concluded the tale, but the notice of such an event as we have it in AT 8.39-40 does not appear to be original to the AT but dependent on the MT shape of the story.

The whole of the original Mordecai tale, as it has been reconstructed here, extends over a mere two days. Haman is elevated one morning, and angered by Mordecai's insubordination that day; that evening he decides to execute Mordecai, and the next morning he visits the king, is compelled to honour Mordecai, and returns home only to find the sentence of death has been passed against him. It is a simple tale structurally and morally. Haman is proud and jealous of his honour; Mordecai's refusal of obeisance may be arbitrary or spiteful, but it is no reason for having him killed. Mordecai turns out, in any case, to be in the morally superior position, since he has actually done the king some service (and Haman hasn't, so far as we know) and, secondarily, having failed hitherto to gain recognition or even gratitude, he now deserves to have some compound interest added to his reward. So the tale of a conflict of courtiers has a straightforward moral thrust: Haman's character is diseased by his pride (we recall that he can take no pleasure in his own honour if there is one person who does not outwardly acknowledge it), whereas Mordecai's only possible fault is a certain wilfulness, though presumably he is also breaking a royal command (as in AT 4.2-3; MT 3.2-3). Even if we judge that Mordecai's refusal to bow is just as much an expression of pride as Haman's insistence that he should bow, Mordecai still has the moral advantage, since he has no designs on Haman's life.

We cannot discern whether in its original form the Mordecai tale involved racial conflict as well as a conflict of personalities, or even whether Mordecai was represented as a Jew. In the Esther tale, there is a Jewish Mordecai who plays a minor, though significant role; if we doubt that the Mordecai of the Mordecai tale was Jewish we might also doubt whether he was indeed called Mordecai, and whether both his name and his racial identity were derived from the Jewish Esther tale rather than the (? Persian) court story.

One further element of the Mordecai story deserves our consideration. The most critical event in it, the event that brings about the reversal of fortunes, is a chance event. Not only is the night of Haman's scheming the very night that the king cannot sleep, but the reading of the royal chronicles (? to fill up the time; ? to send him to sleep) by pure chance lights upon the Mordecai episode. Now whether this chance is intended to be understood as mere luck or as some kind of providence is hard to say. When it is combined with other equally fortuitous events in, say, the Masoretic form of the story it will be hard to resist the impression that more lies behind the events than mere chance. Here at least the centrality of the chance event makes it impossible to designate the tale as merely a courtly 'success' story, for it has something of the 'deliverance' story about it. Mordecai's life is in fact saved by the chance reading—and that motif of 'deliverance through coincidence' will make the tale a peculiarly apt one to be combined with the Esther tale of deliverance of the Jewish people.

The Esther tale is not so simple to categorize. E. Bickerman regarded it as an exemplification of the story type of the queen who brings about the downfall of the vizier; that is, he sees it as another kind of courtly conflict story.[4] But against that view, I would argue that it is not primarily a story of conflict between Esther and Haman, but a story of success achieved against all odds. Bickerman indeed finds it necessary to say that 'in the present text' the conflict between queen and vizier is accidental, in that Haman does not know that Esther is Jewish, and that some other motive for Esther's hostility to Haman must be postulated. Oriental Jews, he notes, followed by the Muslim scholar al-Biruni, imagined that Esther's purpose was to save Mordecai from Haman's vengeance. The rabbis sometimes supposed that Haman came into conflict with Esther because he had wished to marry his daughter to the king, and for this reason he (identified with Memucan in 1.16) had advised the king to repudiate Vashti.

Yet, while there is undoubtedly conflict between Esther and Haman and it is she who finally unmasks Haman and brands him 'a foe and an enemy' (MT 7.6) or 'this deceiver' (AT 8.8), it is not convincing to regard her story as primarily one of courtly rivalry. What is special about the Esther story—and in this respect there is no

need to project an Esther tale different from its deposit in the
Masoretic text—is its preoccupation with the fate of the Jewish
people. The Esther tale has in this primary respect an affinity with
the Exodus story,[5] in which also the royal connections of the hero,
Moses, are not dramatized as a conflict between the pharaoh and a
princeling but between a Gentile king and Moses as representative of
the Jewish people.

The function of Esther is to nullify the threat of Haman, whose
enmity she can remove only by devising Haman's personal destruction.
She encompasses that end by a variety of means—so that the Esther
tale appears primarily as an achievement or success story.

Her most obvious achievement is her stratagem played out at the
second banquet. She has arranged for a scene of disclosure at which
only Ahasuerus and Haman will be present with her (the ubiquitous
courtiers are excluded, and only the principals will act).[6] She has
lulled Haman into such a sense of security with her, by using the first
banquet as a purely social occasion, that even when she has denounced
him to the king Haman still imagines that it can be worth pleading
for his life from her (MT 7.7). Moreover, the stratagem of the second
banquet has been prepared for by the skilful bargaining that went on
at the first banquet (MT 5.6-8), by which she had obliged the king to
more than he imagined (see further, Chapter 2, section III above).

Behind the opportunity for her verbal dexterity as hostess at the
banquets had lain her courageous decision to approach the king
unbidden. We can have some confidence that we know how the
narrative of this crucial moment went in the Esther tale, since it has
changed very little from the earliest version we can reconstruct (the
pre-Masoretic version) to the latest we have. In the earliest version,
represented by AT 5.7, 11, we read: 'You know as well as everyone
that if anyone enters the king's presence unbidden, and if he does not
stretch out his golden rod to him, that person is sentenced to
death . . . I will enter the king's presence unbidden, even if I must
die.' And in the latest version, that of the LXX (4.11, 16), the wording
remains similar: 'All the nations of the kingdom know that any man
or woman who enters the king's presence in the inner chamber
unbidden has no hope of safety; except that anyone to whom the king
extends the golden rod will be safe . . . I will enter the king's presence
contrary to the law, even if I should perish.'

A further achievement of hers, lying behind the opportunity for
her courageous act, was her charm which had in the first place won

her her place at court and her throne. From her first entry into the palace she wins the favour of the eunuch in charge of the women, who gives her attendants of her own beside those usually assigned to the maidens (AT 3.8-9; MT 2.9). And she wins by her charm the favour of the king also: AT 3.9, 14, 17 'When she was taken to the king, she pleased him greatly. When evening came, she would be taken to him, and in the morning she would leave. And when the king had examined all the maidens, Esther proved the most outstanding (ἐπιφανεστάτη)'; cf. MT 2.16-17 'And when Esther was taken to King Ahasuerus . . . the king loved Esther more than all the women, and she found grace and favour in his sight more than all the virgins'.

In short, Esther's success is achieved by a combination of charm, courage, rhetoric, and strategy. She deserves to succeed not because she is good but because she is resourceful. Hers is a different story to Mordecai's, whose only positive act lies outside the temporal frame-work of his story; apart from the somewhat vague 'benefit' he has done the king in the matter of the eunuchs (according to AT 7.3-5; we recall that AT has no account of the conspiracy such as in MT 2.21-23), before the story begins, he actually does nothing at all, and does not speak a word (except perhaps to tell the courtiers he is a Jew, AT 4.4—if that is original to the Mordecai tale). Esther, on the other hand, develops very fast from the orphan girl who is submissively 'taken' into the palace and 'taken' into the king's chambers (תלקח in 2.8, 16) into the decisive female who has Mordecai do everything she orders him (MT 4.17) and the scheming queen who will determine the primary movements of the plot, and will do more of the talking than anyone else. (In the MT of chs. 2–8 Esther has 49 lines of RSV text, Ahasuerus 37, and Haman 35—and some of the speeches of Ahasuerus and Haman now in MT would have belonged only to the Mordecai source.)

Then is there a theme of chance or providence in the Esther tale, as we have noted for the Mordecai tale? The more the outcome hangs on the character's own resources, the less opportunity might be thought to be available for providence to act. But as it is, there are three crucial points at which the plot encounters unpredictability. There is Esther's reception by the king; she has been allowed to set before us the reasons why her unsummoned appearance before him is a risky business: the general law (AT 5.7; MT 4.11) and the specific fact that she at the moment enjoys no special favour with the king, having not been called to his presence for thirty days (AT 5.8 = MT

4.11). Then there is the reaction of the king to Esther's denunciation of Haman: in the AT and so perhaps also in the Esther source she makes it all the more difficult for the king to decide instantly in her favour by saying, 'Haman *your friend* is this deceiver, this wicked man' (8.8) (in the MT, on the other hand, she distances Haman from the king by saying: 'A foe and an enemy! This wicked Haman!' [7.6]). The king must certainly take time for reflection because he does not face a clear-cut decision. In the AT the king springs to his feet and begins to walk about (8.9), apparently outside the room (as in MT 7.8), since at AT 8.11 he 'returns' to the banquet. The reader has little doubt, by this point in the story, how the king will choose, but the story does endeavour to make his response not entirely predictable. (There is a further degree of explicitness in the MT, where Haman 'sees that evil is determined against him by the king' [7.7]—though even here the reader must await the king's return from the garden to be sure how he will act.) Finally, there is the most important coincidence of all: the Jewish girl is Persian queen. Without that timely coincidence there would be no Esther story at all; and Mordecai draws attention to it, in the AT (5.10) as well as the MT (4.14): 'Who knows whether it was for such an opportunity as this that you came to the throne?' This is not the language of chance, but a restrained affirmation of the providential nature of Esther's position.

The Esther tale, then, is a blend of a success story, in which the heroine wins her way by her own qualities and initiatives, and a deliverance story, in which a happy outcome is determined by providential and unpredictable occurrences. This tale was built upon the same synergistic assumptions that we will find to lie behind every future version of the story: both the providential coincidences and the contributions of human courage and ingenuity co-operate in the salvation of the Jewish people.

II. *The Pre-Masoretic Story*

The pre-Masoretic story I have defined in Chapter 8 as the Hebrew *Vorlage* of the AT Esther, up to the point at which Ahasuerus puts into Mordecai's hands the affairs of the kingdom (AT 8.17, roughly equivalent to MT 8.2). Our witnesses to this story are on the one hand the Greek AT and on the other the later Hebrew text, which I have called the proto-Masoretic story.

The significance of the pre-Masoretic story depends somewhat on whether we accept the analysis of distinct Esther and Mordecai tales as presented in Chapter 9 and in the previous section of this chapter. If we do, the achievement of the pre-Masoretic story is that it made a successful combination of two distinct tales, with comparatively little redactional alteration or addition. If we do not, we designate this pre-Masoretic story the oldest reconstructable version of the Esther story, and regard its author as the primary storyteller. In either case, a good deal of what has been said in the preceding section about the individual tales of Mordecai and Esther will hold good for the pre-Masoretic story, whether it is essentially a conflation or a creation.

Suppose that the author of the pre-Masoretic story brought together Mordecai and Esther tales; what induced him to do so? The most obvious connection is the presence of three of the four principal characters in each of the tales, Ahasuerus, Haman and Mordecai in the Mordecai tale, and these three plus Esther in the Esther tale. We cannot of course be sure that when the tales were separate the dramatis personae were so named. Then is there enough similarity of plot as distinct from the names of the characters? If the 'Mordecai' tale told of the providential escape of *a Jew* from a plot against him by a Persian official, and the 'Esther' tale of the providential deliverance of the *Jews* from a plot against them by a Persian official, there would be grounds enough for regarding the two tales as essentially one, and for interweaving them. This seems the most likely probability, for if 'Mordecai' was no Jew the main element in common between the two tales would be the shared motif of 'deliverance through coincidence'—which is not evidently sufficient ground for combining the tales.

What developments arise from the interweaving of the two plots? First and foremost, by linking the hostility between Haman and Mordecai (Mordecai source) with the plot of Haman against the Jews (Esther source), an explanation is given for the hostility of Haman against the Jewish people. Were it not for the Mordecai tale (or alternatively, we could say, for Mordecai's role in the pre-Masoretic story of ch. 3), Haman's racial enmity would be motiveless; even so it is of course utterly disproportionate for him to seek to destroy 'Mordecai and all his people' (AT 4.5) for the sake of one act (as it appears) of disrespectfulness on Mordecai's part. The narrative raises the suspicion that we are not being told the whole truth about Haman, since it can hardly be feasible at the Persian court to plot genocide every time a subordinate steps out of line. We cannot tell whether the AT's gentilic for Haman, 'the Bougaean' (Βουγαῖος), or

'the Gogaean' (Γωγαῖος), may contain some clue to anti-Jewish
racial hostility,[7] but when we discover in the next phase of the story,
the proto-Masoretic layer, which is the first extant Semitic form we
have, that Haman is really an Agagite, a born enemy of the Jews,
everything is explained, both on Mordecai's side and on Haman's.
However that may be, already by the pre-Masoretic stage we have in
Mordecai's insubordination the common cause of the threat to him
and the threat to his people.

The second development from the interweaving of the plots is in
the dramatic shape of the narrative. In between the two banquets of
Esther, which would follow naturally in sequence without any
intervening material (and did so in the postulated Esther source) are
interposed two or three scenes that relate primarily to Mordecai: the
means by which Mordecai will die and the immediacy of his death
(he cannot be allowed to linger on until the thirteenth of Adar when
he would perish along with his entire race!) are determined (AT 6.21-
24 = MT 5.11-14); Mordecai's recognition by the king and the failure
of Haman's plan to ask the king for his execution (he can hardly ask
for Mordecai's life in the same interview in which the king has
exhorted him to 'run quickly' and honour Mordecai, 'not letting a
word fall to the ground' [AT 7.12 = MT 6.10]); and the mournful little
scene where Haman must report his failure to his far from sympathetic
family (AT 7.21-22 = MT 6.13).

The impact of this interposition on the Esther story is twofold: on
the one hand, the outcome of Esther's second and crucial banquet is
much delayed, with resulting narrative suspense, and on the other, its
successful outcome is foreshadowed, though not in the least prejudged,
by Mordecai's temporary elevation to the seat of honour on the king's
horse. The interweaving brings the two major threads of the plot to
their penultimate scene at the same moment, the evening of the
second banquet.

Furthermore, just as the Esther narrative has been interrupted by
the Mordecai, so the Mordecai narrative will be interrupted by the
Esther. We will not learn how Haman's threat against Mordecai is
removed, and what permanent reward will accrue to him, until after
Haman has been unmasked as an enemy of the Jewish people (cf. MT
7.4)—in which, of course, both Mordecai and Esther are included.
These interruptions do not only make for narrative tension but also
for a more sophisticated story-line that invites the reader to envisage
at each moment the relationship of the two principal plots.

What the Mordecai story does for the Esther plot is to speed up its movement; the danger anticipated in the combined story in its pre-Masoretic shape is not just the decree that hangs over the distant thirteenth of Adar but the immediate present in which the gallows stands ready for Mordecai. And what the Esther story does for the Mordecai plot is to develop Mordecai's character, and to parallel its plot of danger to a hero by a more far-reaching one of danger to a people.

Mordecai's character in the Mordecai tale was wafer-thin: he intrigued us a little by his refusal to bow to Haman, but without any sure means of establishing his motivation that interest soon evaporated. Thereafter he behaves like an automoton, speaking not a word, and arousing sympathy only for his situation, not for himself. In the Esther story he becomes a true individual. Here, in the first place, we learn from his own lips his reason for refusing prostration before Haman: he is a Jew (AT 4.4 = MT 3.4). At least, it seems at first hearing to be a reason, but we soon realize that it is an answer that contains questions of its own. Are Jews naturally proud, or are they unwilling to give homage to any but God, or is there something about Haman that makes it reasonable for Mordecai as a Jew not to bow to *him*? The pre-Masoretic story does not tell us explicitly, even if it actually contained the sobriquet 'the Agagite'.[8] Whatever it is, it is a good enough reason for Mordecai, and we are encouraged to keep alert for further explanation. I have noted in Chapter 1 how in the Masoretic text the full significance of 'the Agagite' is only gradually unfolded; the revelation of the underlying tension is even slower in the pre-Masoretic story. For here there is nothing corresponding to MT's 'the Agagite, the enemy of the Jews' (3.10); but at AT 6.23 Haman's wife says, 'He is from the race of the Jews; since the king has agreed with you to destroy the Jews, and the gods have given you a day of destruction for taking revenge on them, let a tree of fifty cubits be cut down . . . ' And at AT 7.22 she recommends Haman to 'Keep quiet, for God is among them'. Thus, less obviously than in the MT, there are in the narrative of the pre-Masoretic story certain signs of racial conflict developed by way of answer to the initial question about Mordecai's behaviour.

The chief point, however, in the pre-Masoretic text at which Mordecai is developed as a fully-fledged character is in the scene in which he persuades Esther to enter the king's presence on behalf of her kinsfolk. The scene is not so elaborated as in the Masoretic

version: there is less reference to the use of messengers, which in the
MT intensifies the sense of distance between Mordecai outside the
palace in mourning garb and Esther inside the palace with palace
clothes at her disposal (4.4). And in the pre-Masoretic story Mordecai
does not inform her of 'all that had happened to him, and the exact
sum of money that Haman had promised to pay into the king's
treasury' (MT 4.7). But the dialogue, insofar as we can be sure that
the AT reproduces the pre-Masoretic story faithfully,[9] is quite similar
to that found in the MT, except that Mordecai's initial charge to
Esther is reported in direct speech (AT 5.4; contrast MT 4.8). The
force of his rhetoric is the same as in the MT, though it is not so
memorably expressed: 'If you neglect to help your people, then God
will be their help and salvation, but you and your father's house will
perish. And who knows whether it was for this moment that you
came to the throne?' (AT 5.9-10). Mordecai comes to life in this scene
as an interestingly complex personality, a hard-headed idealist who
unsentimentally but movingly demands of others the same racial
loyalty as he himself has shown, reckless of his own personal
security.

Moreover, Mordecai's stubbornness (or principle) in refusing to
put off his sackcloth is an interesting extension of the personality we
have met in the confrontation with Haman. And the way the scene
finishes, with Mordecai taking his orders from his niece in exchange
for her having listened to his entreaty (AT 5.12) functions in the same
way as the equivalent sentence in MT (4.17) to signify the transfer of
authority and responsibility from Mordecai to Esther (see Chapter 2,
section II, above).

One further major element in the pre-Masoretic story was due to
the initiative of its author alone and was not found in either his
Mordecai or his Esther source: namely the material of ch. 1, the
Vashti story. I have discussed above, in Chapter 1, some of the ways
in which ch. 1 adumbrates themes that are later to be developed in
the Esther story proper, and have said enough there of its more
evidently satirical tone than that of the subsequent chapters. The
Vashti story, though no doubt not 'original' to the Esther story, is
certainly 'ben trovato', in its plot, its characterization, and its
tonality. Its plot leaves the Persian throne vacant, thus explaining
how a Jewish girl can have become the Persian queen; its characterization reveals a vain and indecisive, but not malign, monarch; and
its tonality hints to the reader that the story of grave danger to the

Jewish people will prove to be no tragedy but will contain upsets and reversals that will lead to a 'comic', upbeat conclusion.

The basic shape of the Esther story as we know it from the Masoretic text was already laid down in this pre-Masoretic phase. Whether the author of this version composed the story as a unity or combined it from separate tales he achieved a satisfying dramatic unity which was indeed patient of extension and elaboration, of which we still can trace three distinct forms (see sections III, IV, V below).

Its meaning is essentially identical with what I have earlier suggested as the meaning of the postulated Esther tale: deliverance from danger is realized through a combination of providential coincidences and human initiatives. The inclusion of the Mordecai story within the Esther story—or, we might prefer to say, the conception of an Esther story of national deliverance which also included the Mordecai story of personal deliverance and success—tended to emphasize all the more the role of the coincidental.

III. *The Proto-Masoretic Story*

The proto-Masoretic revision of the story made one major and several minor additions to its plot (see Chapter 8).

The most notable addition was the introduction of the concept of the irrevocability of Persian law. The *pre*-Masoretic story as attested by the AT had no such reference at (MT) 1.19 or at (MT) 8.8, and it was there assumed that merely 'putting imperial affairs in the hands of Mordecai' (καὶ ἐνεχείρισεν αὐτῷ ὁ βασιλεὺς τὰ κατὰ τὴν βασιλείαν, AT 8.17) was enough to ensure that Haman's decree would be rendered harmless. Now the *proto*-Masoretic story injects a further tension into the drama, with the concept that the decree of Haman, being the law of the Persians and Medes, is unalterable. It alerts us to this new dimension of the plot by spelling it out in the first, paradigmatic chapter, in reference to the deposition of Vashti. Where the pre-Masoretic text had simply 'Let a letter be written to all lands and to all peoples, and let it be known that Vashti has refused the command of the king' (AT 2.18), the proto-Masoretic text has 'Let a royal order go forth from him, and let it be written among the laws of the Persians and the Medes so that it may not be altered, that Vashti is to come no more before King Ahasuerus' (MT 1.19). And the effect of this new conception of the law becomes fully evident in the much elaborated ending of the story as told by the proto-Masoretic narrator in (MT) 8.3-17. First, conceptually, there is an intellectual puzzle to be solved, viz. how an unalterable law can be altered without it seeming so. Then, on the level of the narrative, there is further dramatic tension to be created in Esther's renewal of her appeal to the king (8.3-6). Next, there is the question of the weight and space to be given to the issuance of the second decree in order to make it balance (and in fact outweigh) the first decree (8.9-14). And finally, there is the matter of the reception of the second decree, with the recognition on the part of the citizens of the empire that the intention of the first decree has effectively been stifled (8.15-17).

All these extensions were carried out by the proto-Masoretic author in the style of the pre-Masoretic version, largely re-using parallel material from the earlier chapters of that version; I have examined these extensions in detail in Chapter 8, section I, above, and nothing further needs to be added here.

As for the minor additions to the plot, the most noticeable is the story of Mordecai's discovery of the conspiracy of the two eunuchs at MT 2.21-23 (see for details, Chapter 8, section II, above). The proto-Masoretic narrator, in expanding a plot element he found in embryo form at AT 7.3-4 (corresponding to MT 6.2), composed a superb little scene at the end of ch. 2 which has ramifications throughout the plot. It prepares the account of the reading of the royal chronicles (6.1) but it does not pre-empt it. It suggests a relationship between Esther and Mordecai that will soon be called in question (in ch. 4) and then be delicately reaffirmed and reversed at the same time (Mordecai becomes obedient to Esther, just as she had been obedient to him; but what remains fixed is their loyalty to each other). It establishes Mordecai's loyalty to the king by way of anticipation of his disobedience to the king's command in 3.3. And, in the place where it is set, it raises a tantalizing question whether Haman's promotion and Mordecai's disrespect, which immediately follow, have anything to do with the conspiracy of the eunuchs. All in all, it is a brilliant scene.

We should probably also put to the account of the proto-Masoretic narrator the omission of religious language. Not all the religious references in the AT are to be ascribed also to its *Vorlage*, the pre-Masoretic text, as I have argued above (Chapter 8, section III). But it is impossible to deny that the pre-Masoretic story had some such references, including probably allusions to prayer at AT 5.11, 7.17, and 8.2 (MT 4.16; 6.11; 7.3), to divine help at AT 5.9 and 8.2 (MT 4.14;

7.3), and to Haman's gods at AT 4.7 and 6.23 (MT 3.7; 5.14)—plus perhaps also AT 7.22 (MT 6.13), where Haman's wife says, 'God is among them'. In eliminating all explicitly religious language, the narrator was moving in sympathy with the tendency the plot had always had to keep silence about the causality of its constitutive coincidences. If the presence of a Jewish girl on the Persian throne at the one and only time that Jewish survival was threatened by the Persian bureaucratic machine is not providential, what is? And if readers may be trusted to credit divine providence for that circumstance when they read merely, 'Who knows whether you have not come to the kingdom for such a time as this?' (4.14), what need is there to spell out for them that on the critical night 'the Almighty took away the king's sleep' (AT 7.1; similarly LXX 6.1) when the coincidence itself will point unerringly to the workings of providence? Removal of explicitly religious language does not conceal the divine causality, not if the holes that are left are God-shaped. To the religious believer 'chance' is a name for God.

To the unbeliever, on the other hand, to the pagan, 'chance' is a name for chance, without any design or tendency or reliability. If Haman has the 'good luck' to be promoted to the viziership and the 'good luck' to persuade the king to fall in with his evil plan, it matters nothing whether his gods have given him a day of destruction for taking vengeance on the Jews or not (AT 6.23; cf. 4.7); for his gods have no hand in causality and 'gods' is a name for chance. Our storyteller simply follows the logic of his own narrative. It is not a necessary route to take, of course; for if to the Jew 'chance' is a name for God, one storyteller may well speak often of God where another narrates only coincidences. And if for the pagan 'gods' means no more than fickle fortune, one Jewish writer may well belittle pagan deities by naming them, another by ignoring them.

What we do not need, in this matter of the omission of religious language, is a 'historical' explanation for an aspect of the story its own internal logic can account for perfectly well. Is the absence of God to be explained on the grounds that the author himself was an atheist?[10] Or shall we say that the author 'regarded mere forms and rites [like fasting, and sackcloth and ashes] as the sum total of religion' and that for him 'religion was only a garment to be discarded whenever it hindered the pursuit of worldly aims'.[11] Or is the author perhaps not to blame for the secularity of his writing, being something of a victim of his times, his book 'the product of a nationalistic spirit . . . which has lost all understanding of the demands and obligations of Yahwism, especially in its prophetical form'?[12] Or is the clue to be found in the circumstances of its composition in Persia,[13] or in 'the absence of any wish on the part of the author, either to represent the actors in the history as having more fear of God than they really had, or yet to present the whole occurrences . . . in a point of view that was foreign to their own nature and strange to his contemporaries'?[14] Or is it, more positively, that the author 'summons Jewry in a lengthy and enduring diaspora existence to a particular behaviour: to be active and devoted to a non-Jewish people—in order to remain faithful to their own people and traditions'?[15] Or is it to be sought rather in the circumstances in which it was envisaged that the book would be read?—'at the annual merrymaking of Purim, for which the Mishna lays down the rule that people are to drink until they are unable to distinguish between "Blessed be Mordecai!" and "Cursed be Haman!" On such occasions the name of God might be profaned, if it occurred in the reading; and, therefore, it was deemed best to omit it altogether.'[16] Or is it to be located in the consciousness that Purim was originally a non-Jewish festival, and ought not therefore to be closely associated with the name of God?[17] Or shall we locate the absence of God's name in the genre of the book as an example of wisdom literature in which 'the concept of an unspecified and remote deity devoid of any individual character' may often be found?[18]

Some of these explanations are evidently more plausible than others but none is as satisfying, in my view, as the opinion that no external pressure but the logic of the author's belief in providence accounts for the verbal 'secularity' of the book.

It is not so much the absence of the name of God from the book as the presence in it of critical coincidences working for the good of the Jewish people that defines its theological position. I would identify two primary elements in the book's theological statement: (i) the providence of God is to be relied on to reverse the ill-fortunes of Israel; (ii) divine action and human initiatives are complementary and both indispensable for success or 'salvation'.

(i) The narrative of the Esther scroll (whether in its proto-Masoretic or Masoretic form) recounts the gravest threat to the survival of the Jewish people since the pharaoh gave orders for the slaughter of the Israelites' male children. No Jewish author could have told the Esther story without a consciousness that the exodus story lay in the background as a prototype. The exodus story too had Israelites in a foreign land, threatened by a royal decree, represented at court by one from their own nation, and ultimately safely delivered. In the Exodus story the causality of the deliverance is entirely explicit: the Israelites are 'brought out' (Exod. 12.51) by the 'strong hand' (13.9) of Yahweh the 'man of war' (15.3); in the Esther story the causality is implicit, but none the less patent.

The causality is indicated by the coincidences of the plot and by the overall shape of the plot. In the first place, whether it is the vacancy for a queen at the Persian court, the accession of a Jewish queen, Mordecai's discovery of the plot, Esther's favourable reception by the king, the king's insomnia, Haman's early arrival at the palace or even his reckless plea for mercy at Esther's feet, the chance occurrences have a cumulative effect. 'Each of these incidents regarded by itself might well appear to be the result of chance, and to have no bearing whatever upon the success or otherwise of the great plot. But *taken together, the element of chance disappears*; they all converge upon one point; one supplements the other.' The whole course of events is shaped by 'the guiding hand of the Great Unnamed'.[19]

In the second place, the shape of the whole plot as one grand reversal of fortune[20] from danger to deliverance, from lowly beginnings to ultimate success, is a pattern that points to divine activity. Without attempting to perceive formal chiastic structures in the book as a whole—as some have done[21]—we can certainly conclude that the book is 'ordered according to the theme of reversal'.[22] Reversal of situations or peripety does not of course necessarily point to *divine* causality;[23] most reversal stories we have ever heard have nothing religious about them. But the Esther story belongs firmly within a religious context, partly because of its subject matter (the deliverance of Israel), partly because of its prototype (the exodus story), and partly because of its literary setting (the Hebrew Bible). In such a context, it is yet another exemplification of the old belief that

> Yahweh makes poor and makes rich;
>> he brings low, and also exalts.
> He raises up the poor from the dust;
>> he lifts the needy from the ash heap (1 Sam. 2.7-8).

The storyteller is no theological sophisticate promoting a 'religionless

Judaism', but an Old Believer whose ultimate act of faith is to take
the protective providence of God for granted.

Let me distinguish my perception of where the narrator stands
theologically from that of several other recent writers. Sandra Berg
sees in the narrative a belief in 'a hidden causality behind the surface
of human history, both concealing and governing the order and
significance of events'.[24] And J.A. Loader writes that 'the motif of
God's intervention is present in the book, but ... it is veiled ...
Motifs that suggest a religious quality are introduced, but they are
made to function in such a way that any theological significance is
immediately veiled again.'[25] In my view, there is nothing *hidden* or
veiled about the causality of the events of the Esther story: it is
indeed *unexpressed* but it is unmistakable, given the context within
which the story is set.

I would even more strongly dissent from G. Gerleman's conception
of the tale as 'a deliberate and thorough desacralization and
detheologization of one of the central traditions of salvation-history'.[26]
In emphasizing the centrality of the exodus traditions rather than
pagan folk or court narratives for the materials of the book, he finds
himself compelled to explain Esther's evident 'secularity' as an
entirely conscious rejection of the religiosity of the exodus narratives.
To that we may reply that if indeed there was no space in the Esther
story for God to act, or if what could justly be assigned to a divine
causality were tangential to or else remote from the movement of the
plot, we could no doubt speak of a 'de-theologization'; but as it is,
when so many major developments of the plot are directly due to
chance-providence, we must affirm that the story makes a deliberate
theological statement—admittedly indirectly. And that statement is
not primarily about divine *causality* as such, but about the *reliability*
of divine causality where Israel's fortunes are concerned, regardless
of the manner—open or indirect—in which that causality operates.

(ii) Not everything in the Esther story is, however, due to that
divine causality which may be relied on; for divine action and human
initiatives are complementary and both indispensable for the
deliverance of the Jewish people. This is a theological perception of
the narrator's which has shaped the outworking of the plot: Esther's
bravery and charm, Mordecai's loyalty to the crown and diplomatic
skills are elements as vital for the plot as are the providential
coincidences. Without the protagonists' courage and craft the
coincidences would have fallen to the ground; and without the

coincidences, all the wit in the world would not have saved the Jewish people.

For this reason it is mistaken to read the story as merely a tale of human wisdom and cunning. Such is the direction, though perhaps not the intention, of W. Lee Humphreys's paper, 'A Life-Style for Diaspora: A Study of the Tales of Esther and Daniel',[27] which characterizes the Esther tale as a story of conflict between courtiers, 'played out within the context of court intrigue and in terms of the dynamics and rules of court life', and centring on the relative rank of the two courtiers Mordecai and Haman.[28] To similar effect is S. Talmon's representation of the story as a 'historicized wisdom-tale',[29] a portrayal of applied wisdom, wisdom in action, 'with the covert, but nevertheless, obvious implication, that . . . ultimate success derives from the proper execution of wisdom maxims, as set forth, e.g. in Proverbs and to a certain degree, in Ecclesiastes'.[30] The tendency of both these essays is to obscure any supernatural dimension in the narrative; Talmon explicitly relates the absence of the name of God and of cultic acts like prayer to the humanistic wisdom ideology infusing the book.[31]

As against such a tendency, the genuine complementarity of the divine and the human is rightly recognized by J.A. Loader, who concludes: 'The Book of Esther should be read as a story of God's intervention on behalf of his people, but also as a story of human wisdom and initiative'.[32] But there is no need to follow him in allocating the divine and the human to different *levels* of meaning,[33] the level of divine action being 'deliberately veiled' by the possibility of reading the story simply as a tale of human initiative and therewith a deliberate 'veiling' of God. For the divine and human causalities function upon the *same* level: namely the plot of the story. There is in Esther no story of human actions leading to success that does not depend in large measure upon the divine 'chances'.

For our storyteller there is no theological problem or narrative tension between the human and divine. For him, divine-human co-operation is the most natural thing in the world. And, since both God and the Jewish people have an equal stake in the preservation of the nation, divine and human interests coincide, and they each contribute their best talents to encompassing that end.[34] It is perhaps not surprising that a writing that commends Jewish-Persian co-operation should take for granted a divine-human synergism. As will now be evident, the proto-Masoretic story not only gave—by its new conception of the second decree—the definitive shape to the plot of the core of the Esther story but also—by its removal of religious language—gave the definitive cast to the book's unique theological structure. Nothing of value was lost, on either count, by the addition of 9.1–10.3 in the Masoretic form of the story, but new perspectives were developed, as we shall see in the succeeding section.

IV. *The Masoretic Story*

Most of what has been said about the proto-Masoretic story of Esther (section III above), and indeed much of what has been said on the yet earlier layers of the story (sections I and II), is true also of the Masoretic shape of the story; but obviously it does not bear repetition. In the present section, therefore, I will concentrate only upon what the Masoretic shape adds to the proto-Masoretic Esther (viz. 9.1– 10.3) and upon what differences this new ending gives to the story as a whole.

Already the earlier chapters of this study have sufficiently depreciated the narratival and logical skills of the author(s) of 9.1– 10.3; but having there demonstrated, I hope, that these last two chapters do form a series of appendices to the story proper, I can now concentrate upon the more positive aspect of this material, viz. what it is that the appendices contribute to the Masoretic book as a whole.

a. *The narrative (9.1-19)*
In the first place we should consider the narrative of 9.1-19. Its existence must be due to a conviction on its author's part that the narrative of chs. 1–8 was altogether too cerebral and in need of translation into some form of action. In the story of chs. 1–8 no one got hurt (except for the expendable Haman, who thoroughly deserved his fate); but serious matters of life and death had been at the heart of the conflict and some more dramatic finale than a royal signature or a national holiday might well seem called for. Further, the story of chs. 1–8 left unsettled a perfectly reasonable question: What actually did happen on the thirteenth of Adar?

Narrative problems need narrative solutions. If there is racial conflict, let it be actualized in a scene of real blood-letting. If there is a struggle for power, let there be a clear demonstration of where, in the end, the power lies. The supplementer responsible for 9.1-19 was not very sensitive to the more intellectual and bloodless resolution of the plot given by his predecessor's story, but he was alert to certain constraints which prevented his much more concrete and 'realistic' narrative from subverting the unique character of the older story.

(i) What 'really' happened on the thirteenth of Adar was, of course, in the Masoretic story a massive purge of anti-Semitic elements from the Persian empire, resulting in the death of more than 75,000 non-Jews but in no injury whatsoever to any Jewish partisan. The event is massive in its physical actuality. Nevertheless, this 'realization' of the plot is expressed in the Masoretic story conceptually as well as physically: it is not just a matter of 'laying hands on' (9.2) or 'smiting' and 'slaying' (vv. 5, 6), but essentially of 'getting the mastery' (v. 1)— the note that is struck at the very beginning of the narrative of this chapter.

(ii) The enemies of the Jews are for the most part anonymous and unidentifiable: they no longer survive after the days of massacre as an object of hate or fear for the Jewish people (though we ourselves might 'realistically' ask how many others were wounded or were further inflamed by the massacre). The specific mention by name of the ten sons of Haman (vv. 7-9) contrasts strongly with the vague identity of all the other victims of the Jews: they are just 'their enemies' (vv. 1, 5), 'those who sought their hurt' (v. 2), 'those who hated them' (vv. 5, 16), 'five hundred men' (v. 6), 'three hundred men' (v. 15), 'seventy-five thousand' (v. 16). There is no anti-Jewish group or nation or party which might survive in part to fight another day. Those groups that *are* mentioned in this supplementary narrative are all groups that are favourable to the Jews: all peoples, all ethnarchs, satraps, governors and royal officials, the court, the provinces (vv. 2-4); the enemies of the Jews may as well have been isolated individuals of whom the empire has now been entirely purged.

(iii) There is a retributionist morality at work in the Jewish slaughter: those who are mastered are those who hoped to master (v. 1), those who are slaughtered and destroyed (v. 5) are those who carried the royal permission to destroy, to slay, and to annihilate (3.13). Cruel it may be, but hardly unjust.

(iv) On the other hand, even the talionate retribution stops short of its just due. The enemies of the Jews had been allowed to plunder the Jews' goods (3.13), and the Jews themselves had been specifically permitted by the second decree to plunder the goods of any attackers (8.1). But the narrator of ch. 9 thrice assures us (vv. 7, 15, 16) that the

Jews took no plunder. No doubt there is an ethical motivation for this narrative detail; the slaughter is cast as essentially self-preservation with no intention of self-aggrandisement (like the motivation in Gen. 14.22f.; and the holy war renunciation of 'banned' goods in Jos. 7 and Deut. 20.16ff.).[35]

(v) The Jewish revenge on their enemies is represented as being confined to strictly legal bounds. Though I believe the narrator of ch. 9 misrepresents the intention of the second decree, which according to 8.11 only allowed Jews to defend themselves against armed attack, he himself believed that it gave permission for vengeance upon their enemies whether or not they had made any attack upon the Jews. Superficially, indeed, 8.13 had permitted that very thing ('the Jews were to be ready on that day to avenge themselves upon their enemies'); but what determined the meaning of that generalization had been the precise wording of the imperial decree of v. 11 which envisaged only Jewish *resistance*. The narrator of ch. 9 took his cue from his predecessor's generalization in 8.13 rather than the wording of the royal letter in 8.11, and no doubt genuinely believed that a massacre of 'enemies' was entirely within the scope of the royal edict. The narrative stresses that everywhere—except in Susa—the killing took place only on the prescribed day, for on the following day the Jews 'rested' (נוח) and made holiday. In the one place, Susa, where the massacre was extended to the following day, express royal permission had been granted (vv. 13-14), and there also the letter of the secondary royal decree (v. 14) was faithfully followed.

(vi) The elimination of 'those who hated them' is not celebrated as victory or vengeance, nor as a militaristic achievement glorifying Jewish might. The diction relating to the killing and its sequel is especially significant for the interpretation it puts upon the events of those days of Adar. No words are minced at the moments when the killing itself has to be narrated: they 'smote all their enemies with the stroke of the sword, and slaughter, and destruction' (וַיַּכּוּ . . . בְּכָל־ אֹיְבֵיהֶם מַכַּת־חֶרֶב וְהֶרֶג וְאַבְדָן, v. 5), they 'slew and destroyed' (. . . הָרְגוּ וְאַבֵּד, v.6), they 'slew' the sons of Haman (הָרְגוּ, v. 10), they 'slew' (וַיַּהַרְגוּ) in Susa three hundred men (v. 15), they 'slew' (הָרוֹג) in the provinces seventy-five thousand men (v. 16). But before and after the actual description quite different language is used—not from squeamishness or a bad conscience but as a critical evaluation of the significance the killing is meant to hold for future generations.

Thus the initial term for the events of the massacre is 'getting the

mastery' (שלט), over those who hated them (v. 1), as if to say: this is
not primarily a story about blood-letting but about power. In v. 2
also, in a prefatory summary of the events, what is referred to is a
'laying hands on' (שלח יד ב')—which does not necessarily imply
killing[36]—those who 'sought their hurt' (מבקשי רעתם), itself a term
without a necessary implication of physical violence; and, following
the same transposition from the key of slaughter to the key of power,
death of their enemies is called an inability to 'stand [innocent term!]
before them' (איש לא-עמד בפניהם). In the same key, all the imperial
officials 'support (מנשאים [benign and vague term]) the Jews', rather
than slaying and slaughtering the Jews' enemies.

Likewise, after the actual description of events, backward references
to them modulate the language of killing. In v. 16 we read of the
slaughter by the provincial Jews as a matter of their 'gathering to
defend their lives' (נקהלו ועמד על-נפשם), a reflection of 8.11 (not of
8.13, on which the narrator of ch. 9 has taken his stand!), where the
edict permitted them to 'gather and defend their lives'. This is the
first time in ch. 9 that the massacre has been represented as an act of
self-defence. In an even more remote key from that of slaughter, the
massacre is next portrayed as a 'gaining relief' (נוח)[37] from enemies
(vv. 16, 17). In v. 18 even the 'gathering to defend their lives' has
become a mere 'gathering' (נקהלו) as if for a social occasion (like the
holiday that followed) or—perhaps more to the point—for all the
world like a solemn cultic festal assembly.[38]

Finally, the celebrations of the day(s) following the killing are
reported in language that is totally demilitarized: it is a day of
banqueting (משתה, vv. 17, 18, 19; also 22), of rejoicing (שמחה, vv. 17,
18, 19; also 22), of holiday (יום טוב, v. 19; also v. 22), of exchanging
gifts (משלח מנות, v. 19; also v. 22; and sending gifts to the poor
[מתנות לאביונים, v. 22]). As the act of slaughter recedes into the past,
the memory that is sustained is of festival, carnival and petty
domestic pleasure.[39]

The narrative of 9.1-19 has thus added two new dimensions to the
Esther story of chs. 1–8, dimensions which indeed strongly conflict
with one another. On the one hand it has made the story more
'realistic', less cerebral, more bloody; on the other it has shifted the
focus of the story away from notions of victory (whether intellectual
or physical), military prowess, and power—all of which it unmistakably
contains—to the hearers' present moment where the significance of
the Esther story lies in the festival activities it has given birth to. The

narrative of 9.1-19 has squarely faced the ultimate meaning that the abstract terms 'power' or 'mastery' must have: they must in the end and concretely mean power over life and death, and no mastery gained by Jews in any Esther story can be worth the name if it does not involve the elimination of any elements that are hostile to the Jews. That, at least, seems to be the narrative's initial perspective. But 'mastery' is, according to 9.1-19, no longer the name of the game played out in the Esther story. Deliverance and success are not ends in themselves (as they were in chs. 1–8); they find their meaning in creating the possibility of joy. The holiday and celebration, the banqueting and acts of generosity—these are the goal of this Masoretic story of Esther. This is different from the proto-Masoretic story of chs. 1–8: it too had come to an end with a depiction of 'gladness and joy among the Jews, a feast and a holiday' (8.17)—but that was in the wave of relief that came wherever the king's edict reached, with its promise that armed conflict would not now take place. The feasting and gladness of ch. 9, on the other hand, is the celebration of Jews who have dipped their hands in blood—not illegally but as a cruel necessity for their national survival—and are celebrating now not their victory but the absence of cause for blood or victory in the future. In this respect the Esther scroll, with its Masoretic appendix, harmonizes well with other Old Testament traditions, as in Deuteronomy 3.20 and 12.9 where the purpose of the war of conquest of the land is conceived of as an ultimate 'rest'.

b. *The Letters of Mordecai and Esther and the Responses thereto (9.20-32)*

The 'documentary' appendixes formed by the letters of Mordecai (9.20-28) and Esther (9.29-32) further reinforce the 'demilitarized' memory of the events of the Esther scroll which we have noted already in the narrative of vv. 1-19, but go further than that narrative did in linking the celebration of those events with the traditional festivals of the Jewish year.

(i) We note first that the focus has moved in vv. 20ff. from the spontaneous celebrations following the successes of the thirteenth (or fourteenth) of Adar (vv. 17ff.) to a regulated, agreed, institutionalized celebration of what is to be definitively remembered as a 'gaining relief from their enemies' (נחו מאיביהם). The days that are to be celebrated are not the thirteenth—when the victory was achieved—but the fourteenth and fifteenth, the days when the rejoicing took place.[40] In Susa, indeed, there still was fighting on the fourteenth (v. 18), but it is not for that reason that the fourteenth becomes a holiday, but only because for the provincial Jews the rejoicing had already begun on that day. And however transparently the purpose of Mordecai's letter may have been to resolve a potential liturgical conflict between Jews of Susa and Jews of the provinces over the date of the celebrations, its net effect is to extend over two days celebrations which had originally been adequately contained with the confines of a single day. The rejoicing has been multiplied, not the *Schadenfreude*.

(ii) Secondly, we observe that in the brief summary of the Esther story embedded in vv. 24-25, the massacre by the Jews, and therewith any conception of military victory, has been entirely eliminated. Perhaps the slaughter is alluded to a little later in the phrase 'what had befallen them' (מה הגיע אליהם) in v. 26—not part of the summary— but then perhaps it may just as well be the deliverance from Haman's plot that is in mind. Certainly, within the summary itself, it is only Haman and his sons who suffer because of his evil plot (מחשבתו הרעה, v. 26). This summary, as a representation of the story at a date later, I presume, than even the narrative appendix of 9.1-19, further reinforces the tendency to play down the idea of 'victory' in favour of the idea of 'deliverance' as the central theme of the Esther scroll.

(iii) Thirdly, the response of the Jews to Mordecai's letter is couched primarily in terms of the 'keeping' of the festival 'Purim'. This too represents a movement away from militaristic conceptions and forms an injunction to future readers of the story to conceive it as primarily a memorial to joy. What the Jews solemnly determine in vv. 26-28 is that 'in every year' (בכל־שנה ושנה) and 'in every generation' (בכל־דור ודור), in 'every family, every province, every city' (משפחה ומשפחה מדינה ומדינה עיר ועיר), these days of celebration shall be observed (עשה) *according to what has been written about them* (כִּכְתָבָם)— viz. in the letter of Mordecai, which had prescribed their dates as the days *after* the victory and their character as 'joy' (שמחה, v. 22) for relief rather than gloating over the slain. 'These days', the days of festive celebration, are 'never to be abrogated by the Jews' (אל יעברו מתוך היהודים, v. 28), and 'the recounting of them is never to cease in future generations' (וזכרם לא־יסוף מזרעם). 'The past is kept alive by the story'[41]—not of the victory or even primarily of the deliverance but essentially of the joy participated in by every Jewish family on that unique occasion.

The very name of the festival, Purim, occurring at 9.26 for the first time, is explicitly related to an event as far removed from the notion of bloody victory as it is possible to be. For the name Purim is meant to conjure up the *plot of Haman*, the day for its execution having been determined by Pur, the lot cast at 3.7 (that event also being mentioned in the summary at 9.24). Although the day fixed by Pur, the thirteenth of Adar,[42] was in the end the day of the Jews' massacre of their enemies, the term Pur is never mentioned in connection with the killing *by* the Jews (it is not in 9.1-19, for example) but only in connection with the planned killing *of* the Jews. And though the day fixed by Pur is the *thirteenth* of Adar, the festival Purim is *not* on that day, but on the *fourteenth* and *fifteenth*, the days when there was 'rest' and no killing.

The name Purim itself, quite apart from the issue of the *dates* on which it is to be observed, may further serve in determining where the emphasis of the story should rightly fall according to the final shape of the Masoretic story of Esther. *Pûr* has been defined in v. 24 as *gôrāl*, 'lot', which has there been understood as the 'lot' cast by (or, for) Haman at 3.7. But the festival is called Purim, 'lots' in the plural. Regardless of the historical origins of the festival or of the name, should we not see here a statement about the *meaning* of the festival that is made by the use of the plural? 'They called these days Purim, after the term Pur' (v. 26). One lot is cast by Haman, but there is another 'lot' for the Jews—cast by God. There were *two*, contradictory fates or 'lots' cast for the Jews in the days of Esther; and the first was overturned by the second, itself a set of 'lots' or chances cast by divine providence.[43]

(iv) The ultimate phase in the 'demilitarization' of the Esther story is represented by the letter of Esther (9.29-32), which concerns itself exclusively with the observance of Purim, making no reference to the events which originally led up to the celebration of the festival. Nothing, in fact, in either the letter of Mordecai or of Esther enjoins upon the Jewish people a reading of the Esther scroll, or a remembrance of the events narrated in it: they are to 'keep' (עשה) these days (v. 21; cf. vv. 27, 28), to 'establish' or confirm (קים) them (v. 31). The Jews themselves determine to 'keep' (עשה, vv. 27, 28) and 'remember' (זכר, v. 28) the days themselves, so that the days of Purim should not fall into disuse among the Jews (לא יעברו מתוך היהודים, v. 28) and its commemoration should not cease (זכרם לא־יסוף, v. 28).[44] I do not suggest that the events of the story of Esther are not intended to be recalled in the Purim observances enjoined by Mordecai and Esther but that the emphasis of Purim lies elsewhere: on the merry-making, gift-giving, and other rituals (v. 31). This fact is all the more striking when viewed from our knowledge of how important a place in the Purim celebrations of antiquity and today has been held by the Esther scroll, its reading and its story.[45] The stress in the appendixes to the Masoretic Esther, which lies so heavily on the rituals of the celebration that the story gains no explicit mention, can only be a reflection of the tendency in these verses to downplay the significance of the military aspect of the story.

Other concerns beside the question of 'demilitarization' come to light in the appendixes of 9.20-32.

1. Along with a weakening of interest in the events of the thirteenth of Adar there has been in these appendixes a minimizing of the roles of Esther and Mordecai—and of providence—in the story. So in the summary (9.24-25), the plot of Haman against the Jews is represented as quashed by the king the moment he came to know of its existence—without any intervention by Mordecai or Esther,[46] or by God. No readers of the book can be imagined as forgetting at this point what the story-line of the preceding chapters has been, but they are being encouraged to set the story as a tale of the heroism of Esther and Mordecai, or even as a narrative of divine-human co-operation, within the framework of a larger story of deliverance of the Jews from an evil plot. This is a different conception of the story from what we have gained from considering chs. 1–8 alone, or even 1.1–9.19. Whether it is any more definitive or authoritative a conception is beside my point to argue. But it is a conception that belongs to the decision to view the Esther story through the lenses of the Purim festival which is being celebrated as joyfulness for a deliverance realized.

2. The authority for observing the Purim festival is of a dual nature. There is the formal authority of the letters of Mordecai and Esther, the former no doubt in his position as 'great in the king's house' (9.4; cf. 8.15), the latter explicitly in her office as 'Queen' Esther (so called three times in vv. 29-32). But no less important is the authority of the community. It was the community, whether of Jews in Susa or of provincial Jews, that originated the celebrations as a spontaneous rejoicing (9.17-19). And further, it is the community that 'ordain and take it on themselves and their descendants' (קִיְמוּ וְקִבֵּל הַיְּהוּדִים עֲלֵיהֶם וְעַל־זַרְעָם, v. 27) to observe the days of Purim.

It seems to be very much because of 'what they had faced in this matter' (מה־ראו על־ככה) and 'what had befallen them' (מה הגיע אליהם) that the letters of Mordecai and Esther receive unqualified support by the community to which they were addressed. This is not a divinely instituted festival, like those prescribed in the Torah, so it is important to know where its authority lies: in the leaders raised up by divine providence, to be sure, but also in the community at large.

3. One feature of Mordecai's letter we have not yet considered is its prescription of giving gifts to the poor (משלוח . . . מתנות לאביונים, v. 22), an element that did not figure in the account of the spontaneous celebrations in vv. 17-19. The function of this note is to link Purim celebrations with other occasions of rejoicing in Israel's economic-liturgical life. The nearest parallel is the occasion of rejoicing portrayed in Nehemiah 8.10, 12, at which the people are instructed by Ezra[47] to send portions (שלחו מנות) to those who have nothing prepared; that is to say, the celebrations of Tishri 1, which is the occasion in question, whether it is New Year or new moon,[48] are to be fully entered into despite the feeling of the people that joyfulness is out of order on a day when they have heard the law read with its solemn warnings (vv. 9-11). Those who have nothing prepared for the holiday can only be the poor; Ezra can hardly be represented as instituting a custom of giving gifts to the poor on holidays, but he is reflecting a concern that has become attached to the observance of days of joyful celebration. In the Deuteronomic legislation, gifts to the poor had been linked with the three-year tithe (Deut. 14.28-29; 26.12-13) and the seven-year law of release (15.7-11), but not apparently with the annual festivals.[49] Here in Mordecai's letter this practice functions as one of the means by which the Masoretic appendix 'draws Purim within the orbit of Israel's religious traditions',[50] creating a new festival to be observed duly and seasonally (כזמנם, v. 27; בזמניהם, v. 29), without however turning a 'secular' festival into a 'religious' one.

4. A further new feature introduced into the Masoretic appendixes is the element of 'fasts and their lamenting' (הצומות וזעקתם, v. 31). As we have noted above (Chapter 4, section I, §5), the phrase sits awkwardly in the sentence, but what seems to be referred to are practices already instituted by the Jews, to which Esther now gives her blessing. She sends letters to the Jews to confirm (לקים) the days of Purim (i) in accord with how Mordecai had given confirmation of them (כאשר קים עליהם מרדכי) and (ii) in accord with how the Jews

themselves had confirmed/established for themselves (וכאשר קימו
על־נפשם) the matters of fasts and the associated laments. Esther had
indeed earlier in the story initiated a fast of her own (4.16), but that
was quite a different occasion, and it is not brought into connection
in any way with the fourteenth of Adar.[51] A closer connection is with
the reference in Mordecai's letter to the 'turning' of the month from
sorrow to gladness and from mourning to a holiday (9.22)—but even
there no ritual custom is in view.[52]

The entry of this spontaneously generated custom into the
Masoretic appendixes serves two functions. (i) It emphasizes the role
of the community in determining its liturgical life. The Jews of chs.
1–8 have been the passive victims of Haman's plot, only two
characters—Mordecai and Esther, together with, of course, the
unnamed Providence—engaging in any positive action on their
behalf. In ch. 9 the Jewish people are liberated by the second decree
(as there understood) so as to change the course of events by their
collective action. But when the twelfth year of Artaxerxes is past,
what becomes of those events? The memory of them, and the
celebration of their significance, is the property of the community;
Mordecai and Esther can only lend their weight to what has
effectively already been instituted by the people. (ii) It provides a
context for the festival of joy.[53] 'The celebration is set in the
framework of fasting and mourning, the full religious meaning of
which has been carefully defined throughout the rest of Israel's
sacred tradition.'[54] The context is both emotional and religious. The
joy is not just a licensed release of high spirits but is participated in
consciously as reversal of grief, deliverance from mourning. And
further, the joy is not just the wave of relief that follows the
resolution of crisis (contrast 8.17), but a joy that fasting and lament—
directed to *God*—has been *heard*. God, everywhere in the book
conspicuous by his absence, is the overarching context of the
memory of the Purim festival.

c. *The Encomium on Mordecai (10.1-3)*
This final appendix of the Masoretic book moves in a quite different
direction from the liturgically and religiously oriented letters of
Mordecai and Esther. Here the issue that is addressed is the
significance of the Esther story for Jewish life under foreign rule.
That is, the story does not only have meaning for the days of the
Purim festival: it interprets non-autonomous Jewish existence by

offering a prescription for every day of the year, a 'life-style for diaspora' as W. Lee Humphreys has aptly termed it.[55]

Mordecai in this appendix means more than the 'historical' Mordecai, the man who has figured in the story of the book. B.S. Childs has rightly detected a 'typifying' tendency that emerges at a few points in the book, Haman being cast as the Agagite, an archetypal enemy of the Jews, Mordecai as a descendant of Kish father of Saul.[56] He might equally well have noted the 'typifying' function of this last notice of Mordecai, in which 'the Jew' is celebrated as grand vizier of the Persian empire, both chronicled in Persian annals and 'great among the Jews', and not only an instrument of deliverance in the twelfth year of Ahasuerus but a continuing 'seeker of the welfare of his people', 'speaking peace to all his race' (דבר שלום לכל־זרעו) like a messianic ruler (Zech. 9.10).[57] Mordecai stands, as Humphreys has put it, for 'both the possibility of a rewarding and creative life in a foreign court and in the same moment of the possibility of service and devoted loyalty to one's people and religious identity'.[58] We can go one step further and see 'the court' as typical for a foreign environment, an alien culture, in which Jews can serve two masters at once—without tension.

The meaning of the Esther story from the perspective of these last verses (10.1-3) is that it can be seen not only as a conflict of courtiers, a story of (divine) deliverance, divine-human co-operation, or as the occasion for a festival of joy, but also as a scriptural authorization for Jewish-Gentile co-operation, for the acceptance of office in an alien world, and for enthusiastic support by the community for those individuals who have compromised the strictest standards of Jewish behaviour for the sake of the greater good, the well-being of Israel.

V. *The Septuagint Story*

The Septuagintal version of the Esther story represents a more thorough and substantial reworking of the story than any version we have hitherto considered in this Chapter. Not only are there revisions (often omissions) in almost every verse as compared with the Masoretic version, but there are also the six very considerable Additions. 'It would be very helpful for one's understanding of the Additions', writes Carey A. Moore, 'if one could know their purpose, that is, why an ancient editor supplied this or that Addition, and what he had hoped the Addition would accomplish. It is, however, much easier and safer to describe the Addition's effect; for the particular effect, which may or may not have been the one intended by the ancient editor, is nonetheless objectively observable, whereas the ancient editor's purpose can only be inferred.'[59] Without subscribing to the view that the 'effect' is 'objectively observable' and not rather a matter of informed but ultimately subjective assessment, I can easily assent to Moore's programme of concentrating on the *effect* of the Septuagintal Additions rather than upon historical reconstruction of the author's purposes.

Whether, on the other hand, it is true to say that 'the Book of Esther is totally transformed by the presence of its Additions' in that they make *God*, not Esther or Mordecai, the 'hero' of the story,[60] is another matter, which must shortly be examined. It is true that most scholars have believed—speaking the language of *purpose* rather than *effect*—that the Additions exist primarily 'to supply the religious element that is so conspicuously absent from the Hebrew edition', secondarily 'to give specimens of fine Greek writing, such as are found in the two letters of Artaxerxes'[61] or perhaps rather to 'strengthen its trustworthiness',[64] and thirdly to further extend the narrative element with the introduction of Mordecai's dream and its interpretation.[60]

Whatever may have been the intentions of the author(s) of the Additions—which may have been rather more complex than simply meeting religious deficiencies, for example—the primary effect of the LXX expansions as a whole is, I would suggest, to *assimilate the book of Esther to a scriptural norm*,[61] especially as found in Ezra, Nehemiah, and Daniel.

1. In the case of the *religious* dimensions of the LXX Esther, the function of the Septuagint's additions is not wholly or even primarily to introduce explicit language of divine causation into a deficient Hebrew original, but to recreate the book in the mould of post-exilic Jewish history. It is distinctive of the 'Persian histories' of Ezra and Nehemiah that they embody only a few, though critical, interventions of God in the historical process: he stirs up the spirit of Cyrus (Ezr. 1.1), and the spirits of the returnees (1.5); he aids them in the work of rebuilding the temple (6.22), and makes them joyfully celebrate passover on its completion (6.22); his hand is upon Ezra (7.6, 9, 28; 8.18, 31), initiating his return, giving him courage, choosing companions, protecting the caravan from danger. God's good hand is on Nehemiah also in ensuring he gets from the king what he needs

(Neh. 2.8; cf. 2.18); God puts into his heart what he is to do for Jerusalem (2.12); he assures his enemies that God will make the Jews prosper (2.20); and God does frustrate the enemies' plan (4.15 [Heb. 4.14]); his enemies see the the wall has been built with the help of God (6.16); God puts it into his mind to prepare a population list (7.5); God makes the people rejoice at the dedication of the wall (12.43).

In the LXX of Esther also, at two critical junctures, we read that 'God changed the spirit of the king to gentleness' (καὶ μετέβαλεν ὁ θεὸς τὸ πνεῦμα τοῦ βασιλέως εἰς πραΰτητα) when Esther entered his presence (D8 = 15.8); and that on the crucial night before the planned impalement of Mordecai, 'the Lord kept sleep from the king' (ὁ δὲ κύριος ἀπέστησεν τὸν ὕπνον ἀπὸ τοῦ βασιλέως, 6.1). In Mordecai's final speech also the whole of the narrative is explicitly said to be 'all God's doing' (παρὰ τοῦ θεοῦ ἐγένετο ταῦτα, F1 = 10.4), a story of 'Israel that cried to the Lord and was delivered' (Ισραηλ οἱ βοήσαντες πρὸς τὸν θεὸν καὶ σωθέντες), F5 =10.8; 'the Lord has saved his people, and has delivered us from all these evils. He has done great miracles and signs such as have not been done among the nations' (καὶ ἔσωσεν Κύριος τὸν λαὸν αὐτοῦ, καὶ ἐρρύσατο Κύριος ἡμᾶς ἐκ πάντων τῶν κακῶν τούτων· καὶ ἐποίησεν ὁ θεὸς τὰ σημεῖα καὶ τὰ τέρατα τὰ μεγάλα ἃ οὐ γέγονεν ἐν τοῖς ἔθνεσιν, F6 = 10.9); God 'remembered his people and vindicated his inheritance' (ἐμνήσθη ὁ θεὸς τοῦ λαοῦ αὐτοῦ, καὶ ἐδικαίωσεν τὴν κληρονομίαν ἑαυτοῦ, F9 = 10.12). In the confessional statement of the king also (Addition E) we meet with the statements that 'God who is Lord of all has speedily brought upon him [Haman] the punishment he deserved' (τὴν καταξίαν τοῦ τὰ πάντα ἐπικρατοῦντος θεοῦ διὰ τάχους ἀποδόντος αὐτῷ κρίσιν, E18 = 16.18), and that 'God, who has all things in his power, has made this a day not of ruin, but of joy, for his chosen people' (ταύτην γὰρ ὁ πάντα δυναστεύων θεὸς ἀντ' ὀλεθρίας τοῦ ἐκλεκτοῦ γένους ἐποίησεν αὐτοῖς εὐφροσύνην, E21 = 16.21).

Nothing is told us in these LXX additions that we do not really know already from the Masoretic story, if we have any kind of perception of the significance of the happy coincidences of the plot. The effect of the explicit ascription of events to God is not to inject a previously lacking dimension into the book but to draw out explicitly what lay implicitly in it and in so doing make it more like the other post-exilic histories.

Another aspect of the 'religious' additions of the LXX is the explicit reference to religious activities or beliefs on the part of the actors in the story. The righteous 'cry aloud' to God (A9), Mordecai 'sees what God had resolved to do' (A11), Mordecai's parting instructions to Esther are to 'fear God and keep his commandments' (2.20). He sends a message to her to 'call upon the Lord' before she enters the king's presence (4.8), and obeys by 'invoking the all-seeing God, her preserver' (ἐπικαλεσαμένη τὸν πάντων ἐπόπτην θεὸν καὶ σωτῆρα, D2 = 15.5). Haman's wife and friends believe that Mordecai must in the end be successful because 'the living God is with him' (θεὸς ζῶν μετ' αὐτοῦ, 6.13), and the king himself acknowledges the justice of 'the all-seeing God' (τοῦ τὰ πάντα κατοπτεύοντος ἀεὶ θεοῦ... δίκην, E4 = 16.4), and that the Jews are 'children of the living God, most high, most mighty' (τοῦ ὑψίστου μεγίστου ζῶντος θεοῦ) who 'maintains the [Persian] empire in most wonderful order' (16.16).

Pre-eminent among the religious activities referred to in the LXX Esther are of course the prayers of Mordecai and Esther which form Addition C (13.8–14.9). They each have secondary functions like explaining why Mordecai would not bow before Haman (C5-7 = 13.12-14) or how Esther could square her participation in Persian life with Jewish conscience (C26-28 = 14.15-17); but their primary function is of course rather to represent the piety of distressed Israelites. These prayers assist in remoulding the book into the form of an *exemplary* tale—which does not only record divine deliverance or divine-human co-operation but also gives advice on how a Jew should behave religiously in a foreign environment or a situation of crisis.

In this respect, the LXX additions conform the book more closely to the pattern established by Ezra, Nehemiah, and Daniel, where also we find exemplary prayers of supplication (Ezr. 9.6-15; Neh. 1.5-11; 9.6-37; Dan. 9.4-19), and appropriate reference to religious practices typical of post-exilic Jewry (e.g. fasts: Ezr. 8.21, 23; Neh. 1.4; observance of dietary laws: Dan. 1.8).

2. As for the *dream of Mordecai and its interpretation*, forming Additions A and F, the effect of superimposing this framework upon the Greek book of Esther, it may be suggested, is to conform it more closely to a scriptural precedent in the book of Daniel. There also the *meaning* of history is conveyed through dreams and their interpretation. In the first place, and primarily, it is the dream of Nebuchadnezzar (ch. 2)—which Daniel effectively also dreams after

him (2.19)—which portrays the course of world history as a succession
of empires which will give way to the institution of an eternal
kingdom of God (2.44). In the second place, and subsidiarily, it is the
seer's visions of chs. 7-12, which elaborate, exegete and develop the
initial dream of ch. 2.[65] The function of the premonitory dream form
is of course to emphasize that no historical disasters or dangers facing
the readers of the book have caught God by surprise: he has
discerned all and has disposed all.

In the Greek Esther, the initial dream and its interpretation
readjusts the conception of God as a saviour who intervenes in
Jewish history at the moment when the survival of the people is
suddenly cast into doubt into an all-seeing designer of history who
has already determined the salvation of the Jews before the thought
of genocide has even occurred to Haman. It is a matter of 'a great
God mak[ing] known what shall be hereafter. The dream is certain,
and its interpretation is sure' (Dan. 2.45).

At the same time the presence of the dream with its interpretation
readjusts the focus of the story from that of conflict between Haman
and Mordecai, or between Haman and the Jews, or between the Jews
and their enemies (all present in the Masoretic version) to a wider
focus: it is a conflict on the cosmic level between the 'righteous
nation' and the rest of mankind (A6 = 11.7).[66]

The effect therefore of these two Additions is to set the narrative of
the Esther scroll in a broader interpretative framework in which the
role of God and the nature of the threat to the Jewish people have
been hugely magnified. From an early phase in the history of the
Esther story the world-wide dimension of the threat to the Jews had
been explicit—and the divine act of deliverance had been, as I have
argued, implicit. The Septuagintal Esther makes its distinctive con-
tribution by drawing the book within the orbit in which the book of
Daniel moves, incorporating the story into a grand 'plan of the ages'
in which 'two lots'—for Jews and for Gentiles—'came to the hour
and the moment' (F7 = 10.10), and portraying a God who does more
than merely deliver distressed Israel (A9 = 11.10): like Daniel's God
who 'delivers and rescues' *and* 'works signs and wonders in heaven
and on earth' (Dan. 6.27), Esther and Mordecai's God deals in cosmic
coinage, with an eschaton-like day of gloom and darkness and every
nation readied for battle (A6-7 = 11.7-8), 'saving' his people and
'rescuing' them indeed but equally 'working great signs and wonders
such as have not occurred among the nations' (F6 = 10.9).[67]

3. Finally, the presence of the *documentary material* in Additions B and E, the edicts of Haman and of Mordecai, is to be explained in the same way as an assimilation of the Esther scroll to a characteristic feature of the post-exilic 'Persian histories' of Ezra and Daniel. It is true, as Moore points out,[68] that the closest affinities in language and style lie with the royal letters in 3 Maccabees (3.12-29; 7.1-9), written in a bombastic and convoluted Greek typical of Alexandrian Atticist litterateurs.[69] But the effect of the incorporation of apparently authentic Persian documents is to give the book the air of closer engagement with Persian official records (such as we note in the MT Esther's reference to the Book of the Chronicles of the kings of Media and Persia, 10.2). Such insertions in the Greek Esther do not, however, have solely or primarily the effect of enhancing the book's trustworthiness—though that is often claimed to be their *purpose*— but rather create a greater correspondence with the biblical 'Persian' books. And the significance of the citation of Persian documents in Biblical books, religiously speaking, is not to add an air of greater authenticity to the Biblical books—for why should a Persian document be supposed (except by a latter-day Biblical critic) to be able to *add* anything to a Biblical narrative?—but as a testimony to the impact of the truth of the Jewish religion upon outsiders, neighbours and overlords.

Thus, if we examine the Persian (or neo-Babylonian) documents in Ezra and Daniel, we find that they witness to such effects of the Jewish faith: to Cyrus's conviction that Yahweh has given him world dominion and a special responsibility to rebuild the Jerusalem temple (Ezr. 1.2), to Artaxerxes' realization that Jerusalem is an ancient city and former capital of a great empire (4.20), to Tattenai's understanding that the exile of the Jews was due to the anger of their God (5.12), to Darius's desire that the Jerusalem temple cult be supported from satrapal revenues and that prayers should be made by its priests for the life of the king and his successors (6.8-10), to Nebuchadnezzar's assurance that there is no other god who is able to deliver as the God of Daniel's three friends has done (Dan. 3.29), to Darius's intention that throughout his empire citizens should tremble and fear before the God of Daniel (6.26-27). Especially worthy of note is the letter of Nebuchadnezzar in the form of a 'confession of faith', sent to 'all peoples, nations, and languages' (Dan. 3.31–4.34 [EVV 4.1-37]) because of its similarity to Artaxerxes' second decree in the LXX Esther (Addition E = 16.1-24).[70]

There is, of course, also an anti-Jewish document among the Greek Additions (the first letter of Artaxerxes, Addition B = 13.1-7). But this is principally a foil to the assertion of Jewish innocence in Addition E, as was the accusatory letter of Rehum and Shimshai in Ezra 4.11-16. In both cases they represent the ignorance and latent hostility of non-Jews which is expressed only to be satisfactorily and thoroughly overwhelmed by the pro-Jewish statements that finally emerge from the Persian court. There is more than a trace here of Jewish nervousness and a not wholly misplaced anxiety over their own status in the eyes of their neighbours and rulers, and undoubtedly one function of these 'Persian' documents is to reassure a self-conscious community that it is possible for a Gentile administration to look with comparative favour on the Jewish people, peculiar and deviant though their way of life may seem (cf. Est. 3.8). But whether the 'documentary' Additions B and E of the LXX Esther were made to meet such a particular need in their own time or whether the Additions were not rather created simply in order rather to pay homage to the shape and content of the Biblical histories is hard to say. If imitation is the sincerest form of flattery, it would not be surprising if the Greek-speaking revisers of the Hebrew Esther believed they could best present it to their readers in the lineaments of the other sacred 'Persian' histories.

Whatever the intentions of those responsible for the Greek Additions to Esther, the effect of making the book unlike its Hebrew original was to make it more like its nearest counterparts within the Hebrew Bible. A transformation of its canonical shape had the effect of affirming its canonical status.

And if the effect of the Additions was to assimilate the book to the norm established by Ezra, Nehemiah and Daniel, that was no mis-shaping of the book's central core. I have argued above (section III) that the primary elements of the book's theological statement are that the providence of God is to be relied on to reverse the ill-fortunes of Israel and that divine action and human initiatives are complementary and both indispensable for 'salvation'. The Septuagint Esther, by establishing a connection with the 'Persian histories', invites us to consider the appropriateness of such a statement for these writings as a group, and presents, if you like, the Esther story as an interpretative tool for appreciating those books that have now become its kin. But that is another story.

NOTES

NOTES TO CHAPTER 1

1. W. Dommershausen, *Die Estherrolle: Stil und Ziel einer alttestament-lichen Schrift* (Stuttgarter Biblische Monographien, 6; Stuttgart, 1968), p. 99.

2. 9.1-19 does not exhibit the same scenic structure, and I leave it out of account here.

3. It is hard to believe that Ahasuerus seriously believes Haman is trying to rape Esther.

4. On the meaning of the phrase ופני המן חפו (7.8), see below, Chapter 9, note 12.

5. 'Eine neue Schwierigkeit ist entstanden, zugleich auch eine neue Spannung des Hörers', writes Dommershausen (*Estherrolle*, p. 103), echoing H. Gunkel, *Esther* (Religionsgeschichtliche Volksbücher, II/19-20; Tübingen, 1916), p. 40.

6. The commentators have consistently decided that the 'for' clause must refer *either* to the irreversibility of the first decree already issued by Haman, *or* to the second about to be issued by Mordecai. For the former view, see e.g. A. Bertheau, *Die Bücher Esra, Nechemia und Ester* (Kurzgefasstes exegetisches Handbuch zum Alten Testament, 17; 2nd edn by V. Ryssel; Leipzig, 1887), p. 434; L.B. Paton, *A Critical and Exegetical Commentary on the Book of Esther* (International Critical Commentary; Edinburgh, 1908), pp. 270f.; H. Bardtke, *Das Buch Esther* (Kommentar zum Alten Testament, XVII/5); (Gütersloh, 1963), pp. 367f. For the latter, cf. F.W. Schultz, *The Book of Esther* (A Commentary on the Holy Scriptures by J.P. Lange, tr. by P. Schaff, vol. 7 of the Old Testament; Edinburgh, 1868), p. 293. Moore judges that 'The parenthetic aside here is made by either the author or a glossator rather than by the king, since Esther would have known about the law's irrevocability' (*Esther*, p. 79); but, as far as the plot goes, it hardly matters whether Esther knows or whether the king knows that she knows. What is important is that the reference to the law's irrevocability is Janus-like: it offers a reason why Esther's request cannot be fulfilled *and* it guarantees the authority of anything legal that Mordecai may write.

7. Having thus expressed my reading of this sentence, I find the following lines much to my taste:

The king treats the matter in his own right royal fashion ... [Haman] is gone for ever. As to what remains, the preservation, the safety of your people, 'write ye also as it liketh you.' 'As it liketh you!' Don't trouble me with too many particulars. I am a monarch, not a statesman. There are scribes, there are wise men; and thou, Mordecai, art wise. 'As it liketh you!' 'As it liketh you;' only take care of this, that ye make no attempt to repeal that which is unrepealable, and that ye do not touch the dignity of the Empire. (Alexander Raleigh, *The Book of Esther. Its Practical Lessons and Dramatic Scenes* [Edinburgh, 1880], p. 206).

A more severe reading was given by Paulus Cassel (*An Explanatory Commentary on Esther* [Eng. Tr.; Edinburgh, 1888], p. 233):

[']Write,' says he, 'now also to the Jews what you please,' just as he had before left Haman to do what he liked. We observe in him the same arbitrary proceeding, the same carelessness as to the lives of many people, the same tyrannical caprice now for Esther as it was before for Haman,—all is easy in his hands, except to revoke his former edict, which might be regarded as derogatory to the royal dignity.

The last clause quoted is especially interesting, since for other commentators (Bardtke, *Esther*, p. 368 n. 3; Dommershausen, *Estherrolle*, pp. 103f.) it is a matter of some surprise that the narrator does not speak out against the inflexibility of Persian law. Bardtke indeed in the end explains the narrator's absence of criticism as due to a certain sympathy on the part of a post-Ezran Jew, himself under inflexible law (divine, of course, so that makes all the [moral] difference). In fact, the narrative *is* against Persian law's inflexibility; it mocks it in three distinct ways: 1. Any plot that has an autocrat's authority limited by something of his own creation is necessarily ironic (it is the Frankenstein's monster predicament); 2. The notice of the irreversibility of Persian law in 8.8 inevitably recalls the earlier notice in 1.19 in a plainly frivolous context; 3. The very fact that it is possible to nullify an unalterable law while still paying lip-service to its irrevocability—which is what the remainder of ch. 8 will show Mordecai doing—shows plainly how bogus the doctrine is. The plot itself undermines the irreversibility of (the effects of) the law. So the narrator *does* in fact criticize the law, but he recognizes that the king is a victim of it rather than its willing accomplice, as Cassel's last clause would suggest.

8. Perhaps the devising is represented as requiring lengthy deliberation; so Schultz, p. 85: 'Mordecai himself may have long been in doubt regarding the way to be pursued out of the difficulty ... It may afford us light to know that he waited two months after his elevation before he issued the new edict' (cf. 8.9 with 3.12).

9. For this interpretation of the last half of 8.11, cf. R. Gordis, 'Studies in the Esther Narrative', *JBL* 95 (1976), pp. 43-58 (49-53) (= Moore, *Studies*, pp. 414-18), and see below, p. 179 n. 3. Gordis's interpretation is judged unconvincing, nevertheless, by C.A. Moore, 'Esther Revisited: An Examination of

Some Esther Studies over the Past Decade', *Festschrift for S. Iwry* (forthcoming), ed. A. Kort and S. Morschauser (Winona Lake).

10. E.J. Bickerman, *Four Strange Books of the Bible: Jonah, Daniel, Koheleth, Esther* (New York, 1967), p. 193, correctly observes that 'Haman does not mobilize royal forces against the Jews'. He argues that 'the central government and its satraps would be unable to cope with the task of organizing and carrying out a massacre on the whole terrritory of the empire'. However that may be, it remains the case that the edict is addressed to the king's satraps and provincial governors as well as to the ethnarchs of the various racial groups ('the princes of all the peoples') (3.12).

11. Cf. the permission to returning exiles in Ezr. 1.2-4, which is represented as a Persian decree (oral and written); and the necessity for a 'decree' (טעם) before a routine search in the archives can be carried out (Ezr. 4.19; 6.1).

12. Similarly F. Stummer, *Das Buch Esther* (Echter-Bibel, 2; 2nd edn, Würzburg, 1956), p. 585; B.W. Anderson, 'The Book of Esther. Introduction and Exegesis', (*IB*, vol. 3; Nashville, 1954), p. 870: 'The words *these things* refer to the substance of what has gone before in the Esther narrative, but should not be construed to mean that Mordecai was the author of the foregoing material (Rashi)'.

This issue has been greatly confused by the contention of medieval and other commentators that this clause indicates that Mordecai was the author of the Book of Esther. To say so is to maintain that 9.20 onwards is effectively an *appendix* to the Book of Esther, reflecting back on the narrative of 1.1–9.19. This is a 'critical' step taken by many 'pre-critical' writers, but—regardless of whether it is a step towards 'historical' actuality or not—it is a step away from the text itself. The Masoretic text is hardly the kind of self-conscious narration that *refers to itself*, as a long line of novels have, from *Tom Jones* and *Tristram Shandy* to *Les Faux-monnayeurs*.

The unpersuasive view that 'these things' refers to what is to follow is sometimes sustained as an alternative to the assertion that 9.20 means that Mordecai wrote the book of Esther (so Paton, p. 293). Dommershausen insists (*Estherrolle*, p. 123) that 'wrote these words and sent letters' should be taken as synonymous phrases, and that אלה usually refers to what follows (so Gesenius–Kautzsch, §136*a-b*); BDB, on the other hand, affirm that 'אלה may point indifferently to what follows . . . or to what preceded' (p. 41b). The suggestion of Bardtke (*Esther*, p. 391), Moore (*Esther*, p. 93) and G. Gerleman (*Esther* [Biblischer Kommentar. Altes Testament, 21; Neukirchen-Vluyn, 1973], pp. 137f.) that אלה refers only to the most recent events cannot be disproved, but leaves the point I am making the same: everything of significance must be written down.

13. In Chapter 4, section II, paragraph 2, below I put forward reasons why vv. 23-26a cannot have originally formed a logical sequence, and therewith why vv. 24-26a should not, from the point of view of the *redaction* of the book, be viewed as part of the Mordecai letter. Here, on the other hand, I am

suggesting how vv. 24-26a should be read in the book as it stands, before redaction-critical questions are raised.

14. The custom of referring to the five books, Canticles, Ruth, Lamentations, Qoheleth and Esther as 'the Scrolls' (Megilloth) is doubtless later than the designation of Esther as '*the* Scroll' (Megillah). In Baba Bathra 14b-15a that grouping does not appear, Esther being separated from the other megilloth. It is generally thought that the grouping of the five Megilloth belongs to the post-Talmudic period (M. Haller, *Die fünf Megilloth* [Handbuch zum Alten Testament, 1/18; Tübingen, 1940], p. vii; O. Eissfeldt, *The Old Testament. A Introduction* [tr. P.R. Ackroyd; Oxford, 1966], p. 570). The fact that in Megillah 7a R. Judah (3rd cent. AD), argues that Esther 'does not make the hands unclean', and that his statement is explained as meaning that it was composed to be recited, not written, is indirect support that the prevailing view, that Esther *does* 'make the hands unclean', included the view that Esther was composed in writing (cf. also bYoma 29a). See further S. Segert, 'Zur literarischen Form und Funktion der Fünf Megilloth', *ArOr* 35 (1965), 451-62; S.Z. Leiman, *The Talmudic and Midrashic Evidence for the Canonization of Hebrew Scripture* (PhD, Pennsylvania, 1970; University Microfilms 70-25,680); see esp. pp. 227f. for the texts; E. Würthwein, 'Die Fünf Megilloth als Sammlung', in *Die Fünf Megilloth* (HAT, 18; 2nd edn, Tübingen, 1969), p. iii.

15. B.S. Childs, *Introduction to the Old Testament as Scripture* (London, 1979), p. 599.

16. S.R. Driver, *Introduction to the Literature of the Old Testament* (9th edn; Edinburgh, 1913), p. 481.

17. Cf. C.C. Torrey, 'In the basal Story . . . there is indeed (in our present text) a day appointed, the day for the massacre of the Jews by Haman's order; but the massacre does not take place, the Jews are not molested, nothing happens on that particular date. The real turning point is the day when Esther faced the tyrant, or when sentence was pronounced against Haman; for the Story is one of deliverance, not of victory' ('The Older Book· of Esther', *HTR* 37 [1944], pp. 1-40 [17f.] [= Moore, *Studies*, pp. 464f.]).

18. See Chapter 5 below for a further analysis of 8.15-17.

NOTES TO CHAPTER 2

1. W. Dommershausen, *Die Estherrolle: Stil und Ziel einer alttestamentlichen Schrift* (Stuttgarter Biblische Monographien, 6; Stuttgart, 1968).

2. Dommershausen, *Estherrolle*, p. 11 nn. 1-3. S. Talmon rightly observes, however, that the characters do not undergo any meaningful development ('"Wisdom" in the Book of Esther', *VT* 13 [1963], pp. 419-55 [440]). This

does not mean, however, that the characterization is not complex (see W.L. Humphreys, 'A Life-Style for Diaspora: A Study of the Tales of Esther and Daniel', *JBL* 92 (1973), pp. 211-23 [215]).

3. The depiction of Ahasuerus as a fool (טפש) is frequent in rabbinic sources; cf. bMeg. 12b; Midrash Est. Rabb. 2 on Est. 1.4; Targum Sheni Est. (A. Sperber, *The Bible in Aramaic*, vol. IVA *The Hagiographa* [Leiden, 1968], p. 172, line 13).

4. Cf. P.R. Ackroyd, 'Two Hebrew Notes', *ASTI* 5 (1966-67), pp. 81-84.

5. See S.B. Berg, *The Book of Esther: Motifs, Themes and Structure* (SBL Dissertation Series, 44: Missoula, Montana, 1979), pp. 31-57, for a discussion of banquets as 'a dominant motif' of the book.

6. Another distinction between the two banquets has been suggested by J. Magonet in his paper, 'The Liberal and the Lady: Esther Revisited', *Judaism* 29 (1980), pp. 167-76. He notes that in 5.4 Esther says 'Let the king and Haman come to the banquet I have prepared *for him* [the king]' (יבוא המלך והמן היום אל־המשתה אשר־עשיתי לו), whereas in 5.8 she invites them to the banquet she will prepare *for them* (יבוא המלך והמן אל־המשתה אשר אעשה להם). Here Magonet sees a change from a banquet for the king to a banquet for both of them equally—which is designed to arouse the king's suspicions of Haman as a possible political rival. It is therefore no coincidence that the king cannot sleep, nor that he has the chronicles read to him in order to discover a rival he can set up against Haman. I do not find this reading persuasive, since there is a simpler explanation for the difference in wording between 5.4 and 5.8. In 5.4 Esther is in the king's presence alone, and so naturally speaks of a banquet she has prepared for him (and in her scheme Haman's presence is not entirely necessary at the first banquet). At 5.8, however, she is in the company of both the king and Haman, and must—if only for politeness' sake—invite them to a banquet she will prepare for *them* (moreover, Haman's presence is crucial at the second banquet).

7. Torrey made a similar assertion in his 'The Older Book of Esther' (*HTR* 37 [1944], pp. 1-40 [= Moore, *Studies*, pp. 448-87]), but he did not argue the case.

NOTES TO CHAPTER 3

1. Haller, p. 135, indeed asks, 'What has become of the preparations arranged by Haman in 3¹³?'

2. הַצָּרִים from the infrequent צור, 'be hostile' (BDB, צור III, p. 849a; KB צור II, p. 799a); RSV, NEB, NAB, JB 'attack'; RV 'assault'. For the emendation to הַצֹּרְרִים, see P. Haupt, 'Critical Notes on Esther', *AJSL* (1907-1908), pp. 97-186 (159) (= Moore, *Studies*, p. 63).

3. אתם טף ונשים to be taken as the object of the three verbs (so also R.

Gordis, 'Studies in the Esther Narrative', *JBL* 95 (1976), pp. 43-58 [49-53] [= Moore, *Studies*, pp. 414-418]).

4. Beyond the narrative itself, אויביהם also occurs in 9.22 in the same connection.

5. Paton, p. 280.

6. This can hardly mean 'they passed themselves off as Jews' because there is as yet no guarantee (only a hint to those with open eyes) that the Jewish side is the safest to espouse; cf. Bardtke, *Esther*, pp. 376f.

7. Moore, *Esther*, p. 82.

8. Gerleman, *Esther*, p. 129.

9. J. Hoschander, *The Book of Esther in the Light of History* (Philadelphia, 1923), p. 247.

10. H. Ringgren, *Esther*, in H. Ringgren and A. Weiser, *Das Hohe Lied, Klagelieder, Das Buch Esther* (Das Alte Testament Deutsch, 16; Göttingen, 1958), p. 400.

11. Dommershausen, *Estherrolle*, p. 110.

12. Cf. H.-P. Stähli, *THWAT*, vol. 2, cols. 412f.

13. Gerleman, *Esther*, p. 132, notes this, but makes nothing of it.

14. There is no hint that only the Jews of Susa are meant (against A.B. Ehrlich, *Randglossen zur hebräischen Bibel*, vol. 7 [Leipzig, 1914], *ad loc.*).

15. Paton, p. 211.

16. 'The metropolis Susa' is here plainly to be distinguished from its Jewish population, who are mentioned separately in v. 16.

17. Moore, *Esther*, p. 81.

18. If he is intended to be, 2.5 will have to mean that it was Mordecai who was taken captive in 597 BC, and must therefore be over 110 years old in the third year of Xerxes. However, it is the ancestry of Haman that matters, not of Mordecai—for him it is enough that he is an authentic Jew.

19. Talmon, '"Wisdom" in the Book of Esther', *VT* 13 (1963), pp. 419-55, comparing the figure of Ahasuerus with Sennacherib and Esarhaddon in the Ahiqar story, notes that none of them intentionally does evil. 'Their behaviour rather is immature. They can be led to acknowledge their mistakes, or at least to reconsider their hasty decisions' (p. 44). Similarly W.L. Humphreys, 'A Life-Style for Diaspora: A Study of the Tales of Esther and Daniel', *JBL* 92 (1973), pp. 211-23 (p. 222 n. 38).

20. See Chapter 8, note 15.

21. So Paton, p. 197.

22. See the authors cited by Paton, p. 196. H. Bévenot maintained that the (more original) Greek version correctly envisaged only courtly proskynesis, but that the (secondary) Masoretic text, with its use of the verb השתחוה, introduced an inappropriate religious dimension ('Die Proskynesis und die Gebete im Estherbuch', *Jahrbuch für Liturgiewissenschaft* 11 [1931], pp. 132-39 [132-35]). His argument is vitiated by the use of השתחוה in profane contexts.

23. Bardtke, *Esther*, p. 316, sees this most clearly, though he wants to maintain at the same time that the narrator preserves an irrational element in the behaviour of Mordecai.

24. Paton, p. 198.

25. Paton, p. 198.

26. Bardtke, *Esther*, p. 381.

27. bMegillah, 16b (cf. Soncino Talmud, p. 100 n. 2).

28. Surely he is not joyful. Dommershausen, *Estherrolle*, p. 118, says that the author sets in the king's mouth his own joy over the victory; this would imply that it is because the king is so pleased with the news he has had of the Jews that he invites Esther to make a further request. But while he could understandably be pleased that the Jews had survived the day, there can be no reason why he should welcome the news of a massacre throughout the empire; and his speech to Esther is prompted precisely by news of the *numbers* slain. This is the case even if Gerleman is correct in insisting upon translating מספר in 9.11 not by 'number' but by 'report' (p. 133), since the report manifestly centres on the issue of the numbers.

29. It appears that the author of ch. 9 does not acknowledge the (accurate) distinction made by the author of chs. 1–8 between Susa the acropolis (RSV 'capital') and Susa the metropolis.

30. So Bardtke, *Esther*, p. 387: 'Der König handelt . . . grosszügig und grossmütig . . . Aber diese Grossmütigkeit ist durch die vorgehende Erzählung in keiner Weise begründet. Volk und Verwandschaft der Königin (8,6) sind nicht untergegangen, sondern sind erhalten geblieben . . . Man wird daher folgern müssen, dass, wenn die Grossmütigkeit des Königs nicht in der Erzählung begründet ist, dem Erzähler daran lag, sie hier einzuführen, um damit etwas zu begründen, was er in der Purimfestsitte vorfand, nämlich die Feier am 14. bzw. 15. Adar.' Cf. also his remark on p. 388: 'Wie sehen, wie offenbar dieser abweichende Festbrauch . . . erzählungstechnisch jene Bitte der Esther in V. 13 verursacht hat'.

31. Dommershausen, *Estherrolle*, p. 119.

32. Dommershausen, *Estherrolle*, p. 120.

33. Gerleman, *Esther*, p. 134.

NOTES TO CHAPTER 4

1. J.D. Michaelis, *Deutsche Uebersetzung des Alten Testaments mit Anmerkungen für Ungelehrte*, vol. 13 (Göttingen, 1783).

2. See Paton, pp. 57-60, 292; and Eissfeldt, *Introduction*, pp. 510f. C. Steuernagel, 'Das Buch Ester', in *Die Heilige Schrift des Alten Testaments*, ed. E.F. Kautzsch and E. Bertholet (Tübingen, 1923), vol. 2, pp. 443-56, actually printed 9.20–10.3 under the rubric 'Nachtrag' (pp. 455f.).

3. Anderson, p. 824.

4. Bardtke, *Esther*, p. 396.

5. Gerleman, *Esther*, p. 137.

6. Moore, *Esther*, p. 97.

7. Dommershausen, *Estherrolle*, pp. 128f.

8. Berg, *The Book of Esther: Motifs, Themes and Structure*, p. 38.

9. Certainly so, according to Moore (*Esther*, p. 89), because it contradicts vv. 21-22 and breaks the continuity of v. 18 and v. 20.

10. These readings appear (arguing *e silentio*) in eight of the sixteen miniscules cited by Brooke–McLean.

11. Paton finds it impossible to judge whether the LXX plus is 'a survival, or . . . a happy conjectural emendation' (p. 291).

12. It is probable also that the MT itself contains a gloss, for who are 'those dwelling in the open villages' (הישבים בערי הפרזות) if not precisely 'villagers' (Q הַפְּרָזִים)? The gloss was perhaps introduced to explain K הפרוזים, which could perhaps be misunderstood as הַפְּרוּזִים 'the separated' (cf. Paton, p. 292).

13. For a vigorous, but ultimately ineffectual defence of the appropriateness of v. 19, see Bardtke, *Esther*, p. 389.

14. Some have suggested that עם־הספר, lit. 'with the writing', should be translated 'despite the letter', viz. the letter originally written by Haman (3.12). So P. Haupt, 'Critical Notes on Esther', *AJSL* 24 (1907f.), pp. 97-186 (p. 170) (= Moore, *Studies*, p. 74), and Gerleman, *Esther*, p. 139. Neh. 5.18, where עם־זה means 'despite this', is compared, but it is doubtful if עם would mean 'despite' if it were not in the context of a negative; i.e. עם־זה לחם פחה לא בקשתי can mean 'with this being the case [and so: despite this], I did not seek the food-allowance of a governor', but one wonders, if לא were absent, whether the sentence could mean '*despite* this, I sought . . . ' עם in itself has no *contrastive* sense. The problem remains in Est. 9.25 that Haman's *letter* was not what came upon his head, but his *plot* against Mordecai.

15. Dommershausen, *Estherrolle*, p. 126, thinks that the ישוב, 'let it [his evil plot, מחשבתו הרעה] return', corresponds to מחשבת להשיב את־הספרים, המן, 'to make return the letters, the plot of Haman' in 8.5. This seems incorrect, since להשיב in 8.5 means 'to revoke', just like להעביר in the similar phrase in 8.3 חשב אשר מחשבתו ואת האגגי המן את־רעת להעביר; the notion of 'returning upon one's own head' (ישוב . . . על־ראשו) in 9.25 is quite different.

16. E.g. Bardtke, *Esther*, p. 390.

17. G.R. Driver's suggestion that ובבאה represents an abbreviation of המלכה אסתר ובבוא ('Abbreviations in the Masoretic Text', *Textus* 1 [1960], pp. 112-31 [128]) is not very plausible, though followed by Moore, *Esther*, p. 94, and allowed as a possibility by Bardtke, *Esther*, p. 394.

18. So Bardtke, *Esther*, p. 394.

19. Bardtke, *Esther*, p. 393.

20. Dommershausen, *Estherrolle*, p. 125.

21. Dommershausen refers to the remarks of M. Weiss in his 'Einiges über die Bauformen des Erzählens in der Bibel', *VT* 13 (1963), pp. 456-74 (460ff.).

22. Bardtke's term (*Esther*, p. 394).

23. The comment of BDB, p. 487a, is: 'Est 9²⁶ the 2nd עַל כֵּן (unless dittogr.) points unusually onwards to עַל כָּל דִּבְרֵי הָאִגֶּרֶת *on this account, on account, viz.*, etc.'.

24. Dommershausen, *Estherrolle*, p. 126, speaks of their 'circumstantial documentary style' (*umständlicher Urkundenstil*).

25. See especially S.E. Loewenstamm, 'Esther 9:29-32: The Genesis of a Late Addition', *HUCA* 42 (1971), pp. 117-24 (= Moore, *Studies*, pp. 227-34); so also Moore, *Esther*, p. 95.

26. Loewenstamm, 'Esther 9:29-32', p. 117 (= Moore, *Studies*, p. 227).

27. The gross divergence of the LXX of these verses from MT was obviously recognized at some time in the history of LXX transmission, and a literal rendering of MT vv. 31-32 was incorporated in the miniscules fz at the end of the chapter (LXX 9.31).

28. Paton, p. 302.

29. Brockington, p. 245. The alternative emendation, reading אֶת־כָּל־תֹּקֶף מָרְדֳּכַי '(described) all the might of Mordecai' (so Haupt, *AJSL* 24 [1907f.]), p. 172 [= Moore, *Studies*, p. 76]; Haller, p. 136), is equally unconvincing, since there is no obvious reason why the *power* of Mordecai should be relevant to the observance of Purim; there was no question of its being imposed on the Jews against their will.

30. So Paton, p. 300. The verb וַיִּשְׁלַח in v. 30 is hardly evidence for a mention of Mordecai in v. 29 (why should the feminine verb וַתִּכְתֹּב be followed by the masculine וַיִּשְׁלַח if the same persons are the subject?). It must be an impersonal verb (Dommershausen, *Estherrolle*, p. 134; cf. RSV 'Letters were sent'), or else could be emended to וַיִּשְׁלְחוּ, 'and they sent' (as Syriac), וַתִּשְׁלַח, 'and she sent' (Haupt, p. 173; Paton, p. 300; Bardtke, *Esther*, p. 397), וַיִּשְׁלַח or וַיִּשְׁלְחוּ 'and it/they was/were sent' (G.R. Driver, 'Problems and Solutions', *VT* 4 [1954], pp. 225-45 [237] [= Moore, *Studies*, p. 399]).

31. The same tendency to associate Mordecai and Esther wherever possible is found also in the two LXX miniscules fz in v. 31 where 'and Esther the queen' is appended to the phrase 'Mordecai the Jew' in a quite inappropriate place.

32. So Gerleman, *Esther*, p. 141.

33. So W. Rudolph, 'Textkritisches zum Estherbuch', *VT* 4 (1954), pp. 89-90 (90), regarding them as a corrupted dittography of the next word וַיִּשְׁלַח.

34. So Moore, *Esther*, p. 96; Gerleman, *Esther*, p. 142.

35. It must be admitted that the syntax remains awkward; we must understand, 'Letters were sent to confirm this Purim festival in accord with how the Jews had instituted matters of fasts and their lament(s)'.

36. Haupt, p. 174 (= Moore, *Studies*, p. 78), shows a similar understanding

of the syntax, though he goes beyond the evidence in seeing here an implication that the Jews had adopted the fasting before they adopted the feasting.

37. Cf. T. Witton Davies, *Ezra, Nehemiah and Esther* (Century Bible; Edinburgh, 1909), p. 358: 'This section hangs loosely on to what precedes, and is almost certainly an addition made from a larger record'.

38. Cf. Paton, p. 303: the author 'continues here, as though he were about to give an extended account of Xerxes' reign, but stops abruptly at the end of this v.'.

39. Moore, *Esther*, p. 98.

40. D. Daube, 'The Last Chapter of Esther', *JQR* 37 (1946-47), pp. 139-47.

41. So also Targum I. By way of parallel, we are reminded that Herodotus (3.67) tells us that the pseudo-Smerdis 'gave to all his subjects signal marks of his benevolence . . .; for he sent to every nation under his sway and had proclaimed exemption (ἀτελείη) for a space of three years from military service and from tribute'. As for the LXX translators of Esther, they understood הנחה as ἄφεσις, which probably signifies remission of taxes.

42. O. Eissfeldt indeed argued that 'We must nevertheless reckon with the possibility that there really was such a book, of midrashic kind, compiled by Jews and containing beside historical information all manner of legends and sagas, and in particular concerned with the experiences of Jews at the Persian court' (*The Old Testament. An Introduction*, p. 511). Similarly also Paton, p. 304; Bardtke, *Esther*, p. 403. Moore concurs, comparing 'the midrashic source cited by the Chronicler in II Chron xxiv 27' (*Esther*, p. 99); but although the term מדרש is used there, it is doubtful whether a source distinct from his usual chronicle sources is in mind (cf. H.G.M. Williamson, *1 and 2 Chronicles* [New Century Bible; London, 1982], pp. 17ff., 326). It is even more doubtful that any midrashic work of the kind envisaged by Eissfeldt ever existed.

43. Joined with maqqeph in 1.18, 19.

44. Paton argued ingeniously that Media appears before Persia in Est. 10.2 . because in the order of the Chronicles Media must have preceded Persia; in 1.3, 14, 19 Persia appears first because 'in the time of Xerxes it held the hegemony in the dual kingdom' (p. 304). No other commentator accepts this explanation. Bardtke, *Esther*, p. 403, n. 6, and Dommershausen, *Estherrolle*, p. 136, offer the rather lame explanation that מדי appears first because of the assonance of the *m* with the preceding *m*-sounds in למלכי הימים. Bardtke's categorical proscription, 'Irgendwelche Schlüsse darf man aus diesem Versehen im Ausdruck nicht ziehen', need not deter us from the reasonable inference I have offered. It is noteworthy that Bardtke regards the reversal of the terms Media and Persia as a 'Versehen', an 'oversight'.

45. B.W. Jones, 'The So-Called Appendix to the Book of Esther', *Semitics* 6 (1978), pp. 36-43.

46. I.e. not strict inclusio; the term is borrowed from M. Kessler, 'Inclusio

in the Hebrew Bible', *Semitics* 6 (1978), pp. 44-49 (esp. p. 48).

47. The term was coined by I.M. Kikawada, 'The Shape of Genesis 11:1-9', in *Rhetorical Criticism. Essays in Honor of James Muilenburg* (Pittsburgh Theological Monograph Series, 1; Pittsburgh, 1974), pp. 18-32 (25).

48. Jones, 'The So-Called Appendix', p. 39.

49. Jones, 'The So-Called Appendix', p. 40.

50. Jones, 'The So-Called Appendix', p. 41.

51. Jones, 'The So-Called Appendix', p. 41.

52. Jones, 'The So-Called Appendix', p. 36.

53. Paton, pp. 59f.

54. Jones, 'The So-Called Appendix', p. 42.

55. The terms in question are אח, אגרת, אביונים (of a fellow-Jew), אײם, משנה, מעשה, מס, מה ראו ni. לוה, על־ככה, יגון, זמן, זכר, המם, דרש, דור, אמת, תקף, 'made obligatory' קים, פורים, סוף, מתנה, משפחה. I would not put a great deal of weight on this argument, since it is a form of the argument from silence (viz. the absence of these words from the rest of the book). Most of the items in Paton's list are entirely explicable on the grounds of the subject matter of 9.20–10.3; but the following may be significant of differing authorship: אגרת, על־ככה, קים, תקף. אגרת is late Heb., occurring only elsewhere in Neh. and 2 Chron., a loanword into Aram. from Pers. or Akk. (cf. KB[3], p. 11b); elsewhere in Est. ספר is used. על־ככה is the only occurrence of ככה with a prefixed preposition. קים is usually regarded as an Aramaism, occurring elsewhere only once in Ezek., and twice in Ps. 119 (and once in Ru.), but five times in this passage. תקף occurs twice here (9.29; 10.2) and elsewhere only in Dan. 11.17, but frequently in Aram.

NOTES TO CHAPTER 5

1. If that is the correct interpretation of ופני המן חפו; see further, Chapter 9, note 12.

2. White and violet were the imperial colours, according to Quintus Curtius, *History of Alexander* 6.6.4.

NOTES TO CHAPTER 6

1. C.A. Moore, *Daniel, Esther and Jeremiah: The Additions* (AB, 44; Garden City, N.Y., 1977), p. 162.

2. This useful notation appears to have been due to F.J.A. Hort (cf. H.B. Swete, *An Introduction to the Old Testament in Greek* [Cambridge, 1900], p. 257, n. 4). The numeration employed by Rahlfs in his edition (*Septuaginta, id est Vetus Testamentum graece iuxta LXX interpretes*, 2 vols. [Stuttgart, 1935]) is rather awkward: the first verse of Addition C, for example, which follows MT 4.17, is numbered 4.17^a, the second 4.17^b, and so on. And since Addition C is 30 verses long, Rahlfs must compress those 30 verses into 24 in order to accommodate them within the Roman alphabet (j and v are not used). The Jerusalem Bible follows Rahlfs's system, including also the Vulgate numeration, so that it is possible to see in that translation that, for example, Rahlfs's 4.17^c is in fact two verses in the Vulgate (13.10-11). The RSV and NEB use only the Vulgate numeration; of modern English versions, as far as I can see, only the NAB and C.A. Moore's translation in the Anchor Bible (*Esther*; vol. 44) have adopted the plainer A-F notation.

3. I must confess that I cannot prove this, nor can I reconstruct the process by which the LXX acquired Additions from two sources. Are we to suppose a Greek translation of the Masoretic text alone, to which was added, at separate times the Greek and Semitic Additions, thus forming the LXX we now have? My diagram on p. 140 above assumes this, but it is perhaps not impossible, for example, that the Semitic additions were incorporated into a *Hebrew* text prior to the translation of the LXX.

The important article of E. Tov, 'The "Lucianic" Text of the Canonical and the Apocryphal Sections of Esther. A Rewritten Biblical Book', *Textus* 10 (1982), pp. 1-25, which will be frequently referred to in the pages that follow, argues that it has been misleading not to ascribe the Additions to the Greek translator [of the LXX] himself (p. 10), and that in the A-text (see Chapter 7 below) the Additions should be regarded as part of 'one *organic* whole' together with the translation of the Hebrew Esther (p. 11). There are certain senses in which this latter position is valid (e.g. evident *junctures* have been made between the Additions and the older material), but I cannot see that Tov has advanced any evidence for the former contention, or how it could be true, given that, as he allows, 'modern research has left few doubts that the original language of Add. A, C, D, F, was Hebrew or Aramaic, and that of Add. B and E was Greek' (p. 11).

4. Cf. C.A. Moore, 'On the Origins of the LXX Additions to the Book of Esther', *JBL* 92 (1973), pp. 382-93 (= Moore, *Studies*, pp. 583-94); R.A. Martin, 'Syntax Criticism of the LXX Additions to the Book of Esther', *JBL* 94 (1975), pp. 65-72 (= Moore, *Studies*, pp. 595-602).

5. In the Vulgate's enumeration, 15.1-3 is occupied by the material contained in the LXX at 4.8.

6. In editions of the Greek Bible these Additions are naturally restored to their appropriate places (e.g. by Swete, Brooke–McLean, Rahlfs, Hanhart); in English versions they are either placed together in the Apocrypha (e.g. RSV), or interspersed in the translation of the Hebrew text (e.g. JB, NAB; and

in C.A. Moore's edition of the Additions to Esther in the Anchor Bible). Only the NEB, to my knowledge, takes the preferable decision to translate the Septuagint text (or 'ordinary text', as Brooke–McLean call it, p. 4) in its entirety—as an alternative text to the Masoretic, with the Additions in their appropriate places. This translation in NEB is, however, misleadingly called *The Rest of the Chapters of the Book of Esther*; in fact it contains *all* the chapters of the Greek (Septuagint) Esther.

NOTES TO CHAPTER 7

1. A translation of the Additions in the AT was made by E.C. Bissell, 'Additions to Esther', in *The Apocrypha of the Old Testament* (A Commentary on the Holy Scriptures by J.P. Lange, tr. P. Schaff, vol. 15 of the Old Testament; Edinburgh, 1868), pp. 199-220 [217-20]; but these are the least interesting parts of the AT for our purpose.

2. It is unfortunate also that none of its readings appears in the concordance of E. Hatch and H.A. Redpath, *A Concordance to the Septuagint and other Greek versions of the Old Testament (including the Apocryphal books)*, 2 vols. (Oxford, 1897).

3. In 93 (e_2) and 108 (*b*) both texts of Esther appear in the manuscript (cf. R. Hanhart, *Septuaginta. Vetus Testamentum graecum auctoritate academiae scientiarum gottingensis editum*, VIII, 3 [Göttingen, 1966], p. 15).

4. 'Der "*L*-Text" des Est-Buches nichts zu tun haben kann mit der Textform der Bücher der LXX, die als die "lukianische Rezension" bekannt ist' (Hanhart, p. 92).

5. Cf. Tov, 'The "Lucianic" Text', p. 2. The now current doubts about the 'Lucianic' text go back a long way before 1965, of course; for a forthright statement à propos of Esther, cf. E.J. Bickerman, 'Notes on the Greek Book of Esther', *Proceedings of the American Academy for Jewish Research* 20 (1950), pp. 101-33: 'Without any cogent reason this recension [the AT] was fathered now upon Theodotion now upon Lucian by modern scholars' (p. 103 [= Moore, *Studies*, p. 490]). According to Hanhart, p. 95, the application of the term 'Lucianic' to the AT of Esther is probably due to B. Jacob in 1890, since Ceriani, Field and Lagarde, who maintained the Lucianic character of mss 19, 93 and 108, did not apparently extend this categorization to include Esther.

6. Moore, *Additions*, p. 164. For a concise statement of the arguments, see his 'A Greek Witness to a Different Hebrew Text of Esther', *ZAW* 79 (1967), pp. 351-58 (= Moore, *Studies*, pp. 521-28).

7. Moore concludes that 'the AT borrowed all its Additions from the LXX rather than the reverse (although one cannot ignore the possibility that each

version contributed some Additions to the other)' (*Additions*, p. 165). This is
a matter, however, that does not concern the present enquiry. Tov regards
'the canonical sections in L [= AT] and the so-called Additions as one
organic whole' ('The "Lucianic" Text', p. 11), but I do not think he means to
imply that the Additions did not exist prior to the AT. J.A.F. Gregg, 'The
Additions to Esther', in *The Apocrypha and Pseudepigrapha of the Old
Testament*, ed. R.H. Charles (Oxford, 1913), vol. 1, pp. 665-84, observed that
'The Additions are not a homogeneous whole, and are bound together by no
community of style', but went on to declare, 'This does not prevent them
from being the work of one hand' [!] (p. 669).

8.   Moore argues, no doubt correctly, that 'Addition E was not at first a
part of the AT but was borrowed from the LXX, since Addition E has a
different place in the AT (8.22-32) and repeats in expanded form the content
of 8.35-37 of the AT, the latter being the AT's original version of the second
royal letter' (*Additions*, p. 165).

9.   διεδέχετο, understood similarly by W.H. Brownlee, 'Le livre grec
d'Esther et la royauté divine. Corrections orthodoxes au livre d'Esther', *RB*
73 (1966), pp. 161-85 (163).

10.   C.C. Torrey, 'The Older Book of Esther', *HTR* 37 (1944), pp. 1-40 (7)
(= Moore, *Studies*, p. 454). His argument that the Semitic original was
Aramaic rather than Hebrew is an issue that need not detain us here.

11.   Quotations in this paragraph from Torrey come from pp. 15-16 of his
article (= Moore, *Studies*, pp. 462-63). Torrey's incautious mode of expression
has proved a pitfall to some later writers: we find, for example, the statement
(for which Torrey is cited in support) that 'One of the LXX textual traditions
does, in fact, end here [the end of ch. 8], for from this point on it is the same
as the second LXX tradition' (W.L. Humphreys, *JBL* 92 [1973], p. 213).
Quite apart from the fact that the AT, the text in question, is *not* a LXX text,
no candid reader of the two texts of ch. 9 could claim that the 'textual
tradition' of the AT and the LXX is the *same*.

12.   Tov, 'The "Lucianic" Text', p. 4. As for Tov's general position, I
would submit that the existence of some agreements of AT and LXX against
MT and of some inferior readings in AT that can best be explained as inner-
Greek corruption are no kind of match for the consistently different wording
of the two texts even when they do not presuppose different *Vorlagen*. The
statistical observation of Moore (*Additions*, p. 164) is very telling: 'of the 163
verses in the canonical portion of the LXX, only 45 of them have some phrase
preserved by the AT'. In the light of that, how can it be claimed that the AT 'is
based on the LXX' and that 'since it also differs from the LXX, it must reflect a
revision of the LXX' (Tov, 'The "Lucianic" Text', p. 10)?

The question of the dependence of the text of the Additions in AT upon the
LXX text of those Additions is a different matter entirely. Tov (p. 4) refers to
the examples of Hanhart (p. 88) drawn from Additions C and E, and I have
no wish to dispute AT's dependence upon LXX *in the Additions*. Moore also

believes that 'it is probable that the AT borrowed all its Additions from the LXX rather than the reverse' (*Additions*, p. 165), but discriminates between the text of the Additions and the text of the canonical Esther.

13. The two cases from canonical Esther mentioned by Tov will be discussed fully in section IV.

14. I am not saying that I agree with Tov that the AT of 8.22-52 (Addition F excepted) *was* dependent on LXX, but only that I am not disputing it.

15. H.J. Cook, 'The *A*-text of the Greek Versions of the Book of Esther', *ZAW* 81 (1969), 369-76.

16. Cook, 'The *A*-text', pp. 374f.

17. My italics.

18. Cook, 'The *A*-text', p. 374.

19. Moore, 'Greek Witness', pp. 356f. (= Moore, *Studies*, pp. 526f.).

20. Cook, 'The *A*-text', p. 372.

21. Cook, 'The *A*-text', p. 372.

22. Cook, 'The *A*-text', p. 373.

23. Cook, 'The *A*-text', p. 374.

24. Cook's account of the plot as 'the struggle of Haman with Mordecai, which may have affected Jews in Susa' (p. 372) is somewhat one-sided.

25. Though AT 8.17 marks the point in the narrative sequence at which I think the original of the AT ended, the wording of 8.17 hardly qualifies as a suitable ending because of what it omits.

26. Cook, 'The *A*-text', p. 374. Long ago B. Jacob observed that the revision constituted by the AT (as he regarded it) was in ch. 9 much less careful and consistent than in the previous chapters ('Das Buch Esther bei den LXX', *ZAW* 10 [1890], pp. 241-98 [259]).

27. J. Langen already supposed that AT 8.34-38 was a secondary insertion into the AT ('Die beiden griechischen Texte des Buches Esther', *TTQ* 42 [1860], pp. 244-72 [254f.]).

28. In this particular AT 8.37 agrees with Addition E (AT 8.28 = LXX 16.18); but the relationship between this element of AT and Addition E is not very clear. It may be added that Addition E contradicts the MT and LXX on another aspect of this episode: according to MT, Haman was impaled on the twenty-third of the third month (8.9), but his sons were not impaled until the fourteenth of the twelfth month (9.13).

29. E. Tov maintains that AT is here proved to be dependent on LXX and that τῶν Ἰουδαίων probably reflects a second rendering of מתיהרים ('The "Lucianic" Text', p. 6); neither claim appears tenable to me. Tov does not recognize the peculiar nature of AT 8.17-21, 33-52.

30. Not so absurd against a second-century background, no doubt.

31. Tov, 'The "Lucianic" Text', p. 5.

32. μυριάδας ἑπτὰ καὶ ἑκατὸν ἄνδρας must mean 70,100, not 10,107 as Moore has (*Additions*, p. 242). Josephus, who is several times in agreement with the peculiarities of AT, also has 70,000.

33. Whatever that may be. Have we a trace of a link of this story with Passover (14 Nisan)?

34. One witness to AT (ms 319 = Brooke–McLean: y) does have ἀπέστειλαν, 'they sent', but it still does not sound like a regular festival custom.

35. This appears to be the correct translation; cf. Brownlee, 'Le livre grec d'Esther et la royauté divine', *RB* 73 (1966), p. 176. NEB appears to avoid the obvious sense of διεδέχετο in translating 'acted for'—so also in LXX 10.3 (in NEB 'The Rest of the Chapters of the Book of Esther').

36. The AT ms y does indeed have Ασσυηρον—which is to be explained as the easier reading.

37. Except at 8.47, where Lagarde and Brooke–McLean print Αρταξερξου; e₂ has αρξερξου, b ξερξου, and y ασσυηρου. At 3.14 (Addition B) e₂ has αρταξερξης against the other mss ασσυηρος.

38. I.e., omitting Additions E and F in 8.22-32 and 8.53-59.

39. Moore, *Additions*, p. 164.

40. Misleading statements like the following abound: 'The general scope of the narrative in both is the same, and not infrequently there is literal agreement . . . the changes [in the AT] are always clearly recognizable as such, and, by a careful comparison, the reasons which might have suggested them generally discoverable' (Bissell, *Apocrypha*, p. 200).

41. Paton, p. 38.

42. 'Der "*L*-Text" ist nicht eine Rezension des o'-Textes, sondern eine Neugestaltung der griech. Est-Überlieferung, die in starkem Mass auf dem o'-Text beruht' (p. 87).

43. Cf. Hanhart, pp. 91f. The relation of the ending of AT to the LXX is a more complicated issue.

44. 4.27 in Hanhart's numbering.

45. Hanhart, p. 88. The use of τράπεζαν as a direct object of ἐσθίω is very unusual, but can be paralleled in the Theodotionic Daniel 1.15. It is not entirely clear to me, however, that LXX is indeed prior to AT here; for it is hard to see how Esther ever could have been in the position of eating *Haman's* food. The LXX itself presents, on grounds of narrative logic, an unacceptable reading; and since the rule of *difficilior lectio* does not always apply, the direction of dependence (if any) should no doubt be reconsidered.

On the general principle, one can now refer to the excellent treatments by B. Albrektson, 'Difficilior Lectio Probabilior. A Rule of Textual Criticism and its Use in Old Testament Studies', *OTS* 21 (1981), pp. 5-18; and E. Tov, 'Criteria for Evaluating Textual Readings: The Limitations of Textual Rules', *HTR* 75 (1982), pp. 429-48 (439-42).

46. The AT undoubtedly has the *lectio facilior* compared with LXX, the nearest parallel that can be adduced being 1 Cor. 8.4, where idols are 'nothing in the world' (οὐδὲν εἴδωλον ἐν κόσμῳ). However, easier readings are not necessarily worse readings; in this case, the context in AT 5.23 (LXX C 22) makes it improbable that the LXX's reading is to be preferred, for it is

not a question of power (σκῆπτρον) over the Jews being given to the *gods* of the heathen, but to the *heathen themselves*; it is the heathen who would laugh at Israel's fall, and upon whose heads Esther prays that their own design should fall. And the heathen cannot be called τοῖς μὴ οὖσιν. The point at issue here is, however, that even if Hanhart is right, dependence of AT upon LXX is only evidenced in *the Additions*.

47. So Hanhart, but here also we may wonder whether LXX has a satisfactory reading. Artaxerxes speaks in his letter of crimes against the state committed by persons in high office as things ἀνοσίως συντετελεσμένα τῇ τῶν ἀνάξια δυναστευόντων λοιμότητι, 'what hath been wickedly done through the pestilent behaviour of them that are unworthily placed in authority' (AV); but it is not clear that ἀνάξια, presumably as an adverbial accusative, can properly modify δυναστευόντων, and the very considerable variety of LXX readings at this point confirms the difficulty of the Greek. (O.F. Fritzsche, *Kurzgefasstes exegetisches Handbuch zu den Apokryphen des Alten Testaments*, Lieferung 1 [Leipzig, 1851]), p. 102, reads ἀναξίᾳ, transferring it to precede τῶν or to follow δυναστευόντων, and thus taking it as an adjective qualifying λοιμότητι, 'the unworthy pestilential behaviour'. This is open to the objections that ἀνάξιος is a weak adjective to qualify the colourful noun λοιμότης, and also that τῶν δυναστευόντων without any qualification is surely too vague. In view of the latter difficulty, V. Ryssel, 'Zusätze zum Buch Esther', in *Die Apokryphen und Pseudepigraphen des Alten Testaments*, ed. E. Kautzsch, vol. 1 (Tübingen, 1900), p. 209, read ἀναξίᾳ as dative of a noun from ἀνάσσω, translating 'die auf [höheren] Befehl die Regierung führen'.) On the other hand, it is not obvious either that at this point the AT preserves a better text when it speaks, apparently, of 'the necessity . . . of giving due heed to the cruelty of those having power' (tr. Bissell, *Apocrypha*, p. 219), ἀξίως τῇ τῶν δυναστευόντων ὠμότητι προσέχειν— since it is hard to see the Persian king speaking in such unflattering terms of those in general who hold power.

48. But this would then be a case where AT does *not* correct LXX in the direction of MT.

49. To be sure, divergence inexplicable on any usual grounds *could* be argued to be deliberate divergence simply for the sake of difference. But the distinction between deliberate divergence and unintentional divergence (through mutual ignorance) would be hard to grasp; only if there was *never* (or hardly ever) any parallel could we suppose the improbable and (I think) unparalleled situation of *deliberate divergence*.

50. An apparent inconsistency arises from his remarks on p. 7 n. 9, where he writes: 'It has been recognized by some scholars (e.g., Cook, p. 371) that in the sections which have been translated from a Semitic *Vorlage* (that is, in the canonical sections as well as some of the Additions), the LXX and L texts reflect two different translations (see below), whereas the sections which have been composed in Greek (at least Additions B and E) . . . ' This sounds

as though he agrees with Cook, but there is no sign that he really accepts
that AT is a different *translation* from the LXX (it is not clear what 'see below'
refers to). He does indeed use the term 'translation' of the AT (pp. 11, 25),
but not in any way that implies it was a translation separate from the LXX. I
can only assume that when he says 'It has been recognized by some scholars'
he means 'It has been claimed by some scholars'.

51. Cf. C.A. Moore, *The Greek Text of Esther* (PhD, Johns Hopkins, 1965;
Ann Arbor, 1965), p. 24: fkz are traditional LXX manuscripts corrected or
contaminated by the Hexapla.

52. Tov, 'The "Lucianic" Text', p. 6.

NOTES TO CHAPTER 8

1. Cook, 'The *A*-text', p. 376.

2. Tov, 'The "Lucianic" Text', p. 25.

3. I have earlier expressed my doubts that v. 17 pure and simple
concluded the actual *text* of proto-AT or its *Vorlage*. But this point in the
narrative marks its conclusion.

4. העביר in MT 8.3.

5. Is Esther depicted as unaware of this crucial Persian custom, or does
her word (doubtless found in the pre-MT text) now give the author just the
opportunity he wants to point out how impossible her request is? Moore,
Esther, p. 79, takes it as a 'parenthetic aside . . . made by either the author or
a glossator rather than by the king, since Esther would have known about
the law's irrevocability'. Similarly L. Soubigou, *Esther traduit et commenté*
(2nd edn; La Sainte Bible; Paris, 1952), p. 658 (cited by Dommershausen,
Estherrolle, p. 102).

6. It is of course not entirely clear that the 'for' clause of v. 8 relates to the
first decree rather than the second; Paton, pp. 270f., Bardtke, *Esther*, p. 367,
and Gerleman, *Esther*, p. 128, agree that it does. It is quite possible that it
refers both to the decree that now stands *and* to the decree about to be
written by Esther and Mordecai.

7. On the difficult Hebrew, see now Gerleman, *Esther*, pp. 128f.

8. The crown, according to MT, is set on the head of the horse; depictions
of decorations on horses' heads (cf. Moore, *Esther*, 65), are not necessarily of
crowns, and it may be preferable to delete the *waw* of ואשר and translate the
last clause as '[a horse] which the king has ridden while the royal diadem has
been on his (the king's) head' (similarly Gerleman, *Esther*, pp. 117f.).

9. So Dommershausen, *Estherrolle*, p. 109.

10. Paton, p. 269.

11. Bardtke, *Esther*, p. 363.

12. They are 'erlebte Rede', or 'contaminated narrative' in which the narrator presents the emotion of his characters through his own purportedly detached narrative. Cf. M. Weiss, 'Einiges über die Bauformen des Erzählens in der Bibel', *VT* 13 (1963), pp. 456-74; R. Wellek and A. Warren, *Theory of Literature* (3rd edn; Harmondsworth, 1963), pp. 224, 306 n. 29.

13. On his speech to Esther in 4.13-14, see above, pp. 35f.

14. It will be a nice irony that in the end the king will yield to her pressure with a similar formula: 'write as is good in your eyes' (כתבו כטוב בעיניכם, 8.8).

15. כשר is not elsewhere in Esther; but it corresponds to שוה, 'fitting', which we have seen at 3.8; 5.13; 7.4. 3.8 is not to be translated 'not for the king's profit to tolerate [the Jews]', but 'not appropriate, fitting . . .'; the appeal is not to economics but to the king's sense of dignity and racial superiority; שוה appears to be the Hebrew equivalent of Aram. אריך, 'fitting, worthy of an Aryan'. Likewise שוה in 7.4 probably means that for Esther to have bothered the king with a trivial danger like the enslavement of her people would have been 'inappropriate, *infra dig.*'. Also at 5.13 Haman's complaint that when he sees Mordecai refusing to do him homage the honour he has received from the king (and queen) is not שוה to him may mean that the honour does not suit him or seem appropriate.

16. Surely there is no practical distinction between 'giving' (נתן, vv. 1, 7) and 'setting over' (שים על, v. 2)?

17. Esther and Mordecai receive the 'plunder' of Haman's house (do they not?)—despite the insistence of the supplementer of MT (9.10, 15, 16) that the Jews got no plunder.

18. Paton made a brave attempt at interpreting this strange phrase by translating 'the saviour of the situation' (p. 245). But more attractively Torrey explained the phrase as a rendering of Aram. משיזב ממריה 'saviour of the words', an error for משיזב מריה 'saviour of his lord'. It is not essential to accept Torrey's precise explanation, that 'Some scribe, accustomed to follow this participle [משיזב] with the preposition *min*, carelessly wrote ממריה; and the translator, compelled to read this as ממריה, of course rendered literally' ('The Older Book of Esther', p. 8 [= Moore, *Studies*, p. 455]).

19. Or 'perceived' (Paton, p. 245)?

20. Tov, 'The "Lucianic" Text', pp. 11f.

21. 'Announce a service and pray to God earnestly, and I and my maidens will do likewise' (not in LXX) may be a reference to the prayer of Esther that will follow in AT 5.19-29 (= LXX 14.14-30, Addition C). But equally LXX 4.8 (AT 5.5), 'Call upon the Lord', could be regarded as such a reference, so there is no difference between AT and LXX on this count.

22. On the fact that this AT plus (and those at 7.1, 22, mentioned below) are shared with LXX, see Chapter 8 above.

23. Most similar in LXX is Joel 1.14; 2.15 κηρύξατε θεραπείαν, translating עצרה.

24. Paton, p. 244.
25. The reality may be even more complex. At AT 7.17, for instance, Tov rightly observes that the word order is neither Greek nor Hebrew, but Aramaic ('The "Lucianic" Text', p. 25 n. 23).
26. Paton, p. 258.
27. Gerleman, *Esther*, p. 121.
28. Bardtke, *Esther*, p. 355.
29. Bardtke, *Esther*, p. 356. Similarly Dommershausen, *Estherrolle*, p. 95.
30. Haller, p. 130.
31. BH³ (*prb*).
32. It may be thought unrealistic to suppose that a slip on the part of the proto-MT narrator has been perpetuated into the present MT; but it is no more nor less unrealistic than the opinions of Bardtke and Dommershausen cited above who believe that the anomaly was intentional.
33. The effectiveness of concentration upon larger issues of coherence has been amply attested in Septuagintal criticism by studies of D.W. Gooding, for example (cf. his 'Ahab according to the Septuagint', *ZAW* 35 [1964], pp. 269-80; 'Pedantic Timetabling in 3rd Book of Reigns', *VT* 15 [1965], pp. 153-66; 'The Septuagint's Version of Solomon's Misconduct', *VT* 15 [1965], pp. 325-35).

NOTES TO CHAPTER 9

1. In *Lex tua veritas. Festschrift für Hubert Junker*, ed. H. Gross and F. Mussner (Trier, 1961), pp. 17-29 (= Moore, *Studies*, pp. 424-36). Cazelles's article is reviewed in detail by H. Bardtke, 'Neuere Arbeiten zum Estherbuch. Eine kritische Würdigung', *JEOL* 19 (1965-66), pp. 519-49 (533-41) (= Moore, *Studies*, pp. 91-121 [105-113]).
2. Cazelles, 'Note sur la composition', p. 28 (= Moore, *Studies*, p. 435).
3. Cazelles's statement of this whole point is difficult to follow, so much so that I think that Bardtke has misunderstood Cazelles to say that the first account is of what happens in the provinces at Esther's direction, the second of a massacre in Susa urged by Mordecai ('Neuere Arbeiten', p. 536 [= Moore, *Studies*, p. 108]).
4. Cazelles, 'Note sur la composition', p. 27 (= Moore, *Studies*, p. 434).
5. Bardtke, 'Neuere Arbeiten', p. 539 (= Moore, *Studies*, p. 101).
6. J. Duchesne-Guillemin, 'Les noms des eunuques d'Assuérus', *Le Muséon* 66 (1953), pp. 105-108 (= Moore, *Studies*, pp. 273-76).
7. Cazelles, 'Note sur la composition', p. 24 (= Moore, *Studies*, p. 431).
8. 'Or le roi au v. 12, connaissant le massacre de Suse, propose à Esther un massacre en province. Celle-ci répond en ne demandant rien pour la province, mais application de l'édit du massacre à Suse' ('Note sur la composition', p. 24 [= Moore, *Studies*, p. 431]).

9. Cazelles, 'Note sur la composition', p. 24.

10. 'Les *deux repas* offerts par Esther à Assuérus et Aman ne sont pas sans surprendre, d'autant que le premier est à peine décrit et que la proposition d'Assuérus reprise en VII,1 se retrouvera en IX,12' (p. 27 [= Moore, *Studies*, p. 434]).

11. The contrast between Mordecai's not 'bowing' (3.8) and not 'rising' (5.9) is significant: far from doing Haman the considerable honour of proskynesis, Mordecai does not even do him the common courtesy of rising.

12. The expression 'they covered Haman's face' (פני המן חפו, 7.8) is problematic. References to a Greco-Roman custom of covering the head of a person condemned to death (Livy 1.26.6, 11; Quintus Curtius, *History of Alexander* 6.8.22; Cicero, *Pro Rabirio* 4.13), often cited by commentators, are misleading. For—quite apart from the fact that the reference in Quintus Curtius is not to a custom (see A. Condamin, 'Notes critiques sur le texte biblique. II. La disgrace d'Aman (Esth. VII,8)', *RB* 7 [1898], pp. 258f.)—that is a covering of the *head*, while here it is the face—and furthermore, no evident sentence of death has been passed. The LXX διετράπη τῷ προσώπῳ, 'he was confounded in the face', may point to a Hebrew חָוְרוּ, 'his face became pale' instead of MT חָפוּ (so W. Rudolph, 'Textkritisches zum Estherbuch', *VT* 4 [1954], pp. 89-90 [90]). Not dissimilar in effect was Condamin's suggestion (*RB* 7 [1898], 258-61) that חָפוּ, 'was covered', means metaphorically 'was troubled'—though Condamin preferred to achieve that sense by emending to חָפְרוּ (as also F. Perles, *Analekten zur Textkritik des alten Testaments* [Munich, 1895], p. 32). But it is probably best to accept G. Gerleman's suggestion that we have here an idiom meaning 'he lost consciousness, fell down in a dead faint', on the analogy of the Arabic idiom *ġuniya* (or, *'uġniya*) *'alaihi*, 'it was covered over him' for 'he lost consciousness' (Gerleman, *Esther*, pp. 123f.). NEB read חָפוּ '[his face] was covered', and translated 'Haman hid his face in despair'. Some kind of seizure or stroke may be intended as the instant punishment of Haman, in which case in the MT the hanging on the gallows may be a post-mortem display of a corpse (as is the case with Haman's sons in 9.13f.).

13. Ringgren, *Esther*, p. 395, also raises this possibility.

14. Gen. 39.10 ויהי כדברה אל־יוסף יום יום ולא־שמע; Est. 3.4 ויהי כאמרם אליו יום ויום ולא שמע (Qere).

15. It may also be a small token of redaction that Haman's first boast (v. 11) is in indirect speech, his second (v. 12) in direct speech.

16. H. Ringgren, for example, maintains that the Esther and Mordecai 'motifs' (traditions) are so 'eng ineinander verschlungen' that they cannot now be mechanistically separated ('man sie mechanisch nicht mehr voneinander trennen kann', *Esther*, p. 374). That 'mechanisch' is a give-away: if he could disentangle the sources, it would be artistic, scientific; if he can't, it would be mechanical to try to do so.

17. Bardtke, *Esther*, p. 250.

18. There was not, as is commonly asserted, any law requiring a Persian king to take a wife only from the Persian nobility. Herodotus 3.84 is almost universally misunderstood in this connection.

19. Cf. Bickerman, *Four Strange Books of the Bible*, p. 184.

20. Bardtke, *Esther*, p. 251.

21. Ringgren, *Das Buch Esther*, pp. 374f.; 'Esther and Purim', *SEÅ* 20 (1955), pp. 5-24 (= Moore, *Studies*, pp. 185-204).

22. Cf. esp. *SEÅ* 20 (1955), p. 23.

23. E. Bickerman, *Four Strange Books of the Bible* (New York, 1967).

24. Bickerman, *Four Strange Books*, p. 172.

25. 'We may wonder whether the hero of the original tale was a Jew' (p. 181).

26. Though the actual fate of Haman—to be hung on the gallows prepared for Mordecai—he acknowledges to come from the Mordecai source (p. 184).

27. AT in fact has 'because he had spoken to the king about the eunuchs' (ὑπὲρ τοῦ λελαληκέναι αὐτὸν τῷ βασιλεῖ περὶ τῶν εὐνούχων).

28. Bickerman, *Four Strange Books of the Bible*, p. 187.

29. W. Lee Humphreys, 'A Life-Style for Diaspora: A Study of the Tales of Esther and Daniel', *JBL* 92 (1973), pp. 211-23 (214). We might mention here the view of G.W.E. Nickelsburg that 'a story about court rivals has become the nucleus of a story about the rescue of the Jewish people and the origin of the Feast of Purim' (*Resurrection, Immortality, and Eternal Life in Intertestamental Judaism* [Cambridge, Mass., 1972], p. 51). See also S. Niditch and R. Doran, 'The Success Story of the Wise Courtier: A Formal Approach', *JBL* 96 (1977), pp. 179-93, effectively denying that Esther can properly be labelled an example of the wise courtier story.

30. Humphreys, 'A Life-Style for Diaspora', p. 216.

31. Humphreys, 'A Life-Style for Diaspora', p. 215.

32. Humphreys, 'A Life-Style for Diaspora', p. 216.

33. Humphreys, 'A Life-Style for Diaspora', p. 216.

34. J.C.H. Lebram, 'Purimfest und Estherbuch', *VT* 22 (1972), pp. 208-22 (= Moore, *Studies*, pp. 205-21).

35. Lebram, 'Purimfest und Estherbuch', pp. 216f. (= Moore, *Studies*, pp. 213f.).

36. Lebram, 'Purimfest und Estherbuch', p. 215 (= Moore, *Studies*, p. 212).

NOTES TO CHAPTER 10

1. So Humphreys, 'A Life-Style for Diaspora', p. 215.

2. The suggestion of the Greek versions (not repeated by Josephus) becomes a firm statement in Josippon, according to whom the eunuchs were

relatives of Haman. See also I. Katzenellenbogen, *Das Buch Esther in der Aggada* (Diss. Würzburg, 1913). I have not yet seen the work of J.M. Brown, 'Rabbinic Interpretations of the Characters and Plot of the Book of Esther (as Reflected in Midrash Esther Rabbah)', Rabbinical thesis, Hebrew Union College—Jewish Institute of Religion (Cincinnati, 1976).

3. It seems preferable to derive this element of the narrative from the text we now have than to speculate, with Bickerman, taking a clue from the Greek Additions, that Mordecai informed the king that Haman had been involved in the conspiracy of the eunuchs (*Four Strange Books*, p. 181).

4. Bickerman, *Four Strange Books*, p. 182. Bickerman cites several medieval examples, and also remarks that 'the chronicles of the court of the Persian kings, as recounted by Ctesias, the Greek physician of Artaxerxes II (405-359), are full of conflicts between royal ministers and the king's wife or mother'.

5. See especially G. Gerleman, 'Esther und Exodus', in *Esther*, pp. 11-23; *id.*, 'Esther und Exodus', in *Studien zu Esther. Stoff–Struktur–Stil–Sinn* (Biblische Studien, 48; Neukirchen, 1966), pp. 7-28 (= Moore, *Studies*, pp. 308-35). Most agree that he drastically overstates his case for a literary relationship between Exodus and Esther (see Lebram, 'Purimfest und Estherbuch', p. 208 n. 4 [= Moore, *Studies*, p. 205 n. 4]; Humphreys, 'A Life-Style for Diaspora', p. 216 n. 17); C.A. Moore, 'Esther Revisited Again: A Further Examination of Certain Esther Studies of the Past Ten Years', *HUCA* (R. Gordis Festschrift) (forthcoming); and for a careful critical evaluation, see M.E. Andrew, 'Esther, Exodus and Peoples', *ABR* 23 (1975), pp. 25-28. The issue of relationship between the Joseph and the Esther stories has been long discussed; see L.A. Rosenthal, 'Die Josephsgeschichte mit den Büchern Ester und Daniel verglichen', *ZAW* 15 (1895), pp. 278-84 (= Moore, *Studies*, pp. 277-83); *id.*, 'Nochmals der Vergleich Ester, Joseph, Daniel', *ZAW* 17 (1897), pp. 125-28; P. Riessler, 'Zu Rosenthals Aufsatz, Bd. XV, S. 278ff.', *ZAW* 16 (1896), p. 182; M. Gan, 'The Book of Esther in the Light of the Story of Joseph in Egypt' [Heb.], *Tarbiz* 31 (1961-62), pp. 144-49; A. Meinhold, 'Die Gattung der Josephsgeschichte und des Estherbuches: Diasporanovelle II', *ZAW* 88 (1976), pp. 72-93 (= Moore, *Studies*, pp. 284-305).

6. The eunuch Harbona of MT 7.9 does not belong to the Esther source (see Chapter 9, section II, above).

7. The reading γωγαιον is according to Brooke–McLean and Lagarde found in 93 (= e$_2$, Brooke–McLean; m, Lagarde), whereas in Hanhart's edition γωγαιον is given as the reading of 93 in its LXX (o') text, not in its *L* ('Lucianic') text. I do not understand this discrepancy.

Assuming that γωγαιον is an AT reading, we could explain it as connected with Gog of Ezek. 38–39 (so Bardtke, 'Zusätze zu Esther', p. 35; Moore, *Esther*, p. 36), but the important thing is that it appears to indicate a Hebrew original (א)גגי. Correction of the Greek manuscript tradition in the light of the Hebrew, which is theoretically possible, would be more likely to produce a more accurate vocalization, or a rendering in harmony with the MT's intention (like Josephus's Αμαλεκίτην, *Ant.* 11.209); γωγαιον implies an interpretative rendering of Heb. יגאי(א) in which the precise significance of the consonants was not understood. For these reasons I think γωγαιον may be the earliest Greek reading of all. Βουγαῖον may have developed through confusion of Haman with the Memucan of 1.16 (AT and MT) who is in AT Βουγαῖος (LXX Μουχαῖος). A further complication, it must be admitted, is the name Γωγαῖος at AT 3.3 for the eunuch in charge of the women (MT 2.3 הגי; LXX *om.* and Βουγαῖος (γωγαιος 93, γογαιος 319) at AT 3.8 (MT 2.8 הגי; LXX Γαι, or γαει, γαιη, γωγαιου [93]) for the same person.

Older scholars devoted much space to these questions without shedding much light; see, for example, J. Hoschander, *The Book of Esther in the Light of History* (Philadelphia, 1923), pp. 21-27.

8. See note 7 above.

9. See Chapter 8, section III, for a discussion of the probable contamination of the AT 5.6 by the corresponding passage of LXX (4.8).

10. Cf. H. Steinthal, *Zu Bibel und Religionsphilosophie* (1890), pp. 53ff., mentioned by Paton, p. 95.

11. R.H. Pfeiffer, *Introduction to the Old Testament* (London, 1952), p. 743.

12. G. Fohrer, *Introduction to the Old Testament* (tr. D. Green; London, 1970), p. 253. Similarly A. Weiser, *Introduction to the Old Testament* (tr. D.M. Barton; London, 1961), p. 312: 'a memorial to the nationalist spirit of Judaism which had become fanatical, and . . . had lost all touch with the great tasks which the prophets had placed before their people'.

13. A. Scholz, *Commentar über das Buch Judith und über Bel und Drache* (2nd edn, Leipzig, 1898), p. xvii, cited by Paton, p. 95.

14. K.F. Keil, *Manual of Historico-Critical Introduction*, II (1870), p. 130.

15. A. Meinhold, *Das Buch Esther* (Zürcher Bibelkommentare, 13; Zürich, 1983), p. 101: 'Esther ist ein religiöses Buch in nichtreligiösen Sprache. Der Grund für einen solchen Vorgang indirekten Theologisierens wird u.a. darin liegen, dass der Estherverfasser mit seinen Novelle eine Judenschaft in langer oder gar bleibender Diasporaexistenz zu einen Verhalten auffordert, dem Fremdvolk gegenüber zugewandt und tätig zu sein, dabei dem eigenen Volk und seinen Traditionen treu zu bleiben'.

16. Paton, p. 95. Similarly Anderson, pp. 829f.; D. Harvey, 'Esther, Book of', *Interpreter's Dictionary of the Bible* (ed. G. Buttrick; Nashville, 1962), vol. 2, pp. 149-51 [150].

17. Bardtke, 'Zusätze', p. 17.

18. S. Talmon, '"Wisdom" in the Book of Esther', *VT* 13 (1963), pp. 419-55 (430); followed by Moore, p. xxxiii-xxxiv.

19. W.E. Beet, 'The Message of the Book of Esther', *The Expositor* (8th Series) 22 (1921-22) pp. 291-330 (298f.) (my italics). A similar statement is

made by W.W. Grasham, 'The Theology of the Book of Esther', *Restoration Quarterly* 16 (1973), pp. 99-111: 'The Book of Esther is definitely a religious story, told in non-religious language' (pp. 109f.) (cited with approval by A. Meinhold, 'Zu Aufbau und Mitte des Estherbuches', *VT* 23 [1983], pp. 435-45 [445 n. 30]).

20. Cf. H. Striedl, 'Untersuchung zur Syntax und Stilistik des hebräischen Buches Esther', *ZAW* 55 (1937), pp. 73-108: 'Die ganze Erzählung ist ein grosses נֶהְפּוֹךְ (9_1)'.

21. So Y.T. Radday, 'Chiasm in Joshua, Judges and Others', *Linguistica Biblica* 3 (1973), pp. 6-13; M.V. Fox, 'The Structure of the Book of Esther', *Festschrift I.L. Seeligmann* (forthcoming); cf. the comments of Berg, *Esther*, pp. 106-13.

22. Berg, *Esther*, p. 106.

23. See E. Hamel, 'Le Magnificat et le renversement des situations. Réflexion théologico-biblique', *Gregorianum* 60 (1979), pp. 55-84.

24. Berg, *Esther*, p. 178. Berg develops the point more fully in her article, 'After the Exile: God and History in the Books of Chronicles and Esther', in *The Divine Helmsman. Studies on God's Control of Human Events* (L.H. Silberman volume), ed. J.L. Crenshaw and S. Sandmel (New York, 1980), pp. 107-20 (114-20). See also A. Meinhold, 'Theologische Erwägungen zum Buch Esther', *TZ* 34 (1978), pp. 321-33.

25. J.A. Loader, 'Esther as a Novel with Different Levels of Meaning', *ZAW* 90 (1978), pp. 417-21 (418).

26. Gerleman, *Esther*, p. 23.

27. Humphreys, 'A Life-Style for Diaspora', pp. 211-23.

28. Humphreys, 'A Life-Style for Diaspora', p. 215.

29. S. Talmon, '"Wisdom" in the Book of Esther', *VT* 13 (1963), pp. 419-55 (426).

30. Talmon, '"Wisdom" in the Book of Esther', p. 427; similarly Moore, *Esther*, pp. xxxiii-xxxiv. On Talmon's essay, see also Bardtke, 'Neuere Arbeiten', pp. 541-45 (= Moore, *Studies*, pp. 113-17). I leave aside here the question of the meaningfulness or otherwise of the concept of 'wisdom'; but cf. J.L. Crenshaw, 'Methods in Determining Wisdom Influence upon "Historical" Literature', *JBL* 88 (1969), pp. 129-42 (esp. pp. 140ff.); and R.N. Whybray, *The Intellectual Tradition in the Old Testament* (Beiheft zur *Zeitschrift für die alttestamentliche Wissenschaft*, 135; Berlin, 1974). I have not been able to see the article of N.A. van Uchelen, 'A Chokmatic Theme in the Book of Esther', in *Verkenningen in een Stroomgebied. Festschrift M.A. Beek* (Amsterdam, 1974), pp. 132-40.

31. Talmon, '"Wisdom" in the Book of Esther', p. 430.

32. Loader, 'Esther as a Novel', p. 421.

33. These somewhat misleading 'levels' are exploited in a short but speculative paper by C.H. Miller, 'Esther's Levels of Meaning', *ZAW* 92 (1980), pp. 145-48.

34. R. Gordis interestingly comments: 'The preservation of the Jewish people is itself a religious obligation of the first magnitude ... Jewish survival is not merely an expression of the human instinct of self-preservation, but a Divine commandment' (R. Gordis, *Megillat Esther* [New York, 1972], p. 13)—one which God himself, we might add, no doubt also feels bound by.

35. On the other hand, the notion of 'spoiling the Egyptians' is perfectly acceptable. Another possible explanation of Jewish refusal to take plunder is that their behaviour against the sympathizers of the Agagite Haman is contrasted with that of Saul against Agag the Amalekite (1 Sam. 15). If that is so, however, it is strange that Haman is not here actually called the Agagite.

The view of W. McKane that taking of plunder would 'compromise the intrinsic superiority of the Jews over the Gentiles ... and demean their dignity' is hard to justify from the text, though he rightly observes that the parallel with 1 Sam. 15 would lead one to expect a dedication of plunder to the destruction of the ban ('A Note on Esther IX and 1 Samuel XV', *JTS* 12 [1961], pp. 260-61 [= Moore, *Studies*, pp. 306-307]).

36. Cf. P. Humbert, '"Étendre la main" (Note de lexicographie hébraïque)', *VT* 12 (1962), pp. 383-95.

37. נוח is not be emended to נחום, 'avenged themselves', as W. Rudolph suggested (*VT* 4 [1954], p. 90).

38. Cf. H.-P. Müller, 'קהל *qāhāl* Versammlung', *THWAT*, II, cols. 609-19 (617), though it must be acknowledged that קהל sometimes occurs in war ideology (e.g. Judg. 21.5; 2 Chr. 28.14; cf. Müller, *THWAT*, II, col. 612).

39. Cf. Childs, *Introduction*: 'The festival ... is not to be understood as a victory celebration, but a rejoicing over the relief from persecution, a celebration of rest' (p. 604).

40. B.S. Childs, *Memory and Tradition in Israel* (London, 1962), p. 72.

41. We may perhaps contrast the Greek custom of celebrating the day of battle itself, noting that at some points in the LXX (B-text) the 'fourteenth' rather than the 'thirteenth' as the date of the battle seems well attested (at 3.7 and 13.6 [= B6]; cf. Bickerman, *Four Strange Books*, p. 220). We should note also that 'Nicanor's Day', the thirteenth of Adar, was a celebration of the defeat of Nicanor *on that day* (2 Macc. 15.36).

42. Of course, no *day* is actually mentioned in 3.7, though the casting of lots is apparently 'for the month and for the day' (מיום ליום ומחדש לחדש). Some indeed believe that a notation that 'the lot fell out for the thirteenth day of the month' should be inserted into the MT (ויפל הגורל על־שלושה עשר יום לחדש) on the basis of LXX's καὶ ἔπεσεν ὁ κλῆρος εἰς τὴν τεσσαρεσκαιδεκάτην τοῦ μηνός—though τεσσαρεσκαιδεκάτην, 'fourteenth', must be a mistake for τρισκαιδεκάτην, 'thirteenth', as in 8.12. So Paton, p. 202; Bardtke, *Esther*, p. 315. Gerleman, *Esther*, p. 93, on the other hand, deletes מיום ליום from 3.7 on the ground that no day is mentioned; but the sequel of the story of ch. 3, in which no further narrative is required to establish that

the thirteenth will be the day of the pogrom (3.13), suggests strongly that the fixing of that day was narrated already in 3.7. We should also note that AT has (at 4.7) καὶ βάλλει κλήρους εἰς τὴν τρισκαιδεκάτην τοῦ μηνός; but it is difficult to know whether this represents an original AT reading, since it is inserted awkwardly between the king's command to Haman to write to the provinces (4.10) and Haman's execution of that command (4.13).

43. This interpretation of 'Purim' was stimulated by the suggestion of A.D. Cohen it is the coincidences of the plot, the 'chance-occurrences', that are the *purim* in the plural ('"Hu Ha-goral": The Religious Significance of Esther', *Judaism* 23 [1974], pp. 87-94 [= Moore, *Studies*, pp. 122-29]). On his view the *pur* cast by Haman was just one of many *purim* recounted in the book; but I think it more probable in the context of 9.23-28 that a contrast between the *pur* cast by Haman and *one* other *pur* is being drawn. I would differ from Cohen also over his attempt to explain the *historical origin* of the festival and its name; it is hard to believe that a popular festival took its rise—and its name—from an essentially conceptual construction of events, whether historical or fictional, rather than from some concrete event, ritual, or custom.

The plural form of Purim has recently received a new explanation by Gerleman (*Esther*, pp. 25ff.). According to him, *pûrîm* means not only the lot that is cast, but also the thing apportioned by lot—which is true as well of the term *gôrāl*. The 'portions' from which Purim takes its name are nothing other than the 'portions' (*mānôt*) which are said at 9.19, 22 to be exchanged as part of the holiday celebrations. The sending of such portions (*mānôt*) is also attested at Neh. 8.10, 12 as a festive custom. The festival thus took its name, he argues, from one of its principal customs; and the connection of *pûr*, the lot, with Haman and his plot in 3.7 and 9.24 is entirely secondary. The difficulties with Gerleman's theory are that he cannot explain why if *pûrîm* originally meant 'portions', 'exchanged gifts', its meaning was so forgotten as to enable the idea of Haman's *pûr* to arise, and, more importantly, that *gôrāl*, the middle term for himbetween *pûr* and *mānôt*, always retains at least an allusion to the act of allotting by 'chance', whereas the 'portions' exchanged as gifts have no such significance. A much simpler explanation of the plural Purim would be that it was a festival of *two* days' duration. Or else the plural could be a matter of assimilation to the plurals by which most Jewish festivals were known, Weeks, Booths, *maṣṣôt* (Ex. 12.17), Lights (Hanukkah).

On the question of the *historical* origin of Purim and its name, I have commented more fully in the Introduction to Esther (section V) in my commentary, *Ezra, Nehemiah, and Esther* (New Century Bible; London, 1984).

44. The RSV (and NEB, JB, NAB) of 9.21f. is potentially misleading if read thus: 'they should keep the fourteenth . . . and . . . fifteenth . . . as the days on which the Jews got relief'; for 'as the days' is כימים, 'like the days', which

means that these days are to be celebrated with the same practices as were observed at the initial celebrations. They are not celebrated *as being* the days of the initial 'rest'—which would require the existence of a *kaph essentiae*, probably unattested in the Hebrew Bible.

45. On the translation of v. 25 as 'when it [the plot] came before the king' (as against RSV, for example 'when Esther came . . . '), see above, Chapter 4, section I.2.f.

46. My debt to the approach of B.S. Childs in his pages on 'The Function of 9.20-32' in his *Introduction*, pp. 603-605, will be evident; he is surely correct in insisting upon an interpetation that takes seriously the final form of the book. Nevertheless, I am not sure that I can accept his argument (p. 604) that the keeping of the festival 'according to what was written' (v. 27), admittedly 'the letter of the king (v. 26) and not the whole book of Esther', has as its point that 'the festival [should] be *regulated* [my italics] by the carefully recorded events of the oppression and the deliverance', since the *regulator* of the festival seems rather to be presented as the spontaneous celebrations of the Jews themselves together with the formal authorization and extensions of those celebrations introduced by the letters of Mordecai and Esther. For this reason also I cannot wholeheartedly agree with the statement, 'That later Jewish tradition understood the festival to be *regulated* [my italics] by the reading of the whole book of Esther is a step not far removed from the intent of ch. 9'; for again it is the regulations explicitly relating to the festival that determine its character rather than the Esther scroll as a whole. What would be most parallel in Jewish tradition to the 'intent of ch. 9' is the intent of the Talmud tractate Megillah—which concerns itself principally with the *rituals* of the festival and only secondarily with the *narrative* of the scroll (curiously enough downplaying the various resolutions of the story).

47. Not by Nehemiah also; see my comments in *Ezra, Nehemiah and Esther, ad loc.*

48. See D.J.A. Clines, 'New Year', *Interpreter's Dictionary of the Bible. Supplementary Volume* (ed. K. Crim; Nashville, 1976), pp. 625-29.

49. Though the prescription that Weeks and Booths are to be celebrated by the fatherless and widow (Deut. 16.11, 14) may imply prior gifts to them.

50. Childs, *Introduction*, p. 605.

51. *Contra* Dommershausen, *Estherrolle*, p. 135: 'Sehr sinnvoll lässt der Verfasser *Esther die Initiatorin* sein, sie hatte ja schon einmal ein Fasten angeordnet'.

52. *Contra* Anderson, p. 873, following Torrey. Whether there may be an unbroken line from the fasting here prescribed to the custom of 'Esther's Fast', attested from the ninth century AD as a ritual of the thirteenth of Adar, is beside the present point.

53. So Childs, *Introduction*, p. 604: 'The traditional fasting and lamentations serve to remind Israel of the background of Purim and provide the proper

context for the season of joy'.

54. Childs, *Introduction*, pp. 604f.

55. Humphreys, *JBL* 92 (1973), pp. 211-23.

56. Childs, *Introduction*, p. 606.

57. Meinhold, *Esther*, p. 101, points out that such a phrase occurs elsewhere only of God (Ps. 85.9 מה־ידבר האל יהוה כי ידבר שלום אל־עמו ואל־חסידיו אשמע).

58. Humphreys, 'A Life-Style for Diaspora', p. 216.

59. Moore, *Additions*, p. 8.

60. Moore, *ibid.*

61. Paton, pp. 44f.

62. Eissfeldt, *Introduction*, p. 592; similarly G.W.E. Nickelsburg, *Jewish Literature between the Bible and the Mishnah: A Historical and Literary Introduction* (London, 1981), p. 173: 'to add a note of authenticity'.

63. Eissfeldt, *Introduction*, p. 592.

64. Cf. Bardtke, 'Zusätze', p. 18: 'Sie [the Additions] gestalten das Buch zu einer Urkunde jüdische Glaubens um'.

65. See especially, on the relation between ch. 2 and chs. 7–12, Childs, *Introduction*, pp. 616f.

66. Cf. Moore, *Additions*, pp. 181, 249.

67. The addition of the dream material further alters the shape of the Masoretic story in that it de-emphasizes the Purim festival by shifting the focus from the ritual of Purim to the apocalyptic-like significance of the conflict presented by the story (so C.A. Moore, 'On the Origins of the LXX Additions to the Book of Esther', *JBL* 92 [1973], pp. 383-93 [390] [= Moore, *Studies*, p. 591]).

68. Moore, *Additions*, pp. 195-99.

69. Cf. C.W. Emmett, '3 Maccabees', in *The Apocrypha and Pseudepigrapha of the Old Testament* (ed. R.H. Charles; Oxford, 1913), vol. 1, pp. 155-73 (161).

70. See especially Bardtke on what he calls the 'Anerkennungserlass' of Addition E, in 'Zusätze', pp. 23f.

BIBLIOGRAPHY

P.R. Ackroyd, 'Two Hebrew Notes', *ASTI* 5 (1966-67), pp. 81-84.

B. Albrektson, 'Difficilior Lectio Probabilior. A Rule of Textual Criticism and its Use in Old Testament Studies', *OTS* 21 (1981), pp. 5-18.

B.W. Anderson, 'The Place of the Book of Esther in the Christian Bible,' *JR* 30 (1950), pp. 32-43 (= Moore, *Studies*, pp. 130-41).

—'The Book of Esther. Introduction and Exegesis' (*IB*, vol. 3; New York and Nashville: Abingdon, 1954), pp. 821-74. Cited as Anderson.

M.E. Andrew, 'Esther, Exodus and Peoples', *ABR* 23 (1975), pp. 25-28.

H. Bardtke, *Das Buch Esther* (Kommentar zum Alten Testament, XVII/5); Gütersloh: G. Mohn, 1963). Cited as Bardtke, *Esther*.

—'Neuere Arbeiten zum Estherbuch. Eine kritische Würdigung,' *Ex Oriente Lux* 19 (1965-66), pp. 519-49 (= Moore, *Studies*, pp. 91-121).

—'Zusätze zu Esther', in W.G. Kümmel (ed.), *Jüdische Schriften aus hellenistisch-römischer Zeit*, Band 1, Lieferung 1: *Historische und legendarische Erzählungen* (Gütersloh: G. Mohn, 1973), pp. 15-59.

W.E. Beet, 'The Message of the Book of Esther', *The Expositor* (8th Series) 22 (1921-22), pp. 291-300.

S.B. Berg, *The Book of Esther: Motifs, Themes and Structure* (SBL Dissertation Series, 44: Missoula, Montana: Scholars Press, 1979).

—'After the Exile: God and History in the Books of the Chronicles and Esther', in *The Divine Helmsman* (ed. J.L. Crenshaw and S. Sandmel, New York: Ktav, 1980), pp. 107-27.

A. Bertheau, *Die Bücher Esra, Nechemia und Ester* (Kurzgefasstes exegetisches Handbuch zum Alten Testament, 17; 2nd edn by V. Ryssel; Leipzig: S. Hirzel, 1887).

H. Bévenot, 'Die Proskynesis und die Gebete im Estherbuch', *Jahrbuch für Liturgiewissenschaft* 11 (1931), pp. 132-39.

E.J. Bickerman, 'Notes on the Greek Book of Esther', *Proceedings of the American Academy for Jewish Research* 20 (1950), pp. 101-33.

—*Four Strange Books of the Bible: Jonah, Daniel, Koheleth, Esther* (New York: Schocken, 1967).

E.C. Bissell, 'Additions to Esther', in *The Apocrypha of the Old Testament* (A Commentary on the Holy Scriptures by J.P. Lange, tr. P. Schaff, vol. 15 of the Old Testament; Edinburgh: T. and T. Clark, 1868), pp. 199-220.

L.H. Brockington, *Ezra, Nehemiah and Esther* (New Century Bible: London: Nelson, 1969). Cited as Brockington.

A.E. Brooke, N. McLean and H. StJ. Thackeray, *The Old Testament in Greek*, Vol. 3, Part 1 (London: Cambridge University Press, 1940).

W.H. Brownlee, 'Le livre grec d'Esther et la royauté divine. Corrections orthodoxes au livre d'Esther', *RB* 73 (1966), pp. 161-85.

P. Cassel, *An Explanatory Commentary on Esther* (tr. A. Bernstein; Edinburgh: T. and T. Clark, 1888).

H. Cazelles, 'Note sur la composition du rouleau d'Esther', in *Lex tua veritas. Festschrift für Hubert Junker* (ed. H. Gross and F. Mussner; Trier: Paulinus Verlag, 1961), pp. 17-29 (= Moore, *Studies*, pp. 424-36).

B.S. Childs, *Memory and Tradition in Israel* (SCM: London, 1962).

—*Introduction to the Old Testament as Scripture* (SCM: London, 1979).

D.J.A. Clines, 'New Year', *Interpreter's Dictionary of the Bible. Supplementary Volume* (ed. K. Crim; Nashville: Abingdon, 1976), pp. 625-29.

—*Ezra, Nehemiah, and Esther* (New Century Bible; London: Marshall, Morgan and Scott, 1984).

A.D. Cohen, '"Hu Ha-goral": The Religious Significance of Esther', *Judaism* 23 (1974), pp. 87-94 (= Moore, *Studies*, pp. 122-29).

A. Condamin, 'Notes critiques sur le texte biblique. II. La disgrace d'Aman (Esth. VII,8)', *RB* 7 (1898), pp. 258-61.

H.J. Cook, 'The *A*-Text of the Greek Versions of the Book of Esther', *ZAW* 81 (1969), pp. 369-76.

J.L. Crenshaw, 'Methods in Determining Wisdom Influence upon "Historical" Literature', *JBL* 88 (1969), pp. 129-42.

D. Daube, 'The Last Chapter of Esther', *JQR* 37 (1946-47), pp. 139-47.

W. Dommershausen, *Die Estherrolle: Stil und Ziel einer alttestamentlichen Schrift* (Stuttgarter Biblische Monographien, 6; Stuttgart: Katholisches Bibelwerk, 1968). Cited as Dommershausen, *Estherrolle.*

—*Ester* (Die Neue Echter Bibel; Würzburg: Echter Verlag, 1980).

G.R. Driver, 'Problems and Solutions', *VT* 4 (1954), pp. 225-45 (= Moore, *Studies*, pp. 387-407).

—'Abbreviations in the Masoretic Text', *Textus* 1 (1960), pp. 112-31.

S.R. Driver, *Introduction to the Literature of the Old Testament* (9th edn; Edinburgh: T. and T. Clark, 1913).

J. Duchesne-Guillemin, 'Les noms des eunuques d'Assuérus', *Le Muséon* 66 (1953), pp. 105-108 (= Moore, *Studies*, pp. 273-76).

A.B. Ehrlich, *Randglossen zum hebräischen Bibel textkritisches, sprachliches, und sachliches* (Leipzig: J.C. Hinrichs, 1914).

O. Eissfeldt, *The Old Testament. A Introduction* (tr. P.R. Ackroyd; Oxford: Blackwell, 1966).

C.W. Emmett, '3 Maccabees', in *The Apocrypha and Pseudepigrapha of the Old Testament* (ed. R.H. Charles; Oxford: Clarendon, 1913), vol. 1, pp. 155-73.

G. Fohrer, *Introduction to the Old Testament* (tr. D. Green; London: SPCK, 1970).

M.V. Fox, 'The Structure of the Book of Esther', *Festschrift I.L. Seeligmann*, ed. A. Rofé (forthcoming).

O.F. Fritzsche, ΕΣΘΗP. *Duplicem libri textum ad optimos codices emendavit et cum selecta lectionis varietate edidit* (Zürich: Orel, 1848).

—*Kurzgefasstes exegetisches Handbuch zu den Apokryphen des Alten Testaments*, Lieferung 1 *Das dritte Buch Esra, die Zusätze zum Buch Esther und Daniel, das Gebet des Manasse, das Buch Baruch und der Brief des Jeremia* (Leipzig: Weidmann, 1851).

—*Libri Apocryphi Veteris Testamenti Graece* (Leipzig, 1871).

M. Gan, 'The Book of Esther in the Light of the Story of Joseph in Egypt' [Heb.], *Tarbiz* 31 (1961-62), pp. 144-49.

G. Gerleman, *Studien zu Esther. Stoff–Struktur–Stil–Sinn* (Biblische Studien, 48; Neukirchen-Vluyn: Neukirchener Verlag, 1966), pp. 1-48 (= Moore, *Studies*, pp. 308-49).

—*Esther* (Biblischer Kommentar. Altes Testament, 21; Neukirchen-Vluyn: Neukirchener Verlag, 1973). Cited as Gerleman, *Esther*.

W. Gesenius, E. Kautzsch, and A.E. Cowley, *Gesenius' Hebrew Grammar*, as edited and enlarged by the late E. Kautzsch; 2nd English edition revised by A.E. Cowley (Oxford: Clarendon, 1913).

D.W. Gooding, 'Ahab according to the Septuagint', *ZAW* 35 (1964), pp. 269-80.

—'Pedantic Timetabling in 3rd Book of Reigns', *VT* 15 (1965), pp. 153-66.

—'The Septuagint's Version of Solomon's Misconduct', *VT* 15 (1965), pp. 325-35.

R. Gordis, *Megillat Esther* (New York: The Rabbinical Assembly, 1972).

—'Studies in the Esther Narrative', *JBL* 95 (1976), pp. 43-58 (= Moore, *Studies*, pp. 408-23).

—'Religion, Wisdom and History in the Book of Esther—A New Solution to an Ancient Crux', *JBL* 100 (1981), pp. 359-88.

W.W. Grasham, 'The Theology of the Book of Esther', *Restoration Quarterly* 16 (1973), pp. 99-111.

J.A.F. Gregg, 'The Additions to Esther', in *The Apocrypha and Pseudepigrapha of the Old Testament* (ed. R.H. Charles; Oxford: Clarendon, 1913), vol. 1, pp. 665-84.

H. Gunkel, *Esther* (Religionsgeschichtliche Volksbücher, II/19-20; Tübingen: J.C.B. Mohr, 1916).

M. Haller, *Die fünf Megilloth* (Handbuch zum Alten Testament, 1/18; Tübingen: J.C.B. Mohr, 1940).

E. Hamel, 'Le Magnificat et le renversement des situations. Réflexion théologico-biblique', *Gregorianum* 60 (1979), pp. 55-84.

R. Hanhart, *Septuaginta. Vetus Testamentum graecum auctoritate academiae scientiarum gottingensis editum*, VIII, 3 (Göttingen: Vandenhoeck und Ruprecht, 1966; 2nd edn, 1983).

D. Harvey, 'Esther, Book of', *Interpreter's Dictionary of the Bible* (ed. G. Buttrick; Nashville: Abingdon, 1962), vol. 2, pp. 149-51.

E. Hatch and H.A. Redpath, *A Concordance to the Septuagint and other*

Greek versions of the Old Testament (including the Apocryphal books), 2 vols. (Oxford: Clarendon, 1897).

P. Haupt, 'Critical Notes on Esther', *AJSL* 24 (1907f.), pp. 97-186 (= Moore, *Studies*, pp. 1-90); also published in *Old Testament and Semitic Studies (William Rainey Harper Memorial Volume)*, II (1908), pp. 115-204.

J. Hoschander, *The Book of Esther in the Light of History* (Philadelphia: Dropsie College, 1923).

P. Humbert, 'Étendre la main (Note de lexicographie hébraïque)', *VT* 12 (1962), pp. 383-95.

W.L. Humphreys, 'A Life-Style for Diaspora: A Study of the Tales of Esther and Daniel', *JBL* 92 (1973), pp. 211-23.

B. Jacob, 'Das Buch Esther bei den LXX', *ZAW* 10 (1890), pp. 241-98.

B.W. Jones, 'Two Misconceptions about the Book of Esther', *CBQ* 39 (1977), pp. 171-81 (= Moore, *Studies*, pp. 437-47).

—'The So-Called Appendix to the Book of Esther', *Semitics* 6 (1978), pp. 36-43.

I. Katzellenbogen, *Das Buch Esther in der Aggada* (Diss. Würzburg, 1913).

K.F. Keil, *Manual of Historico-Critical Introduction to the Canonical Scriptures of the Old Testament* (tr. by G.C.M. Douglas from the Second German Edition; Edinburgh: T. & T. Clark, 1870).

M. Kessler, 'Inclusio in the Hebrew Bible', *Semitics* 6 (1978), pp. 44-49.

I.M. Kikawada, 'The Shape of Genesis 11:1-9', in *Rhetorical Criticism. Essays in Honor of James Muilenburg* (Pittsburgh Theological Monograph Series, 1; Pittsburgh: Pickwick, 1974), pp. 18-32.

P. de Lagarde, *Librorum Veteris Testamenti Canonicorum Pars Prior Graece* (Göttingen, 1883).

J. Langen, 'Die beiden griechischen Texte des Buches Esther', *TTQ* 42 (1860), pp. 244-72.

J.C.H. Lebram, 'Purimfest und Estherbuch', *VT* 22 (1972), pp. 208-222 (= Moore, *Studies*, pp. 205-219).

S.Z. Leiman, *The Talmudic and Midrashic Evidence for the Canonization of Hebrew Scripture* (PhD, Pennsylvania, 1970; Ann Arbor: University Microfilms 70-25,680, 1970).

J.A. Loader, 'Esther as a Novel with Different Levels of Meaning', *ZAW* 90 (1978), pp. 417-21.

S.E. Loewenstamm, 'Esther 9:29-32: The Genesis of a Late Addition', *HUCA* 42 (1971), pp. 117-24 (= Moore, *Studies*, pp. 227-34).

J. Magonet, 'The Liberal and the Lady: Esther Revisited', *Judaism* 29 (1980), pp. 167-76.

R.A. Martin, 'Syntax Criticism of the LXX Additions to the Book of Esther', *JBL* 94 (1975), pp. 65-72 (= Moore, *Studies*, pp. 595-602).

W. McKane, 'A Note on Esther IX and 1 Samuel XV', *JTS* 12 (1961), pp. 260-61 (= Moore, *Studies*, pp. 306-307).

A. Meinhold, 'Die Gattung der Josephsgeschichte und des Estherbuches:

Diasporanovelle II', *ZAW* 88 (1976), pp. 72-93 (= Moore, *Studies*, pp. 284-305).

—'Theologische Erwägungen zum Buch Esther', *TZ* 34 (1978), pp. 321-33.

—'Zu Aufbau und Mitte des Estherbuches', *VT* 23 (1983), pp. 435-45.

—*Das Buch Esther* (Zürcher Bibelkommentare, 13; Zürich: Theologischer Verlag, 1983).

J.D. Michaelis, *Deutsche Uebersetzung des Alten Testaments, mit Anmerkungen für Ungelehrte* (Göttingen: J.C. Dieterich, 1773-83).

C.H. Miller, 'Esther's Levels of Meaning', *ZAW* 92 (1980), pp. 145-48.

C.A. Moore, *The Greek Text of Esther* (PhD, Johns Hopkins, 1965; Ann Arbor: Microfilm-Xerox reprint, no. 65-6880, 1965).

—'A Greek Witness to a Different Hebrew Text of Esther', *ZAW* 79 (1967), pp. 351-58 (= Moore, *Studies*, pp. 521-28).

—*Esther* (Anchor Bible, 7B; Garden City, N.Y.: Doubleday, 1971). Cited as Moore, *Esther*.

—'On the Origin of the LXX Additions to the Book of Esther', *JBL* 92 (1973), pp. 382-93 (= Moore, *Studies*, pp. 583-94).

—*Daniel, Esther, and Jeremiah: The Additions* (Anchor Bible, 44; Garden City, N.Y.: Doubleday, 1977).

—*Studies in the Book of Esther* (New York: Ktav, 1982). Cited as Moore, *Studies*.

—'Esther Revisited: An Examination of Some Esther Studies over the Past Decade', *Festschrift for S. Iwry*, ed. A. Kort and S. Morschauer (Winona Lake: Eisenbraun, 1984) (forthcoming).

—'Esther Revisted Again: A Further Examination of Certain Esther Studies of the Past Ten Years', *HUCA* (Festschrift for Robert Gordis) (forthcoming).

G.W.E. Nickelsburg, *Resurrection, Immortality, and Eternal Life in Intertestamental Judaism* (Harvard Theological Studies, 26; Cambridge, Mass.: Harvard University Press, 1972).

—*Jewish Literature between the Bible and the Mishnah: A Historical and Literary Introduction* (London: SCM, 1981).

S. Niditch and R. Doran, 'The Success Story of the Wise Courtier: A Formal Approach', *JBL* 96 (1977), pp. 179-93.

L.B. Paton, *A Critical and Exegetical Commentary on the Book of Esther* (International Critical Commentary; Edinburgh: T. & T. Clark, 1908). Cited as Paton.

F. Perles, *Analekten zur Textkritik des Alten Testaments* (Munich: T. Ackermann, 1895).

R.H. Pfeiffer, *Introduction to the Old Testament* (London: A. and C. Black, 1952).

Y.T. Radday, 'Chiasm in Joshua, Judges and Others', *Linguistica Biblica* 3 (1973), pp. 6-13.

A. Rahlfs, *Septuaginta, id est Vetus Testamentum graece iuxta* LXX *interpretes*, 2 vols. (Stuttgart; Priviligierte Württembergische Bibelanstalt, 1935).

A. Raleigh, *The Book of Esther. Its Practical Lessons and Dramatic Scenes* (Edinburgh: A. and C. Black, 1880).

P. Riessler, 'Zu Rosenthals Aufsatz, Bd. XV, S. 278ff.', *ZAW* 16 (1896), p. 182.

H. Ringgren, 'Esther and Purim', *SEÅ* 20 (1956), pp. 5-24 (= Moore, *Studies*, pp. 185-204).

—*Esther*, in H. Ringgren and A. Weiser, *Das Hohe Lied, Klagelieder, Das Buch Esther* (Das Alte Testament Deutsch, 16; Göttingen: Vandenhoeck und Ruprecht, 1958). Cited as Ringgren, *Esther*.

L.A. Rosenthal, 'Die Josephsgeschichte mit den Büchern Ester und Daniel verglichen', *ZAW* 15 (1895), pp. 278-84 (= Moore, *Studies*, pp. 277-83).

—'Nochmals der Vergleich Ester, Joseph, Daniel', *ZAW* 17 (1897), pp. 125-28.

W. Rudolph, 'Textkritisches zum Estherbuch', *VT* 4 (1954), pp. 89-90.

V. Ryssel, 'Zusätze zum Buch Esther', in *Die Apokryphen und Pseudepigraphen des Alten Testaments*, ed. E. Kautzsch, vol. 1 (Tübingen: J.C.B. Mohr, 1900), pp. 193-212.

A. Scholz, *Commentar über das Buch 'Esther' mit seinen 'Zusätzen' und über 'Susanna'* (Würzburg: L. Woerl, 1892).

F.W. Schultz, *The Book of Esther* (A Commentary on the Holy Scriptures by J.P. Lange, tr. by P. Schaff, vol. 7 of the Old Testament; Edinburgh: T. and T. Clark, 1868).

S. Segert, 'Zur literarischen Form und Funktion der Fünf Megilloth', *ArOr* 35 (1965), pp. 451-62.

L. Soubigou, *Esther traduit et commenté* (2nd edn; La Sainte Bible; Paris: Cerf, 1952).

A. Sperber, *The Bible in Aramiac*, vol. IVA *The Hagiographa* (Leiden: E.J. Brill, 1968).

H. Steinthal, *Zu Bibel und Religionsphilosophie* (Berlin: G. Reimer, 1890).

C. Steuernagel, 'Das Buch Ester', in *Die Heilige Schrift des Alten Testaments* (ed. E.F. Kautzsch and A. Bertholet; Tübingen: J.C.B. Mohr, 1923), vol. 2, pp. 443-56.

Hans Striedl, 'Untersuchung zur Syntax und Stilistik des hebräischen Buches Esther', *ZAW* 55 (1937), pp. 73-108.

F. Stummer, *Das Buch Esther* (Echter-Bibel, 2; 2nd edn, Würzburg: Echter Verlag, 1956), pp. 555-87.

H.B. Swete, *An Introduction to the Old Testament in Greek* (Cambridge: Cambridge University Press, 1900).

—*The Old Testament in Greek* (Cambridge: Cambridge University Press, 1905), vol. 2.

S. Talmon, 'Wisdom in the Book of Esther', *VT* 13 (1963), pp. 419-55.

C.C. Torrey, 'The Older Book of Esther', *HTR* 37 (1944), pp. 1-40 (= Moore, *Studies*, pp. 448-87).

E. Tov, 'The "Lucianic" Text of the Canonical and the Apocryphal Sections of Esther. A Rewritten Biblical Book', *Textus* 10 (1982), pp. 1-25.

—'Criteria for Evaluating Textual Readings: The Limitations of Textual Rules', *HTR* 75 (1982), pp. 429-48.

J. Usher, *De Graeca Septuaginta interpretum versione syntagma: cum libri Estherae editione Origenica, et vetere Graeca altera, ex Arundelliana bibliotheca nunc primum in lucem producta* (London: J. Crook, 1655).

A. Weiser, *Introduction to the Old Testament* (tr. D.M. Barton; London: Darton, Longman and Todd, 1961).

M. Weiss, 'Einiges über die Bauformen des Erzählens in der Bibel', *VT* 13 (1963), pp. 456-74.

R. Wellek and A. Warren, *Theory of Literature* (3rd edn; Harmondsworth: Penguin, 1963).

R.N. Whybray, *The Intellectual Tradition in the Old Testament* (Beiheft zur Zeitschrift für die alttestamentliche Wissenschaft, 135; Berlin: W. de Gruyter, 1974).

G. Wildeboer, *Das Buch Esther* (Kurzer Hand-Commentar zum Alten Testament, 17; Tübingen: J.C.B. Mohr, 1898). Cited as Wildeboer.

H.G.M. Williamson, *1 and 2 Chronicles* (New Century Bible; London: Marshall, Morgan and Scott, 1982).

T. Witton Davies, *Ezra, Nehemiah and Esther* (Century Bible; Edinburgh: T.C. & E.C. Jack, 1909). Cited as Witton Davies.

E. Würthwein, *Die Fünf Megilloth* (HAT, 18; 2nd edn, Tübingen: J.C.B. Mohr, 1969). (The introduction to Esther [pp. 165-74] is the work of Würthwein, the translation and commentary being a revision of M. Haller's first edition.)

ABBREVIATIONS

AB	Anchor Bible
ABR	*Australian Biblical Review*
ArOr	*Archiv Orientalní*
ASTI	*Annual of the Swedish Theological Institute*
AT	A-text of Esther (see Chapter 7)
AV	Authorised Version (King James Version)
BDB	F. Brown, S.R. Driver, and C.A. Briggs (eds.), *A Hebrew and English Lexicon of the Old Testament* (Cambridge, 1907)
BH³	*Biblia Hebraica* (3rd edn; ed. R. Kittel; Stuttgart, 1937)
CBQ	*Catholic Biblical Quarterly*
HAT	Handbuch zum Alten Testament
HTR	*Harvard Theological Review*
HUCA	*Hebrew Union College Annual*
IB	*The Interpreter's Bible* (ed. G.A. Buttrick; Nashville, 1951-57)
JB	Jerusalem Bible
JBL	*Journal of Biblical Literature*
JEOL	*Jaarbericht Ex Oriente Lux*
JQR	*Jewish Quarterly Review*
JR	*Journal of Religion*
JTS	*Journal of Theological Studies*
K	Kethiv (consonantal text)
KB	L. Koehler and W. Baumgartner, *Lexicon in Veteris Testamenti Libros* (Leiden, 1953)
KB³	W. Baumgartner *et al.* (eds.), *Hebräisches und aramäisches Lexikon zum Alten Testament* (Leiden, 1967–)
LXX	Septuagint; B-text of Esther
MT	Masoretic text
NAB	New American Bible
NEB	New English Bible
OTS	*Oudtestamentische Studiën*
Q	Qere (text read)
RB	*Revue Biblique*
RSV	Revised Standard Version
SBL	Society of Biblical Literature
SEÅ	*Svensk Exegetisk Årsbok*

THWAT	*Theologisches Handwörterbuch zum Alten Testament* (ed. E. Jenni and C. Westermann; Munich, 1971-76)
TTQ	*Tübinger Theologische Quartalschrift*
TZ	*Theologische Zeitschrift*
VT	*Vetus Testamentum*
ZAW	*Zeitschrift für die alttestamentliche Wissenschaft*

THE GREEK ESTHER ACCORDING TO THE A-TEXT

Text & Translation

The *text* is not intended to be a critical edition, but is reprinted from *The Old Testament in Greek*, ed. A.E. Brooke, N. McLean and H.StJ. Thackeray (Cambridge, 1940), Vol. III, Part I, pp. 32-42. That text itself had been reprinted without alteration from that of P.A. de Lagarde, *Librorum Veteris Testamenti Canonicorum Pars Prior Graece* (Göttingen, 1883). On p. 248 I have noted all those places where the text printed by R. Hanhart, *Septuaginta. Vetus Testamentum Graece. Auctoritate Academiae Scientiarum Gottingensis editum*, VIII, 3, *Esther* (2nd edn, Göttingen, 1983) differs from the present text—punctuation and orthographic matters apart.

The *translation* is meant to be reasonably literal. In the Additions, the wording of the RSV's 'The Additions to the Book of Esther' has been followed as closely as possible; any deviation from the RSV wording in these sections represents a difference between the A-text (AT) and the text of the LXX (the B-text or 'Septuagint'). The Additions are distinguished from the basic narrative by being further indented from the left-hand margin.

The *verse-numbering* follows the Larger Cambridge (Brooke-McLean) edition; in Hanhart's edition the chapter number is always one less, because he does not count Addition A as ch. 1.

ΕΣΘΗΡ Α

Α

¹ Ἔτους δευτέρου βασιλεύοντος Ἀσσυήρου τοῦ μεγάλου, μιᾷ τοῦ μηνὸς Αδαρ Νισαν (ὅς ἐστι Δύστρος Ξανθικός), ἐνύπνιον εἶδε Μαρδοχαῖος ὁ τοῦ Ἰαείρου τοῦ Σεμεΐου τοῦ Κισαίου τῆς φυλῆς Βενιαμιν, ἄνθρωπος

2 μέγας ² τῆς αἰχμαλωσίας ἧς ᾐχμαλώτευσε Ναβουχοδονοσορ ὁ βασιλεὺς Βαβυλῶνος μετὰ Ἰεχονίου τοῦ

3 βασιλέως τῆς Ἰουδαίας. ³ καὶ τοῦτο ἦν αὐτοῦ τὸ ἐνύπνιον. καὶ ἰδοὺ φωνὴ καὶ κραυγὴ θορύβου, βρονταὶ καὶ

4 σεισμὸς καὶ τάραχος ἐπὶ τῆς γῆς. ⁴ καὶ ἰδοὺ δύο

5 δράκοντες, καὶ προσῆλθον ἀμφότεροι παλαίειν. ⁵ καὶ ἐγένετο αὐτῶν φωνή, καὶ ἐταράσσετο πάντα ἀπὸ τῆς

6 φωνῆς τῆς κραυγῆς ταύτης. ⁶ μαρτυρομένη πᾶσι τοῖς λαοῖς ἡμέρα σκότους καὶ γνόφου καὶ ταραχὴ πολέμου, καὶ ἡτοιμάσατο πᾶν ἔθνος πολεμῆσαι, καὶ ἀνεβοήσαμεν

7 πρὸς κύριον ἀπὸ φωνῆς τῆς κραυγῆς αὐτῶν. ⁷ καὶ ἐγένετο ἐκ πηγῆς μικρᾶς ὕδωρ πολύ, ποταμὸς μέγας·

8 ⁸ φῶς, ἥλιος ἀνέτειλε, καὶ οἱ ποταμοὶ ὑψώθησαν καὶ

9 κατέπιον τοὺς ἐνδόξους. ⁹ καὶ ἀναστὰς Μαρδοχαῖος ἐκ τοῦ ὕπνου αὐτοῦ, ἐμερίμνα τί τὸ ἐνύπνιον καὶ τί ὁ

10 δυνατὸς ἑτοιμάζει ποιῆσαι. ¹⁰ καὶ τὸ ἐνύπνιον αὐτοῦ κεκρυμμένον ἦν ἐν τῇ καρδίᾳ αὐτοῦ, καὶ ἐν παντὶ καιρῷ

11 ἦν ἀναζητῶν αὐτό· ¹¹ ἐπίκρισις διασαφηθήσεται αὐτῷ ἕως τῆς ἡμέρας ἧς ὕπνωσε Μαρδοχαῖος ἐν τῇ αὐλῇ τοῦ βασιλέως μετὰ Ασταου καὶ Θεδεύτου τῶν δύο εὐνούχων

12 τοῦ βασιλέως. ¹² καὶ ἤκουσε τοὺς λόγους αὐτῶν καὶ τὰς διαβολὰς αὐτῶν, ὡς ἐξηγοῦντο τοῦ ἐπιθέσθαι Ἀσσυ-

THE GREEK ESTHER ACCORDING TO THE A-TEXT

A ¹ In the second year of the reign of Ahasuerus the Great, on the first day of the month Adar-Nisan (that is, Dystros-Xanthikos), Mordecai the son of Jair, son of Shimei, son of Kish, of the tribe of Benjamin, had a
² dream. He was a great man, ² from among the captives taken by Nebuchadnezzar king of Babylon with Jeconiah
³ king of Judea. ³ And this was his dream:

Behold, a noise and the sound of confusion, thunders
⁴ and earthquake and tumult upon the earth! ⁴ And behold,
⁵ two dragons, who came forward to fight! ⁵ Their cry was heard, and everything was troubled by the sound of this
⁶ cry. ⁶ There was witnessed by all nations a day of darkness and gloom and a tumult of battle; and every nation made ready for war. And we cried to the Lord
⁷ because of the sound of their cry. ⁷ And there came from
⁸ a little fountain abundant water, a great river. ⁸ Light, the sun, arose; and the rivers were exalted, and they swallowed up those held in honour.

⁹ ⁹ When Mordecai arose from his sleep, he pondered over the meaning of his dream, and over what the Mighty
¹⁰ One was preparing to do. ¹⁰ His dream was hidden in his heart, and at every opportunity he kept seeking to under-
¹¹ stand it. ¹¹ The interpretation would become plain to him upon the day when Mordecai slept in the king's courtyard beside Astaos and Thedeutes the two eunuchs
¹² of the king. ¹² He overheard their words and their plots, how they were planning to lay hands on Ahasuerus the

13 ἤρῳ τῷ βασιλεῖ τοῦ ἀνελεῖν αὐτόν. ¹³ εὖ δὲ φρονήσας ὁ
14 Μαρδοχαῖος ἀπήγγειλε περὶ αὐτῶν. ¹⁴ καὶ ἤτασεν ὁ
βασιλεὺς τοὺς δύο εὐνούχους, καὶ εὗρε τοὺς λόγους
Μαρδοχαίου. καὶ ὁμολογήσαντες οἱ εὐνοῦχοι ἀπήχ-
15 θησαν. ¹⁵ καὶ ἔγραψεν Ἀσσυῆρος ὁ βασιλεὺς περὶ τῶν
λόγων τούτων. καὶ ἐγράφη Μαρδοχαῖος ἐν τῷ βιβλίῳ
τοῦ βασιλέως περὶ τοῦ μνημονεύειν τῶν λόγων τούτων.
16 ¹⁶ καὶ ἐνετείλατο ὁ βασιλεὺς περὶ τοῦ Μαρδοχαίου, θεραπεύειν αὐτὸν ἐν τῇ αὐλῇ τοῦ βασιλέως καὶ πᾶσαν θύραν
17 ἐπιφανῶς τηρεῖν, ¹⁷ καὶ ἔδωκεν αὐτῷ περὶ τούτων Αμαν
Ἀμαδάθου Μακεδόνα κατὰ πρόσωπον τοῦ βασιλέως.
18 ¹⁸ καὶ ἐζήτει ὁ Αμαν κακοποιῆσαι τὸν Μαρδοχαῖον καὶ
πάντα τὸν λαὸν αὐτοῦ ὑπὲρ τοῦ λελαληκέναι αὐτὸν τῷ
βασιλεῖ περὶ τῶν εὐνούχων, δι' ὅτι ἀνῃρέθησαν.
2 ¹ καὶ ἐγένετο μετὰ τοὺς λόγους τούτους ἐν ἡμέραις
Ἀσσυήρου τοῦ βασιλέως τοῦ μεγάλου, ὑπετάγησαν αὐτῷ
ἀπὸ τῆς Ἰνδικῆς ἕως τῆς Αἰθιοπίας ἑκατὸν εἴκοσι ἑπτὰ
2 χῶραι. ² ἐν τῷ καθῆσθαι Ἀσσυῆρον ἐπὶ τοῦ θρόνου τῆς
3 βασιλείας αὐτοῦ, ³ καὶ ἐποίησεν ὁ βασιλεὺς πότον τοῖς
ἄρχουσι τῆς αὐλῆς Περσῶν καὶ Μήδων, καὶ οἱ ἄρχοντες τῶν
4 χωρῶν κατὰ πρόσωπον αὐτοῦ, ⁴ εἰς τὸ ἐπιδειχθῆναι τὸν
πλοῦτον τῆς δόξης τοῦ βασιλέως καὶ τὴν τιμὴν τῆς καυχήσεως
5 αὐτοῦ ἐπὶ ὀγδοήκοντα καὶ ἑκατὸν ἡμέρας, ⁵ ἕως ἀνεπληρώ-
θησαν αἱ ἡμέραι ἃς ἐποίησεν ὁ βασιλεὺς πᾶσι τοῖς εὑρεθεῖσιν
ἐν Σούσοις τῇ πόλει ἀπὸ μεγάλου ἕως μικροῦ, πότον ἐν
ἡμέραις ἑπτὰ ἔνδον ἐν τῇ αὐλῇ τοῦ βασιλέως, ἄγων τὰ
6 σωτήρια αὐτοῦ. ⁶ ἦν δὲ ἐξεστρωμένα βύσσινα καὶ καρπάσινα
καὶ ὑακίνθινα καὶ κόκκινα ἐμπεπλεγμένα ἐν ἄνθεσιν, καὶ
σκηνὴ τεταμένη ἐν σχοινίοις βυσσίνοις καὶ πορφυροῖς ἐπὶ
κύβοις ἀργυροῖς καὶ στύλοις παρίνοις καὶ περιχρύσοις, καὶ
κλῖναι χρυσαῖ ἐπὶ λιθόστρωτον σμαράγδου, καὶ κύκλῳ ῥόδα,
7 ⁷ καὶ ποτήρια χρυσᾶ ἔξαλλα καὶ οἶνος βασιλικὸς ὃν ὁ
8 βασιλεὺς πίνει, ⁸ καὶ πότος κατὰ τὸν νόμον. οὕτως γὰρ
9 ἐπέταξεν ὁ βασιλεὺς ποιῆσαι τὸ θέλημα τῶν ἀνθρώπων. ⁹ καὶ
Ουαστιν ἡ βασίλισσα ἐποίησε δοχὴν μεγάλην πάσαις ταῖς
10 γυναιξὶν ἐν τῇ αὐλῇ τοῦ βασιλέως. ¹⁰ ἐγένετο δὲ τῇ ἡμέρᾳ τῇ
ἑβδόμῃ ἐν τῷ εὐφρανθῆναι τὸν βασιλέα ἐν τῷ οἴνῳ εἶπεν ὁ

13 king to put him to death. [13] But Mordecai, being well
disposed [to the king], made a report concerning them.
14 [14] Then the king examined the two eunuchs and found
the words of Mordecai [to be true]. And when the
15 eunuchs confessed they were led to execution. [15] Ahasuerus
the king made a written record of these matters; and
Mordecai['s name] was written in the king's book in order
16 that these matters should be remembered. [16] And the
king gave command concerning Mordecai that he should
serve in the king's court and should keep watch conspic-
17 uously on every door. [17] And he gave him, because of
these things, Haman the son of Hammedatha, a Mace-
18 donian, who stood before the king; [18] and Haman sought
to injure Mordecai and all his people because he had
spoken about the eunuchs to the king, so that they were
executed.

2 [1] And it came to pass after these things, in the days of
Ahasuerus the great king, that one hundred and twenty-seven
2 lands were subject to him, from India to Ethiopia. [2] When
3 Ahasuerus sat upon his royal throne, [3] the king made a feast for
the chief officers of his court, from the Persians and Medes.
4 And the rulers of the lands [came] before him, [4] so that they
could be shown the wealth of the king's splendour, and the
honour in which he boasted—for one hundred and eighty days
5 [5] until the days were completed, which the king had made, for
all those in the city of Susa from the greatest to the least, a
banquet for seven days within the royal court, to celebrate his
6 deliverance. [6] There were hangings of linen and flax and blue
and scarlet cloth interwoven with flowers, and an awning was
spread taut by linen and purple cords to silver blocks and gilt
marble columns. There were golden couches upon a pavement
7 of emerald and roses in a circle. [7] The drinking-vessels were of
gold, each different from the other, and the wine was royal wine
8 which the king drinks, [8] and drinking was according to the law—
for the king had ordered that whatever the people should wish
was to be done.
9 [9] And Vashti the queen gave a great reception for all the
10 ladies in the king's court. [10] And on the seventh day, when the

11   βασιλεὺς τοῖς παισὶν αὐτοῦ [11] ἀγαγεῖν Ουαστιν τὴν βασί-
      λισσαν εἰς τὸ συνεστηκὸς συμπόσιον ἐν τῷ διαδήματι τῆς
12   βασιλείας αὐτῆς κατὰ πρόσωπον τῆς στρατιᾶς αὐτοῦ. [12] καὶ
      οὐκ ἠθέλησεν Ουαστιν ποιῆσαι τὸ θέλημα τοῦ βασιλέως διὰ
      χειρὸς τῶν εὐνούχων. ὡς δὲ ἤκουσεν ὁ βασιλεὺς ὅτι
      ἠκύρωσεν Ουαστιν τὴν βουλὴν αὐτοῦ, ἐλυπήθη σφόδρα, καὶ
13   ὀργὴ ἐξεκαύθη ἐν αὐτῷ. [13] καὶ εἶπεν ὁ βασιλεὺς πᾶσι τοῖς
      σοφοῖς τοῖς εἰδόσι νόμον καὶ κρίσιν τί ποιῆσαι τῇ βασιλίσσῃ
      περὶ τοῦ μὴ τεθεληκέναι αὐτὴν ποιῆσαι τὸ θέλημα τοῦ
14   βασιλέως. [14] καὶ προσῆλθον πρὸς αὐτὸν οἱ ἄρχοντες Περσῶν
      καὶ Μήδων καὶ οἱ ὁρῶντες τὸ πρόσωπον τοῦ βασιλέως καὶ οἱ
16   καθήμενοι ἐν τοῖς βασιλείοις. [16] καὶ παρεκάλεσεν αὐτὸν
      Βουγαῖος λέγων Οὐ τὸν βασιλέα μόνον ἠδίκηκεν Ουαστιν ἡ
      βασίλισσα, ἀλλὰ καὶ τοὺς ἄρχοντας Περσῶν καὶ Μήδων· καὶ
      εἰς πάντας τοὺς λαοὺς ἡ ἀδικία αὐτῆς ἐξῆλθεν, ὅτι ἠκύρωσε
18   τὸ πρόσταγμα τοῦ βασιλέως. [18] εἰ δοκεῖ οὖν τῷ κυρίῳ ἡμῶν,
      καὶ ἀρεστὸν τῷ φρονήματι αὐτοῦ, γραφήτω εἰς πάσας τὰς
      χώρας καὶ πρὸς πάντα τὰ ἔθνη, καὶ γνωσθήτω ἠθετηκυῖα τὸν
      λόγον τοῦ βασιλέως Ουαστιν, ἡ δὲ βασιλεία δοθήτω ἄλλῃ,
20   κρείττονι οὔσῃ αὐτῆς. [20] καὶ φαινέσθω ὑπακούουσα τῆς
      φωνῆς τοῦ βασιλέως, καὶ ποιήσει ἀγαθὸν πάσαις ταῖς
      βασιλείαις, καὶ πᾶσαι αἱ γυναῖκες δώσουσι τιμὴν καὶ δόξαν
21   τοῖς ἀνδράσιν αὐτῶν ἀπὸ πτωχῶν ἕως πλουσίων. [21] καὶ
      ἀγαθὸς ὁ λόγος ἐν καρδίᾳ τοῦ βασιλέως, καὶ ἐποίησεν
      ἑτοίμως κατὰ τὸν λόγον τοῦτον.

3   [1] καὶ οὕτως ἔστη τοῦ μνημονεύειν τῆς Ουαστιν καὶ ὧν
2   ἐποίησεν Ἀσσυήρῳ τῷ βασιλεῖ. [2] καὶ εἶπον οἱ λειτουργοὶ τοῦ
      βασιλέως Ζητήσωμεν παρθένους καλὰς τῷ εἴδει, καὶ δοθή-
      τωσαν προστατεῖσθαι ὑπὸ χεῖρα Γωγαίου τοῦ εὐνούχου τοῦ
4   φύλακος τῶν γυναικῶν. [4] καὶ ἡ παῖς ἣ ἐὰν ἀρέσῃ τῷ βασιλεῖ,
      κατασταθήσεται ἀντὶ Ουαστιν. καὶ ἐποίησαν ἑτοίμως κατὰ
5   ταῦτα. [5] καὶ ἀνὴρ Ἰουδαῖος ἐν Σούσοις τῇ πόλει ᾧ ὄνομα
      Μαρδοχαῖος υἱὸς Ἰαείρου τοῦ Σεμεΐου τοῦ Κεισαίου τῆς
7   φυλῆς Βενιαμιν. [7] καὶ ἦν ἐκτρέφων πιστῶς τὴν Εσθηρ
      θυγατέρα ἀδελφοῦ τοῦ πατρὸς αὐτοῦ. καὶ ἦν ἡ παῖς καλὴ τῷ
8   εἴδει σφόδρα καὶ ὡραία τῇ ὄψει. [8] καὶ ἐλήμφθη τὸ κοράσιον
      εἰς τὸν οἶκον τοῦ βασιλέως· καὶ εἶδε Βουγαῖος ὁ εὐνοῦχος ὁ

11 king was merry with wine, the king told his servants [11] to bring
Vashti the queen with her royal crown to the banquet that was
12 in progress [to appear] before his army. [12] But Vashti was not
willing to do what the king had desired of her through the
eunuchs. When the king heard that Vashti had refused his
demand, he was greatly vexed, and his anger burned in him.
13 [13] The king asked all his wise men who knew custom and law
what was to be done to the queen for refusing to do the king's
14 will. [14] And there came to him the chiefs of the Persians and
Medes, and those who were the king's intimates (lit. saw the
face of the king) and those who were officials in the palace.
16 [16] And Bougaios advised him, saying, 'It is not only the king
whom Vashti the queen has wronged, but also the leaders of the
Persians and Medes. Indeed, her wrongdoing, that she refused
the command of the king, has been reported to all peoples.
18 [18] Therefore if it seems good to our lord and is pleasing to his
mind, let a letter be written to all lands and to all peoples, and
let it be known that Vashti has refused the command of the
king; and let the royal position be given to another who is better
20 than she, [20] and let her be shown to be obedient to the king's
voice. [The king] will do a benefit to all kingdoms, and all
women will give honour and respect to their husbands—from
21 poor to rich.' [21] And the speech was good in the king's mind,
and he readily did accordingly.
3   [1] And so he ceased to remember Vashti and what she had
2 done to Ahasuerus the king. [2] And the servants of the king said,
'Let us seek beautiful maidens, and let them be put into the
care of Gogaios the eunuch who is in charge of the women.
4 [4] And whichever girl pleases the king shall take the place of
Vashti.' And they readily did so.
5   [5] There was a Jew in the city of Susa named Mordecai, son of
7 Jair, son of Shimei, son of Kish, of the tribe of Benjamin. [7] And
he was faithfully bringing up his uncle's daughter, Esther. The
8 maiden was very beautiful and lovely to behold. [8] And the
maiden was taken into the king's palace; and Bougaios the

φυλάσσων τὸ κοράσιον, καὶ ἤρεσεν αὐτῷ ὑπὲρ πάσας τὰς

9   γυναῖκας. ⁹ καὶ εὗρεν Εσθηρ χάριν καὶ ἔλεον κατὰ πρόσωπον
αὐτοῦ, καὶ ἔσπευσε προστατῆσαι αὐτῆς, καὶ ἐπέδωκεν ὑπὲρ
τὰ ἑπτὰ κοράσια, τὰς ἄβρας αὐτῆς. ὡς δὲ εἰσήχθη Εσθηρ πρὸς

14 τὸν βασιλέα, ἤρεσεν αὐτῷ σφόδρα. ¹⁴ καὶ ὅταν ἐγένετο

17 ἑσπέρα, εἰσήγετο, καὶ τὸ πρωῒ ἀπελύετο. ¹⁷ ὡς δὲ κατ-
εμάνθανεν ὁ βασιλεὺς πάσας τὰς παρθένους, ἐφάνη ἐπιφανεστάτη Εσθηρ. καὶ εὗρε χάριν καὶ ἔλεον κατὰ πρόσωπον
αὐτοῦ, καὶ ἐπέθηκε τὸ διάδημα τῆς βασιλείας ἐπὶ τὴν

18 κεφαλὴν αὐτῆς. ¹⁸ καὶ ἤγαγεν ὁ βασιλεὺς τὸν γάμον τῆς
Εσθηρ ἐπιφανῶς, καὶ ἐποίησεν ἀφέσεις πάσαις ταῖς χώραις.

4   ¹ καὶ ἐγένετο μετὰ τοὺς λόγους τούτους, ἐμεγάλυνεν ὁ
βασιλεὺς Ἀσσυῆρος Αμαν Αμαδάθου Βουγαῖον, καὶ ἐπῆρεν
αὐτόν, καὶ ἔθηκε τὸν θρόνον αὐτοῦ ὑπὲρ ἄνω τῶν φίλων
αὐτοῦ, ὥστε κάμπτεσθαι καὶ προσκυνεῖν αὐτῷ ἐπὶ τὴν γῆν

2   πάντας. ² πάντων οὖν προσκυνούντων αὐτῷ κατὰ τὸ πρόσ-

3   ταγμα τοῦ βασιλέως, Μαρδοχαῖος οὐ προσεκύνει αὐτῷ. ³ καὶ
εἶδον οἱ παῖδες τοῦ βασιλέως ὅτι ὁ Μαρδοχαῖος οὐ προσκυνεῖ
τὸν Αμαν, καὶ εἶπον οἱ παῖδες τοῦ βασιλέως πρὸς τὸν
Μαρδοχαῖον Τί σὺ παρακούεις τοῦ βασιλέως καὶ οὐ

4   προσκυνεῖς τὸν Αμαν; ⁴ καὶ ἀπήγγειλεν αὐτοῖς ὅτι Ἰουδαῖός

5   ἐστιν. καὶ ἀπήγγειλαν περὶ αὐτοῦ τῷ Αμαν. ⁵ ὡς δὲ ἤκουσεν
Αμαν, ἐθυμώθη τῷ Μαρδοχαίῳ, καὶ ὀργὴ ἐξεκαύθη ἐν αὐτῷ,
καὶ ἐζήτει ἀνελεῖν τὸν Μαρδοχαῖον καὶ πάντα τὸν λαὸν

6   αὐτοῦ ἐν ἡμέρᾳ μιᾷ. ⁶ καὶ παραζηλώσας ὁ Αμαν καὶ κινηθεὶς
ἐν παντὶ τῷ θυμῷ αὐτοῦ ἐρυθρὸς ἐγένετο, ἐκτρέπων αὐτὸν ἐξ
ὀφθαλμῶν αὐτοῦ, καὶ καρδίᾳ φαύλῃ ἐλάλει τῷ βασιλεῖ κακὰ

8   περὶ Ισραηλ ⁸ λέγων Ἔστι λαὸς διεσπαρμένος ἐν πάσαις ταῖς
βασιλείαις, λαὸς πολέμου καὶ ἀπειθής, ἔξαλλα νόμιμα ἔχων,
τοῖς δὲ νομίμοις σου, βασιλεῦ, οὐ προσέχουσι, γνωριζόμενοι
ἐν πᾶσι τοῖς ἔθνεσι πονηροὶ ὄντες, καὶ τὰ προστάγματά σου

9   ἀθετοῦσι πρὸς καθαίρεσιν τῆς δόξης σου. ⁹ εἰ δοκεῖ οὖν τῷ
βασιλεῖ, καὶ ἀγαθὴ ἡ κρίσις ἐν καρδίᾳ αὐτοῦ, δοθήτω μοι τὸ
ἔθνος εἰς ἀπώλειαν, καὶ διαγράψω εἰς τὸ γαζοφυλάκιον

11 ἀργυρίου τάλαντα μύρια. ¹¹ καὶ εἶπεν αὐτῷ ὁ βασιλεὺς Τὸ

10 μὲν ἀργύριον ἔχε, τῷ δὲ ἔθνει χρῶ ὡς ἄν σοι ἀρεστὸν ᾖ. ¹⁰ καὶ
περιείλετο ὁ βασιλεὺς τὸ δακτύλιον ἀπὸ τῆς χειρὸς αὐτοῦ καὶ

eunuch, who was in charge, saw the maiden, and she pleased

9   him beyond all the women. ⁹ Esther found favour and mercy in his eyes, and he hastened to take charge of her, and gave her, beyond the seven attendants, her own handmaids. And when

14   Esther was taken to the king, she pleased him greatly. ¹⁴ When evening came, she would be taken to him, and in the morning

17   she would leave. ¹⁷ And when the king had examined all the maidens, Esther proved the most outstanding. She found favour and mercy in his sight, and he set the royal crown upon

18   her head. ¹⁸ And the king married Esther in all splendour, and he gave remissions to all lands.

4   ¹ And it came to pass after these things that King Ahasuerus promoted Haman the son of Hammedatha the Bougaean, and exalted him, and set his seat above his colleagues, so that all should bow and prostrate themselves to the ground before him.

2   ² Now when all were prostrating themselves before him according to the command of the king, Mordecai did not

3   prostrate himself before him. ³ When the servants of the king saw that Mordecai was not doing prostration before Haman, the servants of the king said to Mordecai, 'Why do you transgress against the king and do not do obeisance to Haman?'

4   ⁴ He told them that he was a Jew. And they made a report

5   about him to Haman. ⁵ When Haman heard, he was angry against Mordecai, and his wrath burned in him, and he sought

6   to destroy Mordecai and all his people on one day. ⁶ Haman, being provoked and disturbed with all his spirit, became red [in the face], ordering him out of his sight. And with evil intention

8   he spoke evil words to the king concerning Israel, ⁸ saying, 'There is a people scattered among all kingdoms, a warlike and disobedient people, with their own strange laws, who do not obey your laws, O king; they are reckoned by all nations to be wicked, and they set at naught your commands in order to

9   diminish your glory. ⁹ Therefore, if it seems good to the king, and the decision is good to his mind, let the people be given to me for destruction, and I will pay into the treasury ten

11   thousand silver talents.' ¹¹ The king said to him, 'Keep the

10   money, but do to the people whatever pleases you'. ¹⁰ And the

ἔδωκε τῷ Αμαν λέγων Γράφε εἰς πάσας τὰς χώρας, καὶ
σφραγίζου τῷ δακτυλίῳ τοῦ βασιλέως· οὐ γὰρ ἔστιν ὃς

7 ἀποστρέψει τὴν σφραγῖδα. ⁷ καὶ ἐπορεύθη Αμαν πρὸς τοὺς
θεοὺς αὐτοῦ τοῦ ἐπιγνῶναι ἡμέραν θανάτου αὐτῶν. καὶ
βάλλει κλήρους εἰς τὴν τρισκαιδεκάτην τοῦ μηνὸς Αδαρ
Νισαν φονεύειν πάντας τοὺς Ἰουδαίους ἀπὸ ἀρσενικοῦ ἕως

13 θηλυκοῦ καὶ διαρπάζειν τὰ νήπια. ¹³ καὶ ἔσπευσε καὶ ἔδωκεν
εἰς χεῖρας τρεχόντων ἱππέων.

B ¹⁴ καὶ ὑπέγραψε τὴν ὑποτεταγμένην ἐπιστολήν·
Βασιλεὺς μέγας Ἀσσυῆρος τοῖς ἀπὸ τῆς Ἰνδικῆς ἕως
τῆς Αἰθιοπίας ἑκατὸν καὶ εἴκοσι καὶ ἑπτὰ χωρῶν

15 ἄρχουσι καὶ σατράπαις τάδε γράφει· ¹⁵ πολλῶν ἐπάρξας
ἐθνῶν καὶ πάσης ἐπικρατήσας τῆς οἰκουμένης ἐβουλ-
ήθην—μὴ τῷ θράσει τῆς ἐξουσίας ἐπαιρόμενος, ἐπι-
εικέστερον δὲ καὶ μετὰ ἠπιότητος ἀεὶ διεξάγων—τοὺς
τῶν ὑποτεταγμένων ἀταράχους διὰ παντὸς καταστῆσαι
βίους, τὴν δὲ βασιλείαν ἥμερον καὶ πορευτὴν ἄχρι
περάτων παρεχόμενος, ἀνανεώσασθαι τὴν πᾶσιν ἀνθ-

16 ρώποις ποθουμένην εἰρήνην. ¹⁶ πυνθανομένου δέ μου
τῶν συμβούλων πῶς ἂν ἀχθείη τοῦτο ἐπὶ πέρας, ὁ
σωφροσύνῃ παρ' ἡμῖν διενηνοχώς, εὐνοίᾳ ἀπαραλ-
λάκτῳ καὶ βεβαίᾳ πίστει τὸ δεύτερον τῶν βασιλειῶν
γέρας ἀπενεγκάμενος Αμαν ὑπέδειξεν ἡμῖν πάροικον ἐν
πάσαις ταῖς κατὰ τὴν οἰκουμένην φυλαῖς ἀναμεμῖχθαι
δυσμενῆ τινὰ λαόν, τοῖς μὲν νόμοις ἀντιδικοῦντα πρὸς
πᾶν ἔθνος, τὰ δὲ τῶν βασιλέων παραπέμποντα διηνεκῶς
προστάγματα πρὸς τὸ μηδέποτε τὴν βασιλείαν εὐ-

17 σταθείας τυγχάνειν. ¹⁷ διειληφότες οὖν μονώτατον τὸ
ἔθνος ἐν ἀντιπαραγωγῇ παντὸς κείμενον τῶν ἀνθρώπων
διὰ τῶν νόμων ξενίζουσαν παραγωγήν, καὶ δυσνοοῦν
τοῖς ἡμετέροις προστάγμασιν ἀεὶ τὰ χείριστα συντελεῖν
κακὰ πρὸς τὸ μηδέποτε κατατίθεσθαι τῇ ὑφ' ἡμῶν
κατευθυνομένῃ μοναρχίᾳ, ¹⁸ προστετάχαμεν οὖν ὑμῖν

18 τοὺς σημαινομένους ὑμῖν ἐν τοῖς γεγραμμένοις ὑπὸ
Αμαν τοῦ τεταγμένου ἐπὶ τῶν πραγμάτων καὶ δευτέρου
πατρὸς ἡμῶν ὁλορριζους ἀπολέσαι σὺν γυναιξὶ καὶ
τέκνοις ταῖς τῶν ἐχθρῶν μαχαίραις ἄνευ παντὸς οἴκτου

king took the ring from his finger and gave it to Haman, saying, 'Write to all lands, and seal [the letter] with the king's ring. For

7 there is none who will reject the [king's] seal.' [7] Haman went to his gods to learn the day of their death. And he cast lots for the thirteenth day of the month Adar-Nisan, to slay all the Jews,

13 from male to female, and to plunder their young. [13] And he hastened and entrusted [the letter] to swift horsemen.

B   [14] And he signed the following letter:

'The Great King, Ahasuerus, to the rulers and satraps of the hundred and twenty-seven lands from India to Ethiopia, writes thus:

15   [15] 'Having become ruler of many nations and master of the whole world, not elated with presumption of authority but always acting reasonably and with kindness, I have determined to settle the lives of my subjects in lasting peace, and, making the kingdom peaceable and open to travel throughout its extent, to re-establish the peace which all men desire.

16   [16] 'When I asked my counsellors how this might be accomplished, Haman, who has excelled among us in sound judgment, his unchanging good will and steadfast fidelity, [and] has attained the second place in the kingdom, pointed out to us that among all the nations in the world there is sojourning and scattered a certain hostile people, who have laws opposed to those of every nation and continually disregard the ordinances of the kings, so that the kingdom is never able to reach a condition of

17   stability. [17] We understand that this people, and it alone, stands constantly in opposition to all men on account of the strange perversity of its laws, and is ill-disposed to our commands, constantly doing all the harm they can so that the monarchy administered by us can never be safely established.

18   [18] 'Therefore we have decreed that those indicated to you in the letters of Haman, who is in charge of affairs and is our second father, shall be utterly destroyed, with their wives and children, by the sword of their enemies, without any pity or mercy, on the fourteenth day of the

καὶ φειδοῦς τῇ τεσσαρεσκαιδεκάτῃ τοῦ μηνὸς τοῦ δωδεκάτου (οὗτος ὁ μὴν Αδαρ, ὅς ἐστι Δύστρος), φονεύειν πάντας τοὺς Ἰουδαίους καὶ ἁρπάζειν τὰ νήπια, ἵνα οἱ πάλαι δυσμενεῖς καὶ νῦν ἐν ἡμέρᾳ μιᾷ συνελθόντες εἰς τὸν ᾅδην εἰς τὰ μετ᾽ ἔπειτα εὐσταθή-σωσιν, καὶ μὴ διὰ τέλους παρέχωσιν ἡμῖν πράγματα.

19   ¹⁹ καὶ ἐν Σούσοις ἐξετέθη τὸ πρόσταγμα τοῦτο.

5   ¹ ὁ δὲ Μαρδοχαῖος ἐπέγνω πάντα τὰ γεγονότα, καὶ ἡ πόλις Σοῦσα ἐταράσσετο ἐπὶ τοῖς γεγενημένοις, καὶ πᾶσι τοῖς
2   Ἰουδαίοις ἦν πένθος μέγα καὶ πικρὸν ἐν πάσῃ πόλει. ² ὁ δὲ Μαρδοχαῖος ἐλθὼν εἰς τὸν οἶκον αὐτοῦ περιείλετο τὰ ἱμάτια αὐτοῦ καὶ περιεβάλετο σάκκον, καὶ σποδωθεὶς ἐξῆλθεν ὡς ἐπὶ τὴν αὐλὴν τὴν ἔξω καὶ ἔστη· οὐ γὰρ ἠδύνατο εἰσελθεῖν εἰς τὰ
3   βασίλεια ἐν σάκκῳ. ³ καὶ ἐκάλεσεν εὐνοῦχον ἕνα καὶ ἀπέστειλε πρὸς Εσθηρ. καὶ εἶπεν ἡ βασίλισσα Περιέλεσθε
4   τὸν σάκκον καὶ εἰσαγάγετε αὐτόν. ⁴ ὃς δὲ οὐκ ἤθελεν, ἀλλ᾽ εἶπεν Οὕτως ἐρεῖτε αὐτῇ Μὴ ἀποστρέψῃς τοῦ εἰσελθεῖν πρὸς τὸν βασιλέα καὶ κολακεῦσαι τὸ πρόσωπον αὐτοῦ ὑπὲρ ἐμοῦ καὶ τοῦ λαοῦ, μνησθεῖσα ἡμερῶν ταπεινώσεώς σου ὧν ἐτράφης ἐν τῇ χειρί μου, ὅτι Αμαν ὁ δευτερεύων λελάληκε τῷ
5   βασιλεῖ καθ᾽ ἡμῶν εἰς θάνατον. ⁵ ἐπικαλεσαμένη οὖν τὸν θεὸν λάλησον περὶ ἡμῶν τῷ βασιλεῖ, καὶ ῥῦσαι ἡμᾶς ἐκ
6   θανάτου. ⁶ καὶ ἀπήγγειλεν αὐτῇ τὴν ὀδύνην τοῦ Ισραηλ.
7   ⁷ καὶ ἀπέστειλεν αὐτῷ κατὰ τάδε λέγουσα Σὺ γινώσκεις παρὰ πάντας ὅτι ὃς ἂν εἰσέλθῃ πρὸς τὸν βασιλέα ἄκλητος ᾧ οὐκ ἐκτενεῖ τὴν ῥάβδον αὐτοῦ τὴν χρυσῆν, θανάτου ἔνοχος
8   ἔσται. ⁸ καὶ ἐγὼ οὐ κέκλημαι πρὸς αὐτόν, ἡμέραι εἰσὶ
9   τριάκοντα· καὶ πῶς εἰσελεύσομαι νῦν, ἄκλητος οὖσα; ⁹ καὶ ἀπέστειλε πρὸς αὐτὴν Μαρδοχαῖος καὶ εἶπεν αὐτῇ Ἐὰν ὑπερίδῃς τοῦ ἔθνους σου τοῦ μὴ βοηθῆσαι αὐτοῖς, ἀλλ᾽ ὁ θεὸς ἔσται αὐτοῖς βοηθὸς καὶ σωτηρία, σὺ δὲ καὶ ὁ οἶκος τοῦ
10   πατρός σου ἀπολεῖσθε. ¹⁰ καὶ τίς οἶδεν εἰ εἰς τὸν καιρὸν
11   τοῦτον ἐβασίλευσας; ¹¹ καὶ ἀπέστειλεν ἡ βασίλισσα λέγουσα Παραγγείλατε θεραπείαν καὶ δεήθητε τοῦ θεοῦ ἐκτενῶς, κἀγὼ δὲ καὶ τὰ κοράσιά μου ποιήσομεν οὕτως· καὶ εἰσελεύ-σομαι πρὸς τὸν βασιλέα ἄκλητος, εἰ δέοι καὶ ἀποθανεῖν με.
12   ¹² καὶ ἐποίησεν οὕτως Μαρδοχαῖος,

twelfth month (that is the month Adar, which is Dystros), so that all the Jews may be slain and their children taken as spoil, so that those who have long been and are now hostile may in one day go together to Hades, to the end that they may thereafter be quiet and may cease completely to trouble us.'

19   ¹⁹ This decree was exhibited in Susa.

5   ¹ Mordecai learned all that had taken place, and the city of Susa was in confusion over what had happened, and among all
2   the Jews there was much bitter grief in every city. ² Mordecai, having gone to his house, took off his garments and put on sackcloth; and when he had strewed his head with ashes, he went out to the outer court and sat down; for he could not enter
3   the palace in sackcloth. ³ He called a eunuch and sent him to Esther. And the queen said, 'Take off his sackcloth and bring
4   him in'. ⁴ But he did not wish it, but said, 'Thus you (pl.) will say to her, "Do not refuse to enter the king's presence and to charm him for my sake and the people's, remembering the days of your humble station when you were brought up by me; for Haman, who is the second, has spoken to the king against us for
5   our death. ⁵ Therefore call upon God and speak on our behalf
6   to the king, and deliver us from death."' ⁶ And he made known
7   to her the tribulation of Israel. ⁷ And she sent to him, saying thus: 'You know as well as everyone that if anyone enters the king's presence unbidden, and if he does not stretch out his
8   golden rod to him, that person is sentenced to death. ⁸ And I have not been called before him for thirty days. How shall I go
9   in now, when I have not been summoned?' ⁹ Mordecai sent to her and said to her, 'If you neglect to help your people, then God will be their help and salvation, but you and your father's
10   house will perish. ¹⁰ And who knows whether it was for this
11   moment that you came to the throne?' ¹¹ And the queen sent, saying, 'Proclaim a service of worship and pray earnestly to God; and I and my handmaids will do likewise. I will enter the
12   king's presence unbidden, even if I must die.' ¹² And Mordecai did so.

C
13

14
15

16

17

18

19

20

21

καὶ ἐδεήθη τοῦ κυρίου, μνημονεύων αὐτοῦ τὰ ἔργα,
καὶ εἶπεν ¹³ Δέσποτα παντοκράτορ οὗ ἐν τῇ ἐξουσίᾳ
ἐστὶ τὰ πάντα, καὶ οὐκ ἔστιν ὃς ἀντιτάξεταί σοι ἐν τῷ
θέλειν σε σῶσαι τὸν οἶκον Ισραηλ, ὅτι σὺ ἐποίησας τὸν
οὐρανὸν καὶ τὴν γῆν καὶ πᾶν τὸ θαυμαζόμενον ἐν τῇ ὑπ'
οὐρανόν, καὶ σὺ κυριεύεις πάντων. ¹⁴ σὺ γὰρ πάντα
γινώσκεις, καὶ τὸ γένος Ισραηλ σὺ οἶδας. ¹⁵ καὶ οὐχ ὅτι
ἐν ὕβρει οὐδὲ ἐν φιλοδοξίᾳ ἐποίησα τοῦ μὴ προσκυνεῖν
τὸν ἀπερίτμητον Αμαν, ἐπεὶ εὐδόκουν φιλῆσαι τὰ
πέλματα τῶν ποδῶν αὐτοῦ ἕνεκεν τοῦ Ισραηλ, ἀλλ'
ἐποίησα ἵνα μηδένα προτάξω τῆς δόξης σοῦ, δέσποτα,
καὶ μηδένα προσκυνήσω πλὴν σοῦ τοῦ ἀληθινοῦ, καὶ οὐ
ποιήσω αὐτὸ ἐν πειρασμῷ. ¹⁶ καὶ νῦν, κύριε, ὁ
διαθέμενος πρὸς Αβρααμ φεῖσαι τοῦ λαοῦ σου ὅτι
ἐπιτέθεινται ἡμῖν εἰς καταφθοράν, καὶ ἐπιθυμοῦσιν
ἀφανίσαι καὶ ἐξᾶραι τὴν ἐξ ἀρχῆς κληρονομίαν σου, μὴ
ὑπερίδῃς τὴν μερίδα σου ἣν ἐλυτρώσω ἐκ γῆς Αἰγύπτου·
¹⁷ ἐπάκουσον τῆς δεήσεως ἡμῶν καὶ ἱλάσθητι τῆς
κληρονομίας σου, καὶ στρέψον τὸ πένθος ἡμῶν εἰς
εὐφροσύνην, ἵνα ζῶντες ὑμνήσωμέν σε. καὶ μὴ ἀφανί-
σῃς στόμα ὑμνούντων σε. ¹⁸ καὶ Εσθηρ ἡ βασίλισσα
κατέφυγεν ἐπὶ τὸν κύριον ἐν ἀγῶνι θανάτου κατ-
ειλημμένη. καὶ ἀφείλατο τὰ ἱμάτια τῆς δόξης ἀφ' ἑαυτῆς
καὶ πᾶν σημεῖον ἐπιφανείας αὐτῆς, καὶ ἐνεδύσατο
στενοχωρίαν καὶ πένθος, καὶ ἀντὶ ὑπερηφάνων ἡδυσ-
μάτων σποδοῦ καὶ κόπρου ἔπλησε τὴν κεφαλὴν αὐτῆς,
καὶ τὸ σῶμα αὐτῆς ἐταπείνωσε σφόδρα, καὶ πᾶν
σημεῖον κόσμου αὐτῆς καὶ ἀγαλλιάματος τερπνῶν
τριχῶν ἔπλησε ταπεινώσεως. ¹⁹ καὶ ἐδεήθη τοῦ κυρίου
καὶ εἶπεν Κύριε βασιλεῦ, σὺ εἶ μόνος βοηθός· βοήθησόν
μοι τῇ ταπεινῇ καὶ οὐκ ἐχούσῃ βοηθὸν πλὴν σοῦ, ὅτι
κίνδυνός μου ἐν τῇ χειρί μου. ²⁰ ἐγὼ δὲ ἤκουσα
πατρικῆς μου βίβλου ὅτι ἐλυτρώσω τὸν Ισραηλ ἐκ
πάντων τῶν ἐθνῶν, καὶ τοὺς πατέρας αὐτῶν ἐκ τῶν
προγόνων αὐτῶν, ἐπιθέμενος αὐτοῖς Ισραηλ κληρονομίαν αἰώνιον. καὶ ἐποίησας αὐτοῖς ἃ ἐλάλησας
αὐτοῖς, καὶ παρέσχου ὅσα ᾔτησαν. ²¹ ἡμάρτομεν ἐν-

C   And he prayed to the Lord, calling to remembrance his works. He said:

13   [13] 'Omnipotent Master, in whose power is the universe and against whom no one can stand if it is thy will to save the house of Israel. For thou hast made heaven and earth and every wonderful thing under heaven, and thou rulest

14   over all. [14] For thou knowest all things, and thou knowest

15   the race of Israel. [15] And [thou knowest] that it was not in insolence or vainglory that I acted in not bowing down to the uncircumcised Haman. For I would have been willing to kiss the soles of his feet for the sake of Israel, but I acted thus so that I might not set any above your glory, O Master, and I will not bow down to any one but to thee, the True One, and I will not do it [even] at a time

16   of testing. [16] And now, O Lord, who didst make a covenant with Abraham, spare thy people; for they have set upon us to annihilate us, and they desire to destroy and remove the inheritance that has been thine from the beginning. Do not neglect thy portion, which thou didst

17   redeem out of the land of Egypt. [17] Hear our prayer, and have mercy upon thy inheritance; turn our mourning into rejoicing, that we may live and sing praise to thee; do not destroy the mouth of those who praise thee.'

18   [18] And Esther the queen, seized with deathly anxiety, fled to the Lord; she took off her splendid apparel and every sign of her glorious rank, and clothed herself with distress and mourning, and instead of costly perfumes she covered her head with ashes and dung, and she utterly humbled her body, and every sign of her adornment and delight on her lovely head she covered with humiliation.

19   [19] And she prayed to the Lord, and said:

     'O Lord, King, thou alone art a helper. Help me, who am humble and have no helper but thee, for my danger is

20   in my hand. [20] I have heard from my father's book that thou didst redeem Israel from all the nations, and their fathers from among their ancestors, bestowing upon them, Israel, an everlasting inheritance. And thou didst do for them that which thou didst promise, and didst

21   provide all that they requested. [21] We have sinned before

αντίον σου, καὶ παρέδωκας ἡμᾶς εἰς χεῖρας τῶν ἐχθρῶν

22 ἡμῶν, εἰ ἐδοξάσαμεν τοὺς θεοὺς αὐτῶν. ²² δίκαιος εἶ,
κύριε· καὶ νῦν οὐχ ἱκανώθησαν ἐν πικρασμῷ δουλείας
ἡμῶν, ἀλλ' ἐπέθηκαν τὰς χεῖρας αὐτῶν ἐπὶ τὰς χεῖρας
τῶν εἰδώλων αὐτῶν, ἐξᾶραι ὁρισμὸν στόματος αὐτῶν,
ἀφανίσαι κληρονομίαν σου, καὶ ἐμφράξαι στόμα αἰνούν-
των σε, καὶ σβέσαι δόξαν οἴκου σου καὶ θυσιαστηρίου
σου, καὶ ἀνοῖξαι στόματα ἐχθρῶν εἰς ἀρετὰς ματαίων,
καὶ θαυμασθῆναι βασιλέα σάρκινον εἰς τὸν αἰῶνα.

23 ²³ μὴ δὴ παραδῷς, κύριε, τὸ σκῆπτρόν σου τοῖς μισοῦσί
σε ἐχθροῖς, καὶ μὴ χαρείησαν ἐπὶ τῇ πτώσει ἡμῶν.
στρέψον τὰς βουλὰς αὐτῶν ἐπ' αὐτούς, τὸν δὲ ἀρξά-

24 μενον ἐφ' ἡμᾶς εἰς κακὰ παραδειγμάτισον. ²⁴ ἐπιφάνηθι
ἡμῖν, κύριε, καὶ γνώσθητι ἐν καιρῷ θλίψεως ἡμῶν, καὶ

25 μὴ θραύσῃς ἡμᾶς. ²⁵ δὸς λόγον εὔρυθμον εἰς τὸ στόμα
μου, καὶ χαρίτωσον τὰ ῥήματά μου ἐνώπιον τοῦ
βασιλέως, καὶ μετάστρεψον τὴν καρδίαν αὐτοῦ εἰς
μῖσος τοῦ πολεμοῦντος ἡμᾶς, εἰς συντέλειαν αὐτοῦ καὶ
τῶν ὁμονοούντων αὐτῷ· ἡμᾶς δὲ ῥῦσαι ἐν τῇ χειρί σου
τῇ κραταιᾷ, καὶ βοήθησόν μοι, ὅτι σὺ πάντων γνῶσιν
ἔχεις, καὶ οἶδας ὅτι βδελύσσομαι κοίτην ἀπεριτμήτου,
καὶ ἐμίσησα δόξαν ἀνόμου καὶ παντὸς ἀλλογενοῦς.

26 ²⁶ σύ, κύριε, οἶδας τὴν ἀνάγκην μου, ὅτι βδελύσσομαι
τὸ σημεῖον τῆς ὑπερηφανίας ὅ ἐστιν ἐπὶ τῆς κεφαλῆς
μου, καὶ οὐ φορῶ αὐτὸ εἰ μὴ ἐν ἡμέρᾳ ὀπτασίας μου, καὶ

27 βδελύσσομαι αὐτὸ ὡς ῥάκος ἀποκαθημένης. ²⁷ καὶ οὐκ
ἔφαγεν ἡ δούλη σου ἐπὶ τῶν τραπεζῶν αὐτῶν ἅμα.

28 ²⁸ καὶ οὐκ ἐδόξασα βασιλέως συμπόσια, καὶ οὐκ ἔπιον
σπονδῆς οἶνον, καὶ οὐκ εὐφράνθη ἡ δούλη σου ἐφ'

29 ἡμέραις μεταβολῆς μου εἰ μὴ ἐπὶ σοί, δέσποτα. ²⁹ καὶ
νῦν, δυνατὸς ὢν ἐπὶ πάντας, εἰσάκουσον φωνῆς ἀπηλ-
πισμένων, καὶ ῥῦσαι ἡμᾶς ἐκ χειρὸς τῶν πονηρευομένων
ἐφ' ἡμᾶς, καὶ ἐξελοῦ με, κύριε, ἐκ χειρὸς τοῦ φόβου μου.

6 ¹ καὶ ἐγενήθη ἐν τῇ ἡμέρᾳ τῇ τρίτῃ ὡς ἐπαύσατο
Εσθηρ προσευχομένη, ἐξεδύσατο τὰ ἱμάτια τῆς θερα-

2 πείας, καὶ περιεβάλετο τὰ ἱμάτια τῆς δόξης. ² καὶ
γενομένη ἐπιφανὴς καὶ ἐπικαλεσαμένη τὸν πάντων

thee, and thou hast given us into the hands of our enemies
if we glorified their gods. [22] Thou art righteous, O Lord!
And now they are not satisfied that we are in bitter
slavery, but they have covenanted with their idols to
abolish what thy mouth has ordained, to destroy thy
inheritance, to stop the mouths of those who praise thee,
and to quench the glory of thy house and thy altar, to
open the mouths of the nations for the praise of vain idols,
and to magnify for ever a mortal king. [23] O Lord, do not
surrender thy sceptre to thy enemies who hate thee; and
do not let them rejoice at our downfall. Turn their plans
against themselves, and make an example of the man who
began this against us for evil. [24] Manifest thyself to us, O
Lord; make thyself known in this time of our affliction,
and do not break us in pieces. [25] Put eloquent speech in
my mouth, and make my words pleasing before the king,
and turn his heart to hate the man who is fighting against
us, so that there may be an end of him and those who
agree with him. But save us by thy mighty hand, and help
me, for thou hast knowledge of all things, and thou
knowest that I abhor the bed of the uncircumcised and I
hate the splendour of the wicked and of any alien.
[26] Thou, O Lord, knowest my necessity—that I abhor
the sign of my proud position which is upon my head, and
I do not wear it except on the days when I appear in
public, and I abhor it like the rag of a woman who sits
apart. [27] And thy servant has not eaten at their table
beside them, [28] and I have not honoured the king's feasts
nor drunk the wine of libation. Thy servant has had no
joy in the days of my removal, except in thee, O Master.
[29] And now, since thou art powerful over all, hear the
voice of the despairing, and save us from the hands of
evildoers. And deliver me, O Lord, from the power of my
fear!'

6 [1] On the third day, when Esther ended her prayer, she
took off the garments in which she had worshipped, and
arrayed herself in garments of splendour. [2] Then, majestically adorned, after invoking the aid of the all-knowing

γνώστην καὶ σωτῆρα θεὸν παρέλαβε μεθ' ἑαυτῆς δύο
ἄβρας, καὶ τῇ μὲν μιᾷ ἐπηρείδετο ὡς τρυφερευομένη, ἡ
δὲ ἑτέρα ἐπηκολούθει ἐπικουφίζουσα τὸ ἔνδυμα αὐτῆς.

3   3 καὶ αὐτὴ ἐρυθριῶσα ἐν ἀκμῇ κάλλους αὐτῆς, καὶ τὸ
πρόσωπον αὐτῆς ὡς προσφιλές, ἡ δὲ καρδία αὐτῆς
4   ἀπεστενωμένη. 4 καὶ εἰσελθοῦσα τὰς θύρας ἔστη ἐνώπιον τοῦ βασιλέως. καὶ ὁ βασιλεὺς ἐκάθητο ἐπὶ τοῦ
θρόνου τῆς βασιλείας αὐτοῦ, καὶ πᾶσαν στολὴν
ἐπιφανείας ἐνδεδύκει, ὅλος διάχρυσος, καὶ λίθοι πολυ-
5   τελεῖς ἐπ' αὐτῷ, καὶ φοβερὸς σφόδρα. 5 καὶ ἄρας τὸ
πρόσωπον αὐτοῦ πεπυρωμένον ἐν δόξῃ ἐνέβλεψεν αὐτῇ
6   ὡς ταῦρος ἐν ἀκμῇ θυμοῦ αὐτοῦ. 6 καὶ ἐφοβήθη ἡ
βασίλισσα, καὶ μετέβαλε τὸ πρόσωπον αὐτῆς ἐν
ἐκλύσει, καὶ ἐπέκυψεν ἐπὶ τὴν κεφαλὴν τῆς ἄβρας τῆς
7   προπορευομένης. 7 καὶ μετέβαλεν ὁ θεὸς τὸ πνεῦμα τοῦ
βασιλέως καὶ μετέθηκε τὸν θυμὸν αὐτοῦ εἰς πραότητα,
8   8 καὶ ἀγωνιάσας ὁ βασιλεὺς κατεπήδησεν ἀπὸ τοῦ
θρόνου αὐτοῦ, καὶ ἀνέλαβεν αὐτὴν ἐπὶ τὰς ἀγκάλας
αὐτοῦ καὶ παρεκάλεσεν αὐτὴν καὶ εἶπεν Τί ἔστιν,
9   Εσθηρ· ἐγώ εἰμι ἀδελφός σου. 9 θάρσει, οὐ μὴ ἀποθάνῃς,
ὅτι κοινόν ἐστι τὸ πρᾶγμα ἡμῶν, καὶ οὐ πρὸς σὲ ἡ
10   ἀπειλή. ἰδοὺ τὸ σκῆπτρον ἐν τῇ χειρί σου. 10 καὶ ἄρας
τὸ σκῆπτρον ἐπέθηκεν ἐπὶ τὸν τράχηλον αὐτῆς, καὶ
11   ἠσπάσατο αὐτήν, καὶ εἶπεν Λάλησόν μοι. 11 καὶ εἶπεν
αὐτῷ Εἶδόν σε ὡς ἄγγελον θεοῦ, καὶ ἐτάκη ἡ καρδία
12   μου ἀπὸ τῆς δόξης τοῦ θυμοῦ σου, κύριε. 12 καὶ ἐπὶ τὸ
πρόσωπον αὐτῆς μέτρον ἱδρῶτος. καὶ ἐταράσσετο ὁ
βασιλεὺς καὶ πᾶσα ἡ θεραπεία αὐτοῦ, καὶ παρεκάλουν
αὐτήν.

13   13 καὶ εἶπεν ὁ βασιλεὺς Τί ἔστιν, Εσθηρ; ἀνάγγειλόν μοι,
14   καὶ ποιήσω σοι· ἕως ἡμίσους τῆς βασιλείας μου. 14 καὶ εἶπεν
Εσθηρ Ἡμέρα ἐπίσημός μοι αὔριον· εἰ δοκεῖ οὖν τῷ βασιλεῖ,
εἴσελθε σὺ καὶ Αμαν ὁ φίλος σου εἰς τὸν πότον ὃν ποιήσω
15   αὔριον. 15 καὶ εἶπεν ὁ βασιλεὺς Κατασπεύσατε τὸν Αμαν,
16   ὅπως ποιήσωμεν τὸν λόγον Εσθηρ. 16 καὶ παραγίνονται
ἀμφότεροι εἰς τὴν δοχὴν ἣν ἐποίησεν Εσθηρ, δεῖπνον
17   πολυτελές. 17 καὶ εἶπεν ὁ βασιλεὺς πρὸς Εσθηρ Ἡ βασίλισσα,

God and Saviour, she took her two maids with her, leaning daintily on one, while the other followed carrying her train. ³ She was radiant with perfect beauty, and her face was as if she was beloved, but her heart was in anguish. ⁴ When she had gone through the doors, she stood before the king. The king was seated on his royal throne, clothed in the full array of his majesty, all covered with gold and precious stones. And he was most terrifying.

⁵ Lifting his face, flushed with splendour, he looked upon her like a bull in fierce anger. ⁶ And the queen was terrified, and her face turned pale from faintness, and she collapsed upon the head of the maid who went before her. ⁷ Then God changed the spirit of the king and turned his rage to gentleness; ⁸ and in alarm he sprang from his throne, and took her in his arms and comforted her, and said, 'What is it, Esther? I am your brother. ⁹ Take courage; you shall not die, for our business is mutual, and the threat was not against you. Behold, the sceptre is in your hand.'

¹⁰ Then he raised the sceptre and touched it to her neck, and he embraced her, and said, 'Speak to me'. ¹¹ And she said to him, 'I saw you like an angel of God, and my heart melted at the glory of your wrath, my lord'. ¹² And on her face was a measure of sweat. And the king was agitated, and all his servants, and they sought to comfort her.

¹³ And the king said, 'What is it, Esther? Tell me, and I shall do it for you, to the half of my kingdom.' ¹⁴ And Esther said, 'Tomorrow is a special day for me; therefore if it seems good to the king, do you come, and Haman your friend, to the banquet which I shall prepare tomorrow'. ¹⁵ And the king said, 'Fetch Haman in haste, so that we may do as Esther has said'. ¹⁶ They both arrived at the banquet which Esther had prepared, a lavish supper. ¹⁷ And the king said to Esther, 'O queen, what is

τί τὸ θέλημά σου; αἴτησαι ἕως ἡμίσους τῆς βασιλείας μου, καὶ

18 ἔσται σοι ὅσα ἀξιοῖς. ¹⁸ καὶ εἶπεν Εσθηρ Τὸ αἴτημά μου καὶ τὸ ἀξίωμά μου, εἰ εὗρον χάριν ἐναντίον σου, βασιλεῦ, καὶ εἰ ἐπὶ τὸν βασιλέα ἀγαθὸν δοῦναι τὸ αἴτημά μου καὶ ποιῆσαι τὸ ἀξίωμά μου, ἐλθέτω ὁ βασιλεὺς καὶ Αμαν εἰς τὴν δοχὴν ἣν ποιήσω αὐτοῖς καὶ τῇ αὔριον· καὶ αὔριον γὰρ ποιήσω κατὰ τὰ

19 αὐτά. ¹⁹ καὶ εἶπεν ὁ βασιλεὺς Ποίησον κατὰ τὸ θέλημά σου.

20 ²⁰ καὶ ἀπηγγέλη τῷ Αμαν κατὰ τὰ αὐτά, καὶ ἐθαύμασεν, καὶ

21 ὁ βασιλεὺς ἀναλύσας ἡσύχασεν. ²¹ ὁ δὲ Αμαν εἰσῆλθεν εἰς τὸν οἶκον αὐτοῦ, καὶ συνήγαγε τοὺς φίλους αὐτοῦ καὶ τοὺς υἱοὺς αὐτοῦ καὶ Ζωσάραν τὴν γυναῖκα αὐτοῦ, καὶ ἐκαυχᾶτο λέγων ὡς οὐδένα κέκληκεν ἡ βασίλισσα ἐν ἐπισήμῳ ἡμέρᾳ αὐτῆς εἰ μὴ τὸν βασιλέα καὶ ἐμὲ μόνον· καὶ αὔριον κέκλημαι.

22 ²² τοῦτο δὲ λυπεῖ με μόνον ὅταν ἴδω τὸν Μαρδοχαῖον τὸν Ἰουδαῖον ἐν τῇ αὐλῇ τοῦ βασιλέως, καὶ μὴ προσκυνεῖ με.

23 ²³ καὶ εἶπεν αὐτῷ Ζωσάρα ἡ γυνὴ αὐτοῦ Ἐκ γένους Ἰουδαίων ἐστίν· ἐπεὶ συγκεχώρηκέ σε ὁ βασιλεὺς ἀφανίσαι τοὺς Ἰουδαίους, καὶ ἔδωκάν σοι οἱ θεοὶ εἰς ἐκδίκησιν αὐτῶν ἡμέραν ὀλέθριον, κοπήτω σοι ξύλον πηχῶν πεντήκοντα, καὶ κείσθω, καὶ κρέμασον αὐτὸν ἐπὶ τοῦ ξύλου, ὀρθρίσας δὲ πρὸς τὸν βασιλέα λαλήσεις αὐτῷ· καὶ νῦν εἰσελθὼν εὐφραίνου

24 πρὸς τὸν βασιλέα. ²⁴ καὶ ἤρεσε τῷ Αμαν, καὶ ἐποίησεν οὕτως.

7   ¹ ὁ δὲ δυνατὸς ἀπέστησε τὸν ὕπνον τοῦ βασιλέως τὴν

2   νύκτα ἐκείνην, καὶ ἦν ἀγρυπνῶν. ² καὶ ἐκλήθησαν οἱ ἀναγνῶσται, καὶ τὸ βιβλίον τῶν μνημοσυνῶν ἀνεγινώσκετο

3   αὐτῷ. ³ καὶ ἦν ὑπόθεσις τῶν εὐνούχων καὶ ὃ ἐποίησε

4   Μαρδοχαῖος εὐεργέτημα τῷ βασιλεῖ. ⁴ καὶ ἐπέστησεν ὁ βασιλεὺς τὸν νοῦν σφόδρα, λέγων Πιστὸς ἀνὴρ Μαρδοχαῖος εἰς παραφυλακὴν τῆς ψυχῆς μου, δι' ὅτι αὐτὸς ἐποίησέ με ζῆν ἄχρι τοῦ νῦν, καὶ κάθημαι σήμερον ἐπὶ τοῦ θρόνου μου, καὶ

5   οὐκ ἐποίησα αὐτῷ οὐθέν· οὐκ ὀρθῶς ἐποίησα. ⁵ καὶ εἶπεν ὁ βασιλεὺς τοῖς παισὶν αὐτοῦ Τί ποιήσομεν τῷ Μαρδοχαίῳ τῷ σωτῆρι τῶν λόγων; καὶ νοήσαντες οἱ νεανίσκοι διεφθόνουν αὐτῷ· ἐνέκειτο γὰρ φόβος Αμαν ἐν τοῖς σπλάγχνοις αὐτῶν.

6   ⁶ καὶ ἐνενόησεν ὁ βασιλεύς. καὶ ἐγένετο ὄρθρος. καὶ

7   ἠρώτησεν ὁ βασιλεὺς Τίς ἐστιν ἔξω; καὶ ἦν Αμαν. ⁷ Αμαν δὲ

your desire? Make your request as much as the half of my
18 kingdom, and you will have whatever you wish.' [18] And Esther
said, 'My request and my wish, if I have found favour before
you, O king, and if it pleases the king to grant my request and to
do my wish, let the king and Haman come to the banquet that I
will make for them tomorrow also; and tomorrow I will do as I
19 have done today'. [19] And the king said, 'Do as you please'.
20 [20] And it was told to Haman in the same way, and he was
21 astonished; and the king went out and retired to rest. [21] Haman
went home, and gathered together his friends and his sons and
Zosara his wife, and boasted, saying, 'The queen invited no one
on her special day except the king and me alone; and I am
22 invited for tomorrow also. [22] But the only thing that vexes me
is when I see Mordecai the Jew in the king's palace and he does
23 not do obeisance to me.' [23] Zosara his wife said to him, 'He is
from the race of the Jews; since the king has agreed with you to
destroy the Jews, and the gods have given you a day of
destruction for taking revenge on them, let a tree of fifty cubits
be cut down, and let it be erected, and hang him on the tree;
and go early in the morning to the king and speak to him. But
24 now go and make merry with the king.' [24] It pleased Haman,
and he did accordingly.
7   [1] Now the Mighty One took away the king's sleep that night,
2   and he was wakeful. [2] The readers were summoned, and the
3   book of the chronicles was read to him. [3] And there was a
conspiracy of the eunuchs and a benefit which Mordecai had
4   rendered the king. [4] The king paid close attention, saying,
'Mordecai is a faithful man for protecting my life. Since he has
kept me alive until now, and I sit today upon my throne, and I
5   have done nothing for him, I have not acted rightly.' [5] The king
said to his servants, 'What shall we do for Mordecai, the
saviour of affairs?' And when they considered it, the servants
envied him; for the fear of Haman had fallen on their hearts.
6   [6] And the king understood. Now morning dawned; and the
7   king asked, 'Who is outside?' And it was Haman. [7] Haman had

ὡρθρίκει λαλῆσαι τῷ βασιλεῖ ἵνα κρεμάσῃ τὸν Μαρδοχαῖον.

8   ⁸ καὶ εἶπεν ὁ βασιλεὺς εἰσαγαγεῖν αὐτόν. ⁹ ὡς δὲ εἰσῆλθεν,
εἶπεν αὐτῷ ὁ βασιλεὺς Τί ποιήσομεν τῷ ἀνδρὶ τῷ τὸν βασιλέα
10   τιμῶντι, ὃν ὁ βασιλεὺς βούλεται δοξάσαι; ¹⁰ καὶ ἐλογίσατο ὁ
Αμαν λέγων ὅτι Τίνα βούλεται ὁ βασιλεὺς δοξάσαι εἰ μὴ ἐμέ;
11   ¹¹ καὶ εἶπεν ὁ Αμαν ῎Ανθρωπος ὃν ὁ βασιλεὺς βούλεται
δοξάσαι, ληφθήτω στολὴ βασιλικὴ καὶ ἵππος βασιλικὸς ἐφ᾽ ᾧ
ὁ βασιλεὺς ἐπιβαίνει, καὶ εἷς τῶν ἐνδόξων, τῶν φίλων τοῦ
βασιλέως, λαβέτω ταῦτα, καὶ ἐνδυσάτω αὐτόν, καὶ ἀνα-
βιβασάτω αὐτὸν ἐπὶ τὸν ἵππον, καὶ περιελθέτω τὴν πόλιν
ἔμπροσθεν αὐτοῦ κηρύσσων Κατὰ τάδε ποιηθήσεται τῷ τὸν
12   βασιλέα τιμῶντι, ὃν ὁ βασιλεὺς βούλεται δοξάσαι. ¹² καὶ
εἶπεν ὁ βασιλεὺς τῷ Αμαν Ταχὺ δράμε καὶ λαβὲ τὸν ἵππον καὶ
στολὴν ὡς εἴρηκας, καὶ ποίησον Μαρδοχαίῳ τῷ Ἰουδαίῳ τῷ
καθημένῳ ἐν τῷ πυλῶνι· καὶ μὴ παραπεσάτω ὁ λόγος σου.
13   ¹³ ὡς δὲ ἔγνω Αμαν ὅτι οὐκ ἦν αὐτὸς ὁ δοξαζόμενος, ἀλλ᾽ ὅτι
Μαρδοχαῖος, συνετρίβη ἡ καρδία αὐτοῦ σφόδρα, καὶ μετ-
14   έβαλε τὸ πνεῦμα αὐτοῦ ἐν ἐκλύσει. ¹⁴ καὶ ἔλαβεν Αμαν τὴν
στολὴν καὶ τὸν ἵππον, ἐντρεπόμενος τὸν Μαρδοχαῖον καθ᾽
15   ὅτι ἐκείνῃ τῇ ἡμέρᾳ ἐκεκρίκει ἀνασκολοπίσαι αὐτόν. ¹⁵ καὶ
16   εἶπε τῷ Μαρδοχαίῳ Περιελοῦ τὸν σάκκον. ¹⁶ καὶ ἐταράχθη
Μαρδοχαῖος ὡς ἀποθνήσκων, καὶ ἀπεδύσατο μετ᾽ ὀδύνης τὸν
17   σάκκον καὶ ἐνεδύσατο τὰ ἱμάτια δόξης. ¹⁷ καὶ ἐδόκει
Μαρδοχαῖος τέρας θεωρεῖν, καὶ ἡ καρδία αὐτοῦ πρὸς τὸν
18   κύριον. καὶ ἐξίστατο ἐν ἀφασίᾳ. ¹⁸ καὶ ἔσπευσεν Αμαν
19   ἀναλαβεῖν αὐτὸν ἔφιππον. ¹⁹ καὶ ἐξήγαγεν Αμαν τὸν ἵππον
ἔξω, καὶ προσήγαγεν αὐτὸν ἔξω κηρύσσων Κατὰ τάδε
ποιηθήσεται τῷ ἀνδρὶ τῷ τὸν βασιλέα τιμῶντι, ὃν ὁ βασιλεὺς
20   βούλεται δοξάσαι. ²⁰ καὶ ὁ μὲν Αμαν ἀπῆλθε πρὸς ἑαυτὸν
ἐσκυθρωπωμένος, ὁ δὲ Μαρδοχαῖος ἀπῆλθεν εἰς τὸν οἶκον
21   αὐτοῦ. ²¹ καὶ διηγήσατο Αμαν τῇ γυναικὶ αὐτοῦ πάντα τὰ
22   γενόμενα αὐτῷ. ²² καὶ εἶπεν ἡ γυνὴ αὐτοῦ καὶ οἱ σοφοὶ αὐτοῦ
᾽Αφ᾽ ὅτε λαλεῖς περὶ αὐτοῦ κακά, προσπορεύεταί σοι τὰ
κακά· ἡσύχαζε, ὅτι ὁ θεὸς ἐν αὐτοῖς. ²³ καὶ αὐτῶν λαλούντων
23   παρῆν τις ἐπὶ τὸν πότον σπουδάζων αὐτόν, καὶ οὕτως
ἱλαρώθη, καὶ πορευθεὶς ἀνέπεσε μετ᾽ αὐτῶν ἐν ὥρα.

risen early to speak to the king so that he could hang Mordecai.
8 [8] The king said to bring him in. [9] And when he had entered,
the king said to him, 'What shall we do to the man who fears
10 the king, whom the king wishes to honour?' [10] Haman thought
to himself, saying, 'Whom does the king wish to honour if not
11 me?' [11] So Haman said, 'As for the man whom the king wishes to
honour, let a royal robe be taken and a royal horse upon which
the king rides, and let one of the nobles, the friends of the king,
take these things, and clothe him, and make him mount the
horse, and go through the city before him, proclaiming, "Thus
shall be done for the man who fears the king, whom the king
12 wishes to honour".' [12] The king said to Haman, 'Run quickly,
and take the horse and the robe as you have said, and do
accordingly to Mordecai the Jew who sits at the gate; do not let
13 your word fall to the ground'. [13] And when Haman realized that
it was not he who was being honoured, but Mordecai, his heart
was utterly crushed, and his spirit was changed by faintness.
14 [14] And Haman took the robe and the horse, doing reverence to
Mordecai even as on that very day he had determined to hang
15 him. [15] And he said to Mordecai, 'Take off the sackcloth'.
16 [16] Mordecai was troubled, as one who is dying, and in distress he
17 put off the sackcloth and put on the garments of glory. [17] And
Mordecai thought he saw a portent; and his heart was toward the
18 Lord; and he became speechless. [18] Haman hastened to mount
19 him upon the horse. [19] And Haman led the horse outside, and
brought him outside, proclaiming, 'Thus shall be done for the
man who fears the king, whom the king wishes to honour'.
20 [20] And Haman went to his own house in melancholy, and
21 Mordecai went to his own house. [21] Haman recounted to his
22 wife all that had happened to him. [22] And his wife and his wise
men said, 'From the moment that you spoke evil concerning
him, evil has been coming upon you; keep quiet, for God is
23 among them'. [23] And while they were speaking, one arrived to
fetch him speedily to the banquet; and so he was gladdened. And
when he had come, he sat down at table with them in good time.

8 ¹ ὡς δὲ προῆγεν ἡ πρόποσις, εἶπεν ὁ βασιλεὺς τῇ Εσθηρ Τί
ἐστιν ὁ κίνδυνος; καὶ τί τὸ αἴτημά σου; ἕως τοῦ ἡμίσους τῆς
2 βασιλείας μου. ² καὶ ἠγωνίασεν Εσθηρ ἐν τῷ ἀπαγγέλλειν,
ὅτι ὁ ἀντίδικος ἐν ὀφθαλμοῖς αὐτῆς, καὶ ὁ θεὸς ἔδωκεν αὐτῇ
3 θάρσος ἐν τῷ αὐτὴν ἐπικαλεῖσθαι αὐτόν. ³ καὶ εἶπεν Εσθηρ
Εἰ δοκεῖ τῷ βασιλεῖ, καὶ ἀγαθὴ ἡ κρίσις ἐν καρδίᾳ αὐτοῦ,
δοθήτω ὁ λαός μου τῷ αἰτήματί μου καὶ τὸ ἔθνος τῆς ψυχῆς
4 μου. ⁴ ἐπράθημεν γὰρ ἐγὼ καὶ ὁ λαός μου εἰς δούλωσιν, καὶ
τὰ νήπια αὐτῶν εἰς διαρπαγήν, καὶ οὐκ ἤθελον ἀπαγγεῖλαι,
ἵνα μὴ λυπήσω τὸν κύριόν μου· ἐγένετο γὰρ μεταπεσεῖν τὸν
5 ἄνθρωπον τὸν κακοποιήσαντα ἡμᾶς. ⁵ καὶ ἐθυμώθη ὁ βασιλεὺς καὶ εἶπεν Τίς ἐστιν οὗτος ὃς ἐτόλμησε ταπεινῶσαι τὸ
σημεῖον τῆς βασιλείας μου ὥστε παρελθεῖν τὸν φόβον σου;
6 ⁶ ὡς δὲ εἶδεν ἡ βασίλισσα ὅτι δεινὸν ἐφάνη τῷ βασιλεῖ, καὶ
μισοπονηρεῖ, εἶπεν Μὴ ὀργίζου, κύριε· ἱκανὸν γὰρ ὅτι ἔτυχον
τοῦ ἱλασμοῦ σου· εὐωχοῦ, βασιλεῦ· αὔριον δὲ ποιήσω κατὰ
7 τὸ ῥῆμά σου. ⁷ καὶ ὤμοσεν ὁ βασιλεὺς τοῦ ἀπαγγεῖλαι αὐτὴν
αὐτῷ τὸν ὑπερηφανευσάμενον τοῦ ποιῆσαι τοῦτο, καὶ μετὰ
8 ὅρκου ὑπέσχετο ποιῆσαι αὐτῇ ὃ ἂν βούληται. ⁸ καὶ θαρσή-
σασα ἡ Εσθηρ εἶπεν Αμαν ὁ φίλος σου ὁ ψευδὴς οὗτοσί, ὁ
9 πονηρὸς ἄνθρωπος οὗτος. ⁹ ἔκθυμος δὲ γενόμενος ὁ βασιλεὺς
10 καὶ πλησθεὶς ὀργῆς ἀνεπήδησε, καὶ ἦν περιπατῶν. ¹⁰ καὶ ὁ
Αμαν ἐταράχθη, καὶ προσέπεσεν ἐπὶ τοὺς πόδας Εσθηρ τῆς
11 βασιλίσσης ἐπὶ τὴν κοίτην ἔτι ἀνακειμένης. ¹¹ καὶ ὁ βασιλεὺς
ἐπέστρεψεν ἐπὶ τὸ συμπόσιον. καὶ ἰδὼν εἶπεν Οὐχ ἱκανόν σοι
ἡ ἁμαρτία τῆς βασιλείας, ἀλλὰ καὶ τὴν γυναῖκά μου ἐκβιάζει
12 ἐνώπιόν μου; ἀπαχθήτω Αμαν, καὶ μὴ ζήτω. ¹² καὶ οὕτως
ἀπήγετο. καὶ εἶπεν Αγαθας εἷς τῶν παίδων αὐτοῦ Ἰδοὺ ξύλον
ἐν τῇ αὐλῇ αὐτοῦ πηχῶν πεντήκοντα, ὃ ἔκοψεν Αμαν ἵνα
κρεμάσῃ τὸν Μαρδοχαῖον τὸν λαλήσαντα ἀγαθὰ περὶ τοῦ
βασιλέως· κέλευσον οὖν, κύριε, ἐπ' αὐτῷ αὐτὸν κρεμασθῆναι.
13 ¹³ καὶ εἶπεν ὁ βασιλεὺς Κρεμασθήτω ἐπ' αὐτῷ. καὶ ἀφεῖλεν ὁ
βασιλεὺς τὸ δακτύλιον ἀπὸ τῆς χειρὸς αὐτοῦ, καὶ ἐσφραγίσθη
14 ἐν αὐτῷ ὁ βίος αὐτοῦ. ¹⁴ καὶ εἶπεν ὁ βασιλεὺς τῇ Εσθηρ Καὶ
Μαρδοχαῖον ἐβουλεύσατο κρεμάσαι τὸν σώσαντά με ἐκ
χειρὸς τῶν εὐνούχων; οὐκ ᾔδει ὅτι πατρῷον αὐτοῦ γένος
15 ἐστὶν ἡ Εσθηρ; ¹⁵ καὶ ἐκάλεσεν ὁ βασιλεὺς τὸν Μαρδοχαῖον,

8 ¹ When the drinking was well advanced, the king said to Esther, 'What is the danger? And what is your request?—to the

2 half of my kingdom.' ² Esther was anxious as she replied, for the adversary was before her eyes; but God gave her courage as

3 she called upon him. ³ Esther said, 'If it seems right to the king, and the decision is good in his heart, let my people be given for

4 my request and the nation for my life. ⁴ For we have been sold, I and my people, into slavery, and their children are for a spoil; but I did not want to report it, lest I should disturb my lord; but it has happened that the man who did us wrong has suffered a

5 reversal.' ⁵ The king was angry and said, 'Who is this who has dared to humble the sign of my kingdom so as to pay no heed to

6 fear of you?' ⁶ And when the queen saw that it seemed to the king a great wrong and that he hated the evil, she said, 'Do not be angry, my lord. It is enough that I have found you merciful. Enjoy yourself, O king; and tomorrow I will do as you say.'

7 ⁷ But the king swore that she should tell him who had behaved so arrogantly as to do this, and with an oath he undertook to do

8 for her whatever she wished. ⁸ And Esther, taking courage, said, 'Haman your friend is this deceiver, this wicked man'.

9 ⁹ And the king, becoming enraged and full of wrath, sprang to

10 his feet and began to walk about. ¹⁰ Haman was terrified, and fell at the feet of Esther the queen as she lay upon the couch.

11 ¹¹ The king returned to the banquet; and when he saw, he said, 'Is it not enough for you to commit a crime against the kingdom; do you also force my wife before my own eyes? Let

12 Haman be taken away, and let him not beg for mercy.' ¹² And so he was led away.

Agathas, one of his servants, said, 'Behold, there is a stake in his courtyard, fifty cubits high, which Haman cut down in order to hang on it Mordecai, who had spoken good concerning the king. Therefore command, my lord, that he should be hung

13 upon it.' ¹³ And the king said, 'Let him be hung upon it'. And the king took his signet ring from his hand, and with it

14 [Haman's] life was sealed. ¹⁴ And the king said to Esther, 'Did he purpose to hang even Mordecai, who saved me from the hand of the eunuchs? Did he not know that Esther is of

15 [Mordecai's] family's race?' ¹⁵ And the king called Mordecai

16 καὶ ἐχαρίσατο αὐτῷ πάντα τὰ τοῦ Αμαν. ¹⁶ καὶ εἶπεν αὐτῷ Τί
θέλεις; καὶ ποιήσω σοι. καὶ εἶπε Μαρδοχαῖος ῞Οπως ἀνέλῃς
17 τὴν ἐπιστολὴν τοῦ Αμαν. ¹⁷ καὶ ἐνεχείρισεν αὐτῷ ὁ βασιλεὺς
18 τὰ κατὰ τὴν βασιλείαν. ¹⁸ καὶ εἶπεν Εσθηρ τῷ βασιλεῖ τῇ
19 ἐξῆς Δός μοι κολάσαι τοὺς ἐχθρούς μου φόνῳ. ¹⁹ ἐνέτυχε δὲ ἡ
βασίλισσα Εσθηρ καὶ κατὰ τέκνων Αμαν τῷ βασιλεῖ, ὅπως
ἀποθάνωσι καὶ αὐτοὶ μετὰ τοῦ πατρὸς αὐτῶν. καὶ εἶπεν ὁ
20 βασιλεὺς Γινέσθω. ²⁰ καὶ ἐπάταξε τοὺς ἐχθροὺς εἰς πληθος.
21 ²¹ ἐν δὲ Σούσοις ἀνθωμολογήσατο ὁ βασιλεὺς τῇ βασιλίσσῃ
ἀποκτανθῆναι ἄνδρας, καὶ εἶπεν Ἰδοὺ δίδωμί σοι τοῦ
κρεμάσαι. Καὶ ἐγένετο οὕτως.
E   ²² καὶ ἔγραψε τὴν ὑποτεταγμένην ἐπιστολήν· Βασιλεὺς
μέγας Ἀσσυῆρος τοῖς ἀπὸ τῆς Ἰνδικῆς ἕως τῆς
Αἰθιοπίας ἑκατὸν καὶ εἴκοσι καὶ ἑπτὰ χωρῶν ἄρχουσι
καὶ σατράπαις τοῖς τὰ ἡμέτερα φρονοῦσι χαίρειν.
23   ²³ πολλοὶ τῇ πλείστῃ τῶν εὐεργετούντων χρηστότητι
πυκνότερον τιμώμενοι, μεῖζον φρονήσαντες, οὐ μόνον
τοὺς ὑποτεταγμένους ἡμῖν ζητοῦσι κακοποιεῖν, τὸν δὲ
κόρον οὐ δυνάμενοι φέρειν καὶ τοῖς ἑαυτῶν εὐεργέταις
ἐπιχειροῦσι μηχανᾶσθαι κακά, καὶ τὴν εὐχαριστίαν οὐ
μόνον ἐκ τῶν ἀνθρώπων ἀναιροῦντες, ἀλλὰ καὶ τοῖς τῶν
ἀπειραγάθων κόμποις παρελθόντες, τὸ τοῦ πάντα
δυναστεύοντος δικαιοκρίτου μισοπόνηρον ἐκφυγεῖν
διειληφότες, τὴν δίκην πολλάκις ἐπ᾽ ἐξουσιῶν τεταγμένοι
τὰ τῶν ἐμπιστευομένων φίλων πράγματα χειρίζειν
αἰτίους ἀθώων αἱμάτων καταστήσαντες περιέβαλον
συμφοραῖς ἀνηκέστοις, τῷ τῆς κακοποιίας ψεύδει
παραλογισάμενοι τὴν τῶν ἐπικρατούντων ἀκέραιον
24 εὐγνωμοσύνην. ²⁴ σκοπεῖν δὲ ἔστιν ἐκ τῶν παρα-
δεδομένων ἡμῖν ἱστοριῶν καὶ ὅσον τὸ παρὰ πόδας
θεωροῦντες ἀξίως τῇ τῶν δυναστευόντων ὠμότητι
προσέχειν εἰς τὰ μετ᾽ ἔπειτα, καὶ τὴν βασιλείαν
ἀτάραχον παρέχειν πᾶσι τοῖς ἔθνεσι μετ᾽ εἰρήνης, οὐ
χρώμενοι ταῖς διαβολαῖς, τὰ δὲ ὑπὸ τὴν ὄψιν ἐρχόμενα
μετ᾽ ἐπιεικείας διεξάγοντες.

16 and bestowed on him all that was Haman's. [16] And he said to
him, 'What do you want? I shall do it for you.' Mordecai said,
17 'That you should revoke the letter of Haman'. [17] And the king
put into his hands the affairs of the kingdom.

18   [18] Moreover Esther said to the king, 'Grant me permission
19 to punish my enemies with slaughter'. [19] And Esther the queen
took counsel with the king also against the sons of Haman, that
they also should die together with their father. And the king
20 said, 'So be it'. [20] And she smote the enemies in great numbers.
21 [21] And in Susa the king made an agreement with the queen to
slay men, and he said, 'Behold, I give them to you to hang.' And
it was so.

E   [22] And he wrote the following letter:
'The Great King, Ahasuerus, to the one hundred and
twenty-seven rulers and satraps of the provinces from
India to Ethiopia, to those who are loyal to our government, greeting.

23   [23] 'The more often they are honoured by the too great
kindness of their benefactors, the more proud many men
having become, they not only seek to injure our subjects,
but in their inability to stand prosperity they even
undertake to lay evil schemes against their own benefactors.
They not only take away thankfulness from among men,
but, transgressing because of the boasts of those who
know nothing of goodness, imagining that they will
escape justice, the evil-hating attribute of the righteous
Judge, who rules over all.* And often, being set in places
of authority to manage the affairs of friends who have
trusted them, they have made them responsible for the
shedding of innocent blood and have involved them in
irremediable calamities, having beguiled by the falseness
of their evil-doing the sincere good will of their sovereigns.

24   [24] 'It can be seen from the records that have been
handed down to us as well as by observing what is close at
hand [that it is necessary] for the future to give due heed
to the cruelty of those who exercise authority, and to
render our kingdom quiet and peaceable for all nations,
by giving no heed to plots but by dealing equitably with
what comes before our eyes.

* *Punctuating the Greek* διειληφότες τὴν δίκην, πολλάκις

25   25 ἐπιξενωθεὶς γὰρ ἡμῖν Αμαν ᾿Αμαδάθου ὁ Βουγαῖος
ταῖς ἀληθείαις ἀλλότριος τοῦ τῶν Περσῶν φρονήματος
καὶ πολὺ διεστὼς τῆς ἡμετέρας χρηστότητος ἔτυχε τῆς
ἐξ ἡμῶν πρὸς πᾶν ἔθνος φιλανθρωπίας ἐπὶ τοσοῦτον,
ὥστε ἀναγορευθῆναι πατέρα ἡμῶν καὶ προσκυνεῖσθαι
ὑπὸ πάντων τὸ δεύτερον τῶν βασιλικῶν θρόνων
26   διατελεῖν. 26 οὐκ ἐνεγκὼν δὲ τὴν ὑπερηφανίαν, ἐπετή-
δευσεν ἡμᾶς τῆς ἀρχῆς καὶ τοῦ πνεύματος μεταστῆσαι,
τὸν δὲ ἡμέτερον σωτῆρα διὰ παντὸς Μαρδοχαῖον καὶ
τὴν ἄμεμπτον τούτου κοινωνὸν Εσθηρ σὺν τῷ παντὶ
τούτων ἔθνει πολυπλόκοις μεθοδείαις διαρτησάμενος
εἰς ἀπώλειαν· διὰ γὰρ τούτων τῶν τρόπων ᾠήθη λαβὼν
ἡμᾶς ἐρήμους ἐξαλλοτρίωσιν τῆς τῶν Περσῶν ἐπι-
27   κρατείας ἕως εἰς τοὺς Μακεδόνας ἀγαγεῖν. 27 τοὺς οὖν
ὑπὸ τοῦ τρισαλιτηρίου παραδεδομένους ὑμῖν ᾿Ιουδαίους
εὑρίσκομεν μὴ ὄντας κακούργους, δικαιοτάτοις δὲ
πολιτευομένους νόμοις, ὄντας δὲ καὶ υἱοὺς τοῦ μόνου
θεοῦ καὶ ἀληθινοῦ, τοῦ κατευθύναντος ἡμῖν τὴν
βασιλείαν μέχρι τοῦ νῦν ἐν τῇ καλλίστῃ διαθέσει.
28   28 καλῶς οὖν ποιήσατε μὴ προσέχοντες τοῖς προ-
απεσταλμένοις ὑμῖν ὑπὸ Αμαν γράμμασιν, διὰ τὸ καὶ
αὐτὸν τὸν τὰ τοιαῦτα ἐργασάμενον πρὸς ταῖς Σούσων
πύλαις ἐσταυρῶσθαι, ἀποδεδωκότος αὐτῷ τὴν κατ᾿
ἀξίαν δίκην τοῦ τὰ πάντα κατοπτεύοντος ἀεὶ κριτοῦ.
29   29 ἐκτεθήτω δὲ τὸ ἀντίγραφον τῆς ἐπιστολῆς ἐν παντὶ
τόπῳ, χρῆσθαί τε τοὺς ᾿Ιουδαίους τοῖς ἑαυτῶν νόμοις
καὶ ἐπισχύειν αὐτοῖς, ὅπως τοὺς ἐν καιρῷ θλίψεως
30   ἐπιθεμένους ἀμύνωνται. 30 ἐκρίθη δὲ ὑπὸ τῶν κατὰ τὴν
βασιλείαν ᾿Ιουδαίων ἄγειν τὴν τεσσαρεσκαιδεκάτην
τοῦ μηνός, ὅς ἐστιν Αδαρ, καὶ τῇ πεντεκαιδεκάτῃ
ἑορτάσαι, ὅτι ἐν αὐταῖς ὁ παντοκράτωρ ἐποίησεν αὐτοῖς
31   σωτηρίαν καὶ εὐφροσύνην. 31 καὶ νῦν μετὰ ταῦτα
σωτηρίαν μὲν εὖ ποιοῦσι τοῖς Πέρσαις, τῶν δὲ ἐπι-
32   βουλευσάντων μνημόσυνον τῆς ἀπωλείας. 32 ἡ δὲ πόλις
καὶ ἡ χώρα ἥτις κατὰ ταῦτα μὴ ποιῆσαι, δόρατι καὶ πυρὶ
καταναλωθήσεται μετ᾿ ὀργῆς, καὶ οὐ μόνον ἀνθρώποις
ἄβατος, ἀλλὰ καὶ θηρίοις καὶ πετεινοῖς ἐκταθήσεται.

25 ²⁵ 'For Haman, the son of Hammedatha, a Bougaean, having become our guest but really being an alien to the Persian spirit and quite devoid of our kindliness, so far enjoyed the good will that we have for every nation that he was called our father and was continually bowed down

26 to by all as the person second to the royal throne. ²⁶ But, unable to restrain his arrogance, he undertook to remove our kingdom and our life, and with intricate deceits busied himself with the destruction of Mordecai our perpetual saviour, and of Esther his blameless partner, together with their whole nation. He thought that in this way he would find us undefended and would accomplish an appropriation of the kingdom of the Persians to the Macedonians.

27 ²⁷ 'Now we find that the Jews, who were consigned to you by this thrice-accursed man, are not evildoers but are governed by most righteous laws, and also are sons of the only true God, who has directed the kingdom for us in the most excellent order.

28 ²⁸ 'Therefore do well by not paying attention to the letters sent to you by Haman, because the man himself who did such things has been hanged at the gate of Susa; for there has been inflicted on him the punishment he deserved by the Judge who always sees everything.

29 ²⁹ 'Therefore let a copy of this letter be posted in every place, that the Jews are to live under their own laws, and that they are to be given reinforcements so that they may defend themselves against those who attack them at the

30 time of their affliction. ³⁰ And it has been decided by the Jews throughout the kingdom to keep the fourteenth day of the month, that is Adar, and to celebrate a festival on the fifteenth, because on those days the Almighty wrought

31 for them salvation and rejoicing. ³¹ And now they do well [to regard it] hereafter as salvation for the Persians, but a reminder of destruction for those who have laid plots.

32 ³² Any city or country which does not act accordingly shall be destroyed in wrath with spear and fire. It shall lie impassable not only for men but also for beasts and birds.'

33   ³³ ἐξετέθη δὲ καὶ ἐν Σούσοις ἔκθεμα περιέχον τάδε, καὶ ὁ
      βασιλεὺς ἐνεχείρισε τῷ Μαρδοχαίῳ γράφειν ὅσα βούλεται.

34   ³⁴ ἐπέστειλε δὲ Μαρδοχαῖος διὰ γραμμάτων, καὶ ἐσφραγίσατο
      τῷ τοῦ βασιλέως δακτυλίῳ, μένειν τὸ ἔθνος αὐτοῦ κατὰ

35   χώρας ἔκαστον αὐτῶν καὶ ἑορτάζειν τῷ θεῷ. ³⁵ ἡ δὲ ἐπιστολὴ

36   ἣν ἀπέστειλεν ὁ Μαρδοχαῖος ἣν ἔχουσα ταῦτα· ³⁶ Αμαν
      ἀπέστειλεν ὑμῖν γράμματα ἔχοντα οὕτως Ἔθνος Ἰουδαίων
      ἀπειθὲς σπουδάσατε ταχέως ἀναπέμψαι μοι εἰς ἀπώλειαν.

37   ³⁷ ἐγὼ δὲ ὁ Μαρδοχαῖος μηνύω ὑμῖν τὸν ταῦτα ἐργασάμενον
      πρὸς ταῖς Σούσων πύλαις κεκρεμάσθαι καὶ τὸν οἶκον αὐτοῦ

38   διακεχειρίσθαι· ³⁸ οὗτος γὰρ ἐβούλετο ἀποκτεῖναι ἡμᾶς τῇ
      τρίτῃ καὶ δεκάτῃ τοῦ μηνὸς ὅς ἐστιν Αδαρ.

39   ³⁹ καὶ ὁ Μαρδοχαῖος ἐξῆλθεν ἐστολισμένος τὴν βασιλικὴν

40   ἐσθῆτα καὶ διάδημα βύσσινον περιπόρφυρον. ⁴⁰ ἰδόντες δὲ οἱ
      ἐν Σούσοις ἐχάρησαν. καὶ τοῖς Ἰουδαίοις ἐγένετο φῶς, πότος,

41   κῶθον. ⁴¹ καὶ πολλοὶ τῶν Ἰουδαίων περιετέμνοντο, καὶ

42   οὐδεὶς ἐπανέστη αὐτοῖς· ἐφοβοῦντο γὰρ αὐτούς. ⁴² οἱ δὲ
      ἄρχοντες καὶ οἱ τύραννοι καὶ οἱ σατράπαι καὶ οἱ βασιλικοὶ
      γραμματεῖς ἐτίμων τοὺς Ἰουδαίους· ὁ γὰρ φόβος Μαρδοχαίου

43   ἐπέπεσεν ἐπ᾽ αὐτούς. ⁴³ καὶ προσέπεσεν ἐν Σούσοις ὀνομασ-

44   θῆναι Αμαν καὶ τοὺς ἀντικειμένους ἐν πάσῃ βασιλείᾳ. ⁴⁴ καὶ
      ἀπέκτεινον ἐν Σούσοις οἱ Ἰουδαῖοι ἄνδρας ἑπτακοσίους καὶ
      τὸν Φαρσαν καὶ τὸν ἀδελφὸν αὐτοῦ καὶ τὸν Φαρνα καὶ τὸν
      Γαγαφαρδαθα καὶ τὸν Μαρμασαιμα καὶ τὸν Ιζαθουθ καὶ τοὺς
      δέκα υἱοὺς Αμαν Αμαδάθου τοῦ Βουγαίου τοῦ ἐχθροῦ τῶν

45   Ἰουδαίων, καὶ διήρπασαν πάντα τὰ αὐτῶν. ⁴⁵ καὶ εἶπεν ὁ
      βασιλεὺς τῇ Εσθηρ Πῶς σοι οἱ ἐνταῦθα καὶ οἱ ἐν τῇ περιχώρῳ

46   κέχρηνται; ⁴⁶ καὶ εἶπεν Εσθηρ Δοθήτω τοῖς Ἰουδαίοις οὓς
      ἐὰν θέλωσιν ἀνελεῖν καὶ διαρπάζειν. καὶ συνεχώρησεν. καὶ

47   ἀπώλεσαν μυριάδας ἑπτὰ καὶ ἑκατὸν ἄνδρας. ⁴⁷ ἔγραψε δὲ
      Μαρδοχαῖος τοὺς λόγους τούτους εἰς βιβλίον, καὶ ἐξαπέστειλε
      τοῖς Ἰουδαίοις οἳ ἦσαν ἐν τῇ Ἀρταξέρξου βασιλείᾳ, τοῖς
      μακρὰν καὶ τοῖς ἐγγύς, στῆσαι τὰς ἡμέρας ταύτας εἰς ὕμνους
      καὶ εὐφροσύνας ἀντὶ ὀδυνῶν καὶ πένθους, τὴν τεσσαρεσ-

48   καιδεκάτην καὶ τὴν πεντεκαιδεκάτην. ⁴⁸ καὶ ἀπέστειλε

49   μερίδας τοῖς πένησιν, καὶ προσεδέξαντο. ⁴⁹ διὰ τοῦτο

33 ³³ And a decree comprising these matters was set out also in Susa, and the king gave permission to Mordecai to write
34 whatever he wished. ³⁴ And Mordecai sent orders in writing, and sealed them with the king's signet ring, that his people should remain each in his own place and should keep festival to
35 God. ³⁵ And the letter which Mordecai sent was as follows:
36 ³⁶ 'Haman has sent to you letters as follows: "Hasten with all speed to send to destruction on my behalf the disobedient
37 race of the Jews". ³⁷ But I, Mordecai, advise you that the man who did this has been hung at the gates of Susa, and his family
38 has been slain. ³⁸ For he planned to kill us on the thirteenth day of the month which is Adar.'
39 ³⁹ And Mordecai went forth clothed in royal garments, and
40 with a headdress of linen edged with purple. ⁴⁰ And when those in Susa saw him they rejoiced. And the Jews had light and
41 drinking and a banquet. ⁴¹ And many of the Jews circumcised themselves, and no one opposed them; for they feared them.
42 ⁴² And the rulers and the lords and the satraps and the royal scribes feared the Jews; for the fear of Mordecai had fallen upon
43 them. ⁴³ And it came about that in Susa Haman was mentioned by name and in all the kingdom those who were opposed.
44 ⁴⁴ And in Susa the Jews slew seven hundred men and Pharsan and his brother and Pharna and Gagaphardatha and Marmasaima and Izathouth and the ten sons of Haman the son of Hammedatha the Bougaean the enemy of the Jews, and they took as plunder all that was his.
45 ⁴⁵ And the king said to Esther, 'How have your people here
46 and in the countryside fared?' ⁴⁶ And Esther said, 'Let permission be given to the Jews to slay and plunder whomever they wish'. And he agreed. And they slew 70,100 men.
47 ⁴⁷ And Mordecai wrote these matters in a book, and sent it to the Jews who were in the kingdom of Artaxerxes, to those who were far and those who were near, that they should keep these days for hymns and rejoicings in the place of pain and
48 grief—the fourteenth and fifteenth. ⁴⁸ And he sent portions to
49 the poor and they accepted them. ⁴⁹ Wherefore these days were

50 ἐκλήθησαν αἱ ἡμέραι αὗται φουρδαια διὰ τοὺς κλήρους τοὺς πεσόντας εἰς τὰς ἡμέρας ταύτας εἰς μνημόσυνον. [50] καὶ ἔγραψεν ὁ βασιλεὺς τὰ τέλη τῆς γῆς καὶ θαλάσσης καὶ τὴν ἰσχὺν αὐτοῦ, πλοῦτόν τε καὶ δόξαν τῆς βασιλείας αὐτοῦ.
51 [51] καὶ ἐδόξασε Μαρδοχαῖος καὶ ἔγραψεν ἐν τοῖς βιβλίοις
52 Περσῶν καὶ Μήδων εἰς μνημόσυνον. [52] ὁ δὲ Μαρδοχαῖος διεδέχετο τὸν βασιλέα Ξέρξην, καὶ μέγας ἦν ἐν τῇ βασιλείᾳ καὶ φιλούμενος ὑπὸ πάντων τῶν Ἰουδαίων, καὶ ἡγεῖτο αὐτῶν, καὶ δόξαν παντὶ τῷ ἔθνει αὐτοῦ περιετίθει.
F   [53] καὶ εἶπε Μαρδοχαῖος Παρὰ τοῦ θεοῦ ἐγένετο
54 ταῦτα. [54] ἐμνήσθη γὰρ τοῦ ἐνυπνίου οὗ εἶδεν. καὶ ἀπετελέσθη καὶ εἶπεν Ἡ μικρὰ πηγὴ Εσθηρ ἐστίν, καὶ οἱ δύο δράκοντες ἐγώ εἰμι καὶ Αμαν· ποταμὸς τὰ ἔθνη τὰ συναχθέντα ἀπολέσαι τοὺς Ἰουδαίους· ἥλιος καὶ φῶς οἳ ἐγένοντο τοῖς Ἰουδαίοις ἐπιφανεία τοῦ θεοῦ, τοῦτο τὸ
55 κρίμα. [55] καὶ ἐποίησεν ὁ θεὸς τὰ σημεῖα καὶ τὰ τέρατα ταῦτα ἃ οὐ γέγονεν ἐν τοῖς ἔθνεσιν. καὶ ἐποίησε κλήρους δύο, ἕνα τῷ λαῷ τοῦ θεοῦ καὶ ἕνα τοῖς ἔθνεσιν.
56 [56] καὶ προσῆλθον οἱ δύο κλῆροι οὗτοι εἰς ὥρας κατὰ καιρὸν καὶ ἡμέρας κυριεύσεως τοῦ αἰωνίου ἐν πᾶσι τοῖς
57 ἔθνεσιν. [57] καὶ ἐμνήσθη ὁ θεὸς τοῦ λαοῦ αὐτοῦ, καὶ
58 ἐδικαίωσε τὴν κληρονομίαν αὐτοῦ. [58] καὶ πᾶς ὁ λαὸς ἀνεβόησε φωνῇ μεγάλῃ καὶ εἶπεν Εὐλογητὸς εἶ, κύριε, ὁ μνησθεὶς τῶν διαθηκῶν τῶν πρὸς τοὺς πατέρας ἡμῶν·
59 ἀμήν. [59] καὶ ἔσονται αὐτοῖς αἱ ἡμέραι αὗται ἐν μηνὶ Αδαρ, ἐν τῇ τεσσαρεσκαιδεκάτῃ καὶ τῇ πεντεκαιδεκάτῃ τοῦ αὐτοῦ μηνός, μετὰ συναγωγῆς καὶ χαρᾶς καὶ εὐφροσύνης ἐνώπιον τοῦ θεοῦ κατὰ γενεὰς εἰς τὸν αἰῶνα ἐν τῷ λαῷ αὐτοῦ Ισραηλ.

called Phourdaia on account of the lots which fell out for these days for a memorial.

50 ⁵⁰ And the king wrote to the ends of the earth and the sea
51 concerning his power, his wealth and his fame. ⁵¹ And Mordecai magnified him, and wrote it in the books of the Persians and
52 Medes for a memorial. ⁵² And Mordecai was successor to king Xerxes, and he was great in the kingdom, and beloved by all the Jews and he ruled over them, and bestowed glory on all his people.

F ⁵³ And Mordecai said, 'These things have come from
54 God'. ⁵⁴ For he remembered the dream which he had had. And it was accomplished, and he said, 'The tiny spring is Esther, and the two dragons are Haman and myself. The river is the nations that gathered to destroy the Jews. The sun and the light which appeared to the
55 Jews are a revelation of God; this is the judgment. ⁵⁵ And God has done these signs and wonders, which have not occurred among the nations. And he made two lots, one
56 for the people of God and one for the nations. ⁵⁶ And these two lots came to the hour and day in the right time of the rule of the Eternal One among all the nations.
57 ⁵⁷ And God remembered his people, and vindicated his
58 inheritance. ⁵⁸ And all the people cried out with a great shout and said, "Blessed art thou, O Lord, who hast remembered the covenants with our fathers. Amen."
59 ⁵⁹ So they will observe these days in the month of Adar, on the fourteenth and fifteenth of that month, with an assembly and joy and gladness before God, from generation to generation for ever among his people Israel.'

LIST OF READINGS
WHERE HANHART'S GÖTTINGEN EDITION DIFFERS
FROM THE TEXT PRINTED HERE

(orthographic variants apart)

3.5   ανηρ] *pr* ἦν H
4.17   εν αντιπαραγωγη] ἐναντίᾳ παραγωγῇ H
5.9   του εθνους] τὸ ἔθνος H
5.22   στοματος αυτων] στόματός σου H
7.9   ποιησομεν] ποιήσωμεν H
7.11   εφ' ω] ἐφ' ὃν H
7.19   εξω 2°] *om* H
8.19   τεκνων] *pr* τῶν H
8.25   μεθοδειαις] μεθόδοις H
8.28   κατ' αξιαν] καταξίαν H
8.34   επεστειλε] ἀπέστειλε H
8.47   Αρταξερξου] Ασσυήρου H
8.49   φουρδαια] Φουραια H
8.52   Ξερξην] Ασσυῆρον H
8.54   οι εγενοντο] ἣ ἐγένετο H

(H = Hanhart's edition)

INDEXES

INDEX OF MODERN AUTHORS

INDEX OF BIBLICAL REFERENCES